Marcel Proust and
the Text as Macrometaphor

Lois Marie Jaeck

MARCEL PROUST AND THE TEXT AS MACROMETAPHOR

UNIVERSITY OF TORONTO PRESS
Toronto Buffalo London

© University of Toronto Press 1990
Toronto Buffalo London
Printed in Canada

ISBN 0-8020-2715-6

Printed on acid-free paper

University of Toronto Romance Series 60

Canadian Cataloguing in Publication Data

Jaeck, Lois Marie, 1946–
 Marcel Proust and the text as macrometaphor

(University of Toronto romance series; 60)
Includes bibliographical references.
ISBN 0-8020-2715-6

1. Proust, Marcel, 1871–1922. À la recherche du temps perdu. 2. Proust, Marcel, 1871–1922. Temps retrouvé. 3. Metaphor. I. Title. II. Series.

PQ2631.R63A835 1990   843'.912   C90-093237-6

This book has been published with the help of a grant from the Canadian Federation for the Humanities, using funds provided by the Social Sciences and Humanities Research Council of Canada.

Contents

Acknowledgments vii

1 Introduction: The Text as Metaphor 3

PART ONE
ON PROUST AND METAPHOR AS THE BASIC TROPE OF ART

2 Metaphor: From Aristotle to Proust 11
3 Proust: From Involuntary Memory to Metaphor 17

PART TWO
A LA RECHERCHE DU TEMPS PERDU:
THE TEXT AS MACROMETAPHOR

4 Structure as Macrometaphor 31
5 Repetition and Cross-Referentiality as Macrometaphor 50
6 Conclusion: Literature as Macrometaphor 183

Notes 201
Bibliography 221
Index 225

Acknowledgments

This book owes its genesis, in part, to Dr Frederic Grover's graduate seminar on Proust at the University of British Columbia, which inspired me to renew a love affair with Proust's work that began in 1968 – the first time I read the *Recherche*. I thank Dr Carlo Chiarenza for introducing me, as a graduate student, to literary and critical theory, and for encouraging me to plunge into comparative literature studies. To my mother I am indebted for her unfailing moral support of all my scholarly research. I thank my son Aaron for revealing to me again, through his own childhood, those inarticulate bonds among ourselves, the world, and its phenomena that we lose sight of as we grow up and that we try to retrieve through literature.

MARCEL PROUST AND THE TEXT AS MACROMETAPHOR

1 Introduction: The Text as Metaphor

In 'Metaphor and the Main Problem of Hermeneutics' (1974), Paul Ricoeur suggests that 'the process of understanding a metaphor is the key for understanding larger texts, say literary works.'[1] In an attempt to establish a common ground between text and metaphor, Ricoeur asks himself two questions: 'to what extent may we treat metaphor as a work in miniature, and ... may a work ... be considered as an expanded metaphor?'[2] I contend that Marcel Proust answered Ricoeur's question in novelistic form through his literary masterpiece, *A la recherche du temps perdu*, fifty years before Ricoeur's theoretical paper on the same subject.

Ricoeur does not discuss Proust in his paper, but he does refer to Proust's 'original source': Aristotle's theory of metaphor as expressed in the *Poetics*. Ricoeur briefly analyses the meaning and relationship of metaphor, lexis, mimesis, poesis, and tragedy in Aristotle's text and concludes that there is a possible connection set forth in the *Poetics*, 'between the function of imitation, as making human actions higher than they actually are, and the structure of metaphor, as transcending the meaning of ordinary language into strange uses.'[3] Ricoeur surmises that the mirror relationship of metaphor and text is implied in Aristotle's *Poetics*; however, neither he nor Aristotle explains why the mimetic text and metaphor give rise to a common effect. I will demonstrate that metaphor and the literary text function in the same manner – they both give rise to an inarticulate impression which transcends the combined fields of signification which engendered it – because their basic structures are analogous. In order to clarify what the common structures of metaphor and mimetic text are, I will first analyse Proust's theory of metaphor as presented in *Le temps retrouvé* (the last volume of *A la recherche du temps perdu*), and then illustrate how the structure of metaphor (as defined by Proust) is the basic model for the structure of his novel, with the result that the text in its entirety functions as a 'macrometaphor.'

Much excellent work has already been done on the individual poetic metaphors in Proust,[4] but little has been done on the comprehensive poetics of the novel as a whole,[5] or on the essential metaphorical nature of the ideas, milieus, symbols, characters, and primary architectural elements of the novel and how they reflect each other. In his conclusion to *Proust's Binoculars* (1963), for example, Roger Shattuck suggested that the 'action which dominates all of the *Recherche* is the action of metaphor: the reconciliation of a duality or, in more complex cases, of a multiplicity.' He proposed that metaphor 'encompasses all aspects of the book, from the aspects of personality to the division of society itself to the stereoscopic assembling of past and present ...' and remarked that it had never been pointed out that the 'deux côtés' represent most basically the action of metaphor itself – different elements folding into one. Despite his acknowledgment of the metaphorical structure of the *Recherche*, however, Shattuck's own critical study did not explore it, apart from mentioning the metaphorical function of the 'two ways.'[6]

In *Allegories of Reading* (1979), Paul de Man suggested that everything in the *Recherche* signifies something other than what it represents, 'be it love, consciousness, politics, art, sodomy or gastronomy,' and proposed that the most adequate term to designate this 'something else' is reading.[7] Although he describes a passage about reading in *Du côté de chez Swann* as the dramatization of metaphor,[8] de Man does not perceive metaphor as the underlying symbol of the work, but suggests instead that Proust's text is an 'allegory of reading'[9] whose multiple elements can all be regarded as reflections of the reading process. I agree with de Man that everything in Proust's novel signifies something other than what it represents, but I propose that the metaphorical process more accurately corresponds to the underlying mechanism of Proust's fictional technique – the reading process, as described by Proust and as experienced by the reader, being but one link (albeit one of the most essential ones) in the interplay of macrometaphors which constitute the text.

Jean Ricardou, in 'La métaphore d'un bout à l'autre' (1978)[10] and in 'Pour une lecture rétrospective' (1980),[11] has presented to date the most comprehensive explanation of the narrative function of metaphor in Proust's text. In both discussions (the latter is a gloss of the first work), Ricardou begins by describing a 'metamorphosis' of the linguistic operation, metaphor. With Proust, he proposes, metaphor ceases to be mainly representative or expressive, and becomes productive. He offers as an example of this new kind of 'productive' metaphor, the invasion of the Guermantes' courtyard in Paris by the Baptistery of St Mark's in Venice, through the element common to both scenes: the uneven paving stone. Unlike traditional 'representative' metaphor, which would have evoked the past scene only for the purpose of representing the paving stone in the Guermantes' courtyard, Proust's 'metaphorical telescoping' of two cells of fiction (Paris/Venice) causes a movement from one place to another through the point that they have in common. The unevenness of the paving stones, according to Ricardou, is no longer of any importance; what is important is the passage from one place to the other.[12] He describes this process of metaphorical telescoping as 'ordinal' metaphor, and stresses that, rather than expressing or representing an aspect of the fiction, it is instead productive of a narrative order.[13]

Between representative (traditional) metaphor and ordinal metaphor, there is, according to Ricardou, not merely a difference in function – the one representing an aspect of the fiction (a paving stone's unevenness, for example), the other ordering two fictional cells (the Guermantes' mansion interrupted by Venice) – but a contradiction in function: whereas he sees representative metaphor as obeying the mechanics of representation, he views ordinal metaphor as an anti-representative function. By causing two fictional cells, remote in time and space, to be telescoped into a single instant, the ordinal metaphor volatizes time and space – the two categories on which the effect of representation depends.[14] His explanation of the effects of 'representative' metaphor does not take into account the 'traditional' view of poetic metaphor as the combination of two entities in a reciprocal, balanced relationship that allows their unvoiced, common factors to intimate themselves. By virtue of being a reciprocal opposition, metaphor has always effected a banishment of time and space – the function which Ricardou attributes to 'ordinal' metaphor, but which he denies that metaphor-understood-as-a-poetic-trope can accomplish. Far from denouncing metaphor as 'representative,' Proust's narrator stresses that the metaphorical process is the only device which is representative in the true sense of the word – the only mechanism available to a writer that allows him to express the atemporal, internal reality of things through his work – the reality which eludes representation through cinematographic, temporal forms of description.

Rather than seeing a rift between the function of metaphor-understood-as-a-poetic-trope and the kinds of metaphorical structures which manifest themselves in the *Recherche*, I propose that their difference resides mainly in the narrative distance over which the metaphor may realize itself: just as the words linked in a 'poetic' metaphor may dovetail phenomena in reality vastly separated in time and space, so events in Proust's text – frequently widely separated in the time and space of the novel – will summon up each other through the intermediary of their common factors and give rise to the same result. For this reason, I regard the large, time/space 'metaphors' in Proust's text as 'macrometaphors' whose structure and function is mirrored in 'miniature' in 'poetic' metaphor.

From the point of view of metaphor and narrative structure, the historical significance of Proust's work resides in it being a 'working model' or structural representation of the theory of art and metaphor which is presented in its context. In his preface to 'Discours du Récit' (*Figures III*), Gérard Genette denies the possibility of treating *A la recherche du temps perdu* as an example of what the novel is in general, but acknowledges nevertheless that Proust's novel is made up of universal elements:

> Il me paraît impossible de traiter la *Recherche du temps perdu* comme un simple exemple de ce qui serait le récit en général, ou le récit romanesque, ou le récit de forme autobiographique, ou Dieu sait quelle autre classe, espèce ou variété: la spécificité de la narration proustienne prise dans son ensemble est irréductible, et toute extrapolation serait ici une faute de méthode; la *Recherche* n'illustre qu'elle-même. Mais d'un autre côté, cette specificité n'est pas indécomposable, et chacun des traits qu'y dégage l'analyse se prête à quelque rapprochement, comparaison ou mise en perspective. Comme toute oeuvre, comme tout organisme, la *Recherche* est faite d'éléments universels, ou du moins transindividuels, qu'elle assemble en une synthèse spécifique, en une totalité singulière. L'analyser, c'est aller non du général au particulier, mais bien du particulier au général.[15]

It is not surprising that Genette should find generalities in the *Recherche*, as its narrator frequently comments on the common factors shared by different works of art, characters, places, and architectural landmarks. After he has begun writing his own novel, Marcel compares his method of discovery to conducting research with a telescope: bringing together separate worlds situated great distances apart but reflected in each other because they manifest the same general laws:

PART ONE

ON PROUST AND METAPHOR AS THE BASIC TROPE OF ART

2 Metaphor: From Aristotle to Proust

In the final volume of *A la recherche du temps perdu* (*Le temps retrouvé*), Marcel Proust's narrator denies the validity of 'realistic' fiction that depicts a scene by describing one after another the innumerable objects which were present at a given moment in a given place, and declares that truth will only be attained by an author through metaphor (III, 889). Although he suggests that metaphor is the fundamental building block of art and that style is essentially metaphor,[1] he does not explain why and how metaphor is synonymous with style. In this chapter, I will analyse in detail Proust's definition of metaphor and the forces it brings into play, and then compare the structure and effect of metaphor to the architectural elements of *A la recherche du temps perdu*, in order to show that the totality of the novel – including its paragraph sequence and chapter organization – is a macrometaphor: a metaphorical structure whose composite binary components are 'macro' entities such as different places, characters, ideas, times, images, and symbols joined together in the text.

To perceive the parallels between the structure of Proust's novel and the metaphorical process, we must first determine exactly what the word 'metaphor,' as used by Proust, means. Gérard Genette's 'La Rhétorique restreinte'[2] looks briefly at the history of the usage of the word 'metaphor' and explains how and where Proust's definition of metaphor fits into that tradition. Genette reminds us that, in 1970, three papers defining metaphor in a general sense appeared almost simultaneously: *La Rhétorique générale* by the Groupe de Liège,[3] 'Pour une théorie de la figure généralisée'[4] by Michel Déguy, and 'La Métaphore généralisée' by Jacques Sojcher.[5] Genette shows how the usage of metaphor has evolved from being understood first in a generalized sense,[6] as defined by Aristotle in his *Poetics* and *Rhetoric*, Book III, to later being used in a specific sense to signify a trope of poetic diction, as classified and defined in 1730 by Jacques Dumarsais

(French grammarian), then back to being understood in a generalized sense, as defined and utilized by Marcel Proust in the first quarter of the twentieth century, and by Michel Déguy and Jacques Sojcher in 1970.

Before proceeding with Genette's commentary on Aristotle's definition of metaphor, let us look at the original definition. In the *Poetics*, Aristotle proposed that 'metaphor consists in the transference of a name (from the thing which it properly denotes) to some other thing, the transference being either from genus to species, or from species to genus, or from species to species, or by analogy and proportion.'[7] In Book III, Chapter 3 of *Rhetoric*, Aristotle also contended that 'the simile also is a metaphor; the difference is but slight.'[8] Genette suggests that the original definition of metaphor by Aristotle was not seen as a general principle; it simply was. Because it was such a fundamental, taken-for-granted concept, Aristotle consecrated only a few pages to it in a large book dedicated to style and composition.[9] Aristotle's general view of metaphor,[10] however, was divided and specialized into a number of individual tropes – metaphor, metonymy, contiguity, synecdoche, analogy, and many others – by Dumarsais in his book *Des Tropes*, published in 1730.[11] Genette proposes that we have felt the need to generalize the concept of metaphor in the twentieth century because we made it too specific earlier in our history.[12] He traces the steps which bring about the reduction of Dumarsais' multiple poetic terminology (of which metaphor was one classification among twenty others) into one trope – generalized metaphor.

In the nineteenth century, Pierre Fontanier wrote two books on poetic language – *Commentaire raisonné des tropes* and *Traité général des figures du discours* – in which, according to Genette, he distinguished himself through a point of view remarkable for its ambiguity: on the one hand, he enlarged the number of tropes which Dumarsais defined, but on the other hand, he finished by reducing the entire army of tropes to three which he considered to be worthy of the name – metonymy, synecdoche, and metaphor.[13] The threefold classification, according to Genette, confirmed Fontanier's position as the founder of modern rhetoric.[14]

Fontanier's reduction of all poetic tropes into three basic classifications was reduced once more in 1923 by the Russian formalist, Boris Eikhenbaum, who established that metonymy equals prose, and metaphor equals poetry.[15] Roman Jakobson later supported Eikhenbaum's reduction in his article on Pasternak in 1935, and again in Part II of his book *Fundamentals of Language* in 1956, wherein he proposed that 'the development of a discourse may take place along two different semantic lines: one topic may lead to another either through their similarity or through their contiguity. The metaphoric way would be the most appropriate term for the first case, and the metonymic way for the second, since they find their most condensed expression in metaphor and metonymy respectively.'[16] In his concluding remarks, Jakobson repeats Eikhenbaum's premise that metonymy equals prose, metaphor equals poetry: 'The principle of similarity underlies poetry: the metrical parallelism of lines on the phonic equivalence of rhyming words prompts the question of semantic similarity and contrast: there exist, for instance, grammatical and anti-grammatical rhymes. Prose, on the contrary, is forwarded essentially by contiguity; thus, for poetry, metaphor, and for prose, metonymy, is the line of least resistance ...'[17]

Genette describes one more major movement of reduction in the history of metaphor whereby metaphor absorbs its ultimate adversary – metonymy – and becomes 'trope des tropes' (Sojcher), 'figure des figures' (Déguy), 'le noyau, le coeur, et finalement l'essence et presque le tout de la rhétorique' (Genette).[18] Jacques Sojcher classifies metaphor as the central trope of all poetic language, on the grounds that the essence of all poetic language is displacement of sense, and displacement of sense is metaphor: 'Si la poésie est un espace qui s'ouvre dans le langage, si par elle les mots reparlent et le sens se résignifie, c'est qu'il y a entre la langue usuelle et la parole retrouvée déplacement de sens, métaphore. La métaphore n'est plus, dans cette perspective, une figure parmi d'autres, mais la figure, le trope des tropes.'[19] In his argument for generalized metaphor, Michel Déguy suggests that all the methods employed by metonymy, synecdoche, and resemblance (contiguity, proximity, and juxtaposition for metonymy; intersection for synecdoche) have metaphorical superimposition as their common denominator, and therefore, all are metaphorical.[20]

Genette pinpoints the characteristic that makes metaphor the central trope of all language – the essentially metaphorical nature of poetic language and of language in general[21] – and suggests that metaphor has been designated as the central figure of all rhetoric because 'il convient à l'esprit, dans sa faiblesse, que toutes choses, fût-ce les figures, aient un centre.'[22] Jacques Sojcher offers a more rationalistic explanation: the displacement of sense brought about by poetic language – be it analogy, metaphor, synecdoche, or metonymy – is the result of the engendering (and consequent perception) of a difference or a digression. The primary element of poetic metaphor is difference, and for this reason, metaphor is chosen to be the term which includes those other divergent tropes – synecdoche and metonymy – whose ultimate effect is analogous to metaphor.[23] Sojcher concludes 'La Métaphore généralisée' with the suggestion that metaphor generally conceived as difference and displacement of sense is not just a figure of style, but an existential figure at the origin of thought and language, which discovers itself in poetic language and, through the latter, allows man to discover himself:

> La métaphore est essentiellement pour nous l'ouverture à l'unité. Mais cette unité est confuse; elle échappe toujours de quelque manière à l'analyse logique, grammaticale. Elle ne se découvre que dans et par le langage poétique, et l'homme en lui la découvre et se révèle à lui-même.
>
> La métaphore est alors plus qu'une figure de style, elle est aussi une figure existentielle, puisqu'elle est à l'origine d'une conversion du regard, du coeur, de la pensée et du langage, sans laquelle il n'y aurait pas conscience métaphorique.[24]

In 'La Rhétorique restreinte,' Genette acknowledges that Proust's work is an example of a discourse in which the term 'metaphor' tends to cover almost the entire analogical field:

> On sait en effet que le terme de métaphore tend de plus en plus à recouvrir l'ensemble du champ analogique: alors que l'éthos classique voyait dans la métaphore une comparaison implicite, la modernité traiterait volontiers la comparaison comme une métaphore explicite ou motivée. L'exemple le plus caractéristique de cet usage se trouve évidemment chez Proust, qui n'a cessé d'appeler métaphore ce qui dans son oeuvre, le plus souvent, est pure comparaison. Ici encore, les mobiles de la réduction apparaissent assez clairement dans la perspective d'une figuratique centrée sur le discours poétique ou à tout le moins (comme chez Proust) sur une poétique de discours: nous n'en sommes plus aux comparaisons homériques, et la concentration sémantique du trope lui assure une supériorité esthétique presque évidente sur la forme développée de la figure.[25]

He asserts that Proust represents a more advanced stage of restriction than Jakobson; that before the previously mentioned publications of the Russian formalists he had already broken down the distinction

15 Metaphor

between metonymy and metaphor and had baptized as metaphor all figures of analogy.[26] He gives an example of a Proustian metaphor that is 'pure metonymy,' and refers to his paper 'Métonymie chez Proust,' in which he attempted to demonstrate that a large number of Proustian metaphors are in fact metonymies[27] or at least metaphors with a metonymical basis:

> On a rappelé tout à l'heure la façon dont Proust baptisait métaphore toute figure d'analogie: il faut maintenant ajouter qu'il lui arrive, par un lapsus tout à fait significatif, d'étendre cette appellation à toute espèce de figure, même la plus typiquement métonymique, comme la locution 'faire catleya' (pour faire l'amour) en utilisant comme accessoire – ou à tout le moins comme prétexte un bouquet de catleyas. J'ai tenté ailleurs de montrer qu'un grand nombre des 'métaphores' proustiennes sont en fait des métonymies, du moins des métaphores à fondement métonymiques.[28]

Genette acknowledges that Proust's definition of metaphor characterizes him as a writer fifty years ahead of his time, but he does not examine or even mention the mirror relationship that Proust's generalized view of metaphor shared with the structure of his novel, even though Proust himself declared that metaphor is the essence of style and the fundamental building block of art.

Leaving Genette's brief history of metaphor behind us, let us examine more closely the factors common to Proust's view of metaphor as expounded in *A la recherche du temps perdu* (1913–27), and Jacques Sojcher's generalized view of metaphor explained in 'La Métaphore généralisée' (1970). Proust, like Sojcher, uses the term metaphor to describe a variety of poetic mechanisms that are usually classified under separate headings in traditional rhetoric. We have already seen that Proust frequently classifies as metaphor poetic devices that are commonly designated as metonymies, analogies, and similes; and affirms in *Le temps retrouvé* that metaphor is the basic building block of any literary work: 'Le rapport peut être peu intéressant, les objets médiocres, le style mauvais, mais tant qu'il n'y a pas eu cela, il n'y a rien' (III, 889). Proust suggests, like Sojcher fifty years later, that metaphor is 'le trope des tropes.' Sojcher extends the concept of metaphor beyond its traditional sense of a trope of literary style and sees it as an 'existential figure' that is mirrored in any change of consciousness, be it a conversion of perception, of the state of the mind (soul, feelings), of thought, or of language. He sees its function as essentially an opening onto a unity beyond logical, grammatical analysis ('la métaphore est essentiellement pour nous ouverture à l'unité')[29] which reveals itself through poetic language and allows one to discover oneself.

Although Proust does not state directly that metaphor is an existential figure or a pattern that reflects itself at the heart of existence, his narrator explains that the rule of metaphor was revealed to him by nature herself ('La nature ne m'avait pas mis elle-même, à ce point de vu, sur la voie de l'art, n'était-elle pas commencement d'art elle-même, elle qui ne m'avait permis de connaître, souvent, la beauté d'une chose que dans une autre ...,' III, 889), and that art must duplicate this natural process if it is to express the truth that eludes intelligence and analysis. Proust does not declare in a preface that one discovers oneself through metaphor, but he does write a seven-volume book about a man who did just that: he discovered his true self – his vocation to be a writer – at the moment that his three experiences of involuntary memory (classifiable as natural metaphors) led him to an awareness of the metaphorical process, how it occurs naturally, and how it must duplicate itself in art. Just as Sojcher suggests that the relationship of a reader with the book is essentially metaphorical ('La métaphore est alors plus qu'une figure de style, elle est aussi une figure existentielle ... Tel est bien l'échange de l'écriture et de la lecture, la change de la circularité.'),[30] so the narrator of the *Recherche* realizes that his book will serve as a magnifying glass that will allow his readers to read what lies inside themselves (VIII, 424).

Having determined how and where Proust's usage of the word 'metaphor' fits into the rhetorical tradition, I must settle down to the main problem of this work and analytically compare Proust's definition of metaphor with the architectural elements of his novel, find their common denominators, and thus demonstrate how metaphor is the basic building block of Proust's text. By doing this, I will also illustrate how metaphorical structure – in Proust's work and in other literary texts – is the basic building block of literary expression itself – the vehicle through which our thoughts and perceptions can retranslate themselves back into the realm of the inexpressible. This process allows us to realize in part Antonin Artaud's project: although we cannot prevent our breath (true self) from being stolen from our body through speech, we can restore it, repossess it, and reawaken the being in us which both transcends and eludes thought and speech,[31] as metaphor gives back to us the unspeakable difference between thought and speech, which eludes expression through the intellect and reason.

3 Proust: From Involuntary Memory to Metaphor

In *Le temps retrouvé*, Proust's analysis of his three consecutive experiences of involuntary memory and the inexplicable happiness they produce culminates in three sentences that explain the intrinsic, reflective relationship of internal reality, art, and metaphor:

> Ce que nous appelons la réalité est un certain rapport entre ces souvenirs qui nous entourent simultanément – rapport que supprime une simple vision cinématographique, laquelle s'éloigne par là, d'autant plus du vrai qu'elle prétend se borner à lui – rapport unique que l'écrivain doit retrouver pour en enchaîner à jamais dans sa phrase les deux termes différents. On peut faire se succéder indéfiniment dans une description les objets qui figuraient dans le lieu décrit, la vérité ne commencera qu'au moment où l'écrivain prendra deux objets différents, posera leur rapport, analogue dans le monde de l'art à celui qu'est le rapport unique de la loi causale dans le monde de la science, et les enfermera dans les anneaux nécessaires d'un beau style; même, ainsi que la vie, quand, en rapprochant une qualité commune à deux sensations, il dégagera leur essence commune en les réunissant l'une et l'autre pour les soustraire aux contingences du temps, dans une métaphore ... Le rapport peut être peu intéressant, les objets médiocres, le style mauvais, mais tant qu'il n'y a pas eu cela, il n'y a rien. (III 889–90)

In this key passage, Proust describes metaphor as a duplication or re-presentation of reality. He does not refer to an external reality or one readily perceived by our senses, but to an internal, essential reality that constitutes the inexpressible connection between apparently dissimilar phenomena, which allows us to apprehend intuitively their innate similarity, even though this common factor eludes expression through logic, intelligence, or ordinary language.

In order to re-present the internal truth that Proust feels is the true subject of all great works of art (III 891), the artist-writer must duplicate the process used by Nature when she presents these truths to us. Proust suggests that the essential mechanisms which reveal internal reality to us in natural, lived experience are superimposition or contiguity: two or more dissimilar phenomena encroach themselves one upon the other, and thus reveal an essential nature common to them both – an internal truth more real than their external differences. The metaphorical process, according to Proust, is the artistic means that allows the artist/writer to duplicate the superimposition or contiguity of dissimilars which occurs spontaneously in nature. This process entails primarily the artist's recognition of the unique relationship between two dissimilar objects and the revelation of that rapport by linking the objects in the work of art in such a way that their textual superimposition or close proximity allows their innate similarity to manifest itself and to free itself from external circumstances.

The steps in the narrator's train of thought leading up to and following this key passage on the relationship of metaphor and art are invaluable for this study, as they are working models of the macrometaphorical process. The indirect but causally linked connections Proust establishes in the Guermantes' library between the superimposition of the past on the present, the interaction of a reader with his book, the translation of life experience into art, and the device of metaphor as the joining together of dissimilar phenomena are the clues which allow us to perceive that, for Proust, metaphorical structure is not just the joining together of two words in a poetic image, but more essentially, the 'rapprochement' of macro-units such as different times, different places, different levels of reality. Like their micro-doubles, these macrometaphors join together dissimilar phenomena in such a way that a common essence is revealed that was not hitherto perceptible or expressible.

The narrator proceeds through eight levels of investigation which follow from each other, and individually all reflect the metaphorical process. In the course of my analysis of these eight levels, we shall see that the metaphorical process catalyses a chain reaction which begins when the internal similarity of dissimilar objects manifests itself, because this internal essence then enters into a mirror relationship with still another entity. Metaphor thus gives rise to a series of doubles recognitions which all reflect one basic model – the metaphorical process.

In the first step of his inquiry, immediately following his three consecutive experiences of involuntary memory that take place in the course of an hour at the Guermantes residence, the narrator realizes that he has just felt the same happiness that had been given to him by various other episodes in his life: by the view of three trees he thought he recognized in the course of a drive near Balbec, by the sight of the twin steeples of Martinville, by the flavour of a madeleine dipped in tea, by many other sensations about which he has spoken, and by the last works of Vinteuil, which seemed to combine the quintessential character of all of the experiences (III, 866): 'La félicité que je venais d'éprouver était bien en effet la même que celle que j'avais éprouvée en mangeant la madeleine et dont j'avais alors ajourné de rechercher les causes profondes. La différence, pûrement matérielle, était dans les images évoquées' (III, 867). By comparing his experience of the uneven paving stone with his experience of the madeleine dipped in tea, he is able to perceive a second common denominator that his present experience shares with the previous one: both bring into the present an identical sensation that he had experienced in the past and, with it, all of the other sensations from the past linked on that day to that particular sensation (III, 870). Thus, in the first step of the inquiry which will lead him to the rule of metaphor, the narrator inadvertently makes use of the metaphorical process: he recognizes a link between dissimilar phenomena, and by means of their comparison, he allows the common factors that are the cause of that inexplicable connection between dissimilars to reveal themselves.

In the second stage of his inquiry, the narrator attempts to discern the essence of the identical pleasures experienced three times within the space of a few minutes (the sensations produced by the feel of the uneven paving stone, the sound of the spoon against the plate, and the texture of the napkin against his mouth): 'Or cette cause, je la devinais en comparant ces diverses impressions bienheureuses qui avaient entre elles ceci de commun que je les éprouvais à la fois dans le moment actuel et dans un moment éloigné, jusqu'à faire empiéter le passé sur le présent, à me faire hésiter à savoir dans lequel des deux je me trouvais ...' (III, 871). In all three cases, a past moment is able to emerge into the context of the present through the intermediary of a sensation common to both times, even though the external circumstances of the past and the present moments are radically different.

The narrator compares his experiences of involuntary memory to analogies: 'Cet être-là n'était jamais venu à moi, ne s'était jamais manifesté, qu'en dehors de l'action, de la jouissance immédiate, chaque fois que le miracle d'une analogie m'avait fait échapper au présent. Seul, il avait le pouvoir de me faire retrouver les jours anciens, le temps perdu, devant quoi les efforts de ma mémoire et de mon intelligence échouaient toujours' (III, 871). He does not expound on the exact nature of the connection between an analogy and an experience of involuntary memory, but his ensuing analysis implies that the superimposition of a past moment onto the present is like the joining of two words in a metaphor. Metaphor gives rise to a field of signification that originates neither from one word nor the other but from an element common to both, which is beyond discourse and reason, in the realm of the inexpressible. Similarly, a past/present reminiscence reveals a moment of time which is atemporal: 'Rien qu'un moment du passé? Beaucoup plus, peut-être; quelque chose qui, commun à la fois au passé et au présent, est beaucoup plus essentiel qu'eux deux' (III, 872).

In the third level of his inquiry, the narrator explores the manner in which he interacts with the past/present analogy that life presented to him, and by doing so, he inadvertently conducts an investigation of the second stage of the movement of signification of metaphor – the interaction of a reader/observer with an analogy that is presented to him in a work of art. Just as an extratemporal moment was able to reveal itself through the duplication of a past sensation in the present, an extratemporal 'being' (the essential nature of the narrator) is able to emerge into consciousness through its recognition of itself in its spatial double – the extratemporal essence disengaged by the past/present analogy:

> Mais qu'un bruit, qu'une odeur, déjà entendu ou respirée jadis, le soient de nouveau, à la fois dans le présent et dans le passé, réels sans être actuels, idéaux sans être abstraits, aussitôt l'essence permanente et habituellement cachée des choses se trouve liberée, et notre vrai moi qui, parfois depuis longtemps, semblait mort, mais ne l'était pas entièrement, s'éveille, s'anime en recevant la céleste nourriture qui lui est apportée. (III, 872–3)

Following the narrator's own methodology, let us compare the first and third levels of his inquiry in order to clarify their common metaphorical structure: in both the past/present analogy and the analogy/narrator interaction, two apparently dissimilar phenomena dovetail as a result of a factor common to them both, and thus allow their essential quality (innate common essence) to reveal itself momentarily and to transcend the external differences of the two juxtaposed phenomena in which it was enshrined.

Having discerned precisely why the three 'intimation' experiences gave him the same inexplicable happiness (they fed the being in him that could nourish itself only on the essence of things), the narrator proceeds to investigate other phenomena which produced an effect similar to that engendered by his experiences of involuntary memory. He critically questions the significance of the 'obscure impressions' which solicited his attention in a manner somewhat similar to his involuntary reminiscences, but which differed from the latter in that they concealed within them not a sensation dating from an earlier time but a new truth:

> Cependant, je m'avisai au bout d'un moment, après avoir pensé à ces résurrections de la mémoire, que, d'une autre façon, des impressions obscures avaient quelquefois, et déjà à Combray du côté de Guermantes, sollicité ma pensée, à la façon de ces reminiscences, mais qui cachaient non une sensation d'autrefois mais une vérité nouvelle, une image précieuse que je cherchais à découvrir par des efforts du même genre que ceux qu'on fait pour se rappeler quelque chose, comme si nos plus belles idées étaient comme des airs de musique qui nous reviendraient sans que nous les eussions jamais entendus, et que nous nous efforcerions d'écouter, de transcrire. (III, 878)

Just as the joining together of dissimilar phenomena in a metaphor allows us to perceive their common essence, so the narrator's comparison permits him to see clearly the common denominators shared by the involuntary reminiscences and the obscure impressions. He notices immediately that they both presented themselves to him involuntarily; he was not free to choose them (III, 879). Their superimposition also causes him to realize that the factor first perceived as their manifest difference is in fact their similarity: whereas the reminiscences brought to him an old truth (a sensation dating from an earlier time), the obscure impressions appeared to bring with them a new truth (III, 878). Closer examination of that new truth, however, leads him and the reader to the realization that the new truth is older than the old truths returned to him through involuntary memory, and that both experiences are engendered by analogous mechanisms. Involuntary memory gave the past back to the narrator through the exact duplication in the present of a sensation that he had experienced in the past – a common sensation that allowed that past moment momentarily to re-emerge into the context of the present moment.

Similarly, the obscure impressions appear to be 'déjà-vu' even though he has never noticed them before, because their outlines duplicate characters in an inner book of unknown symbols carved in relief, which he stumbled on unconsciously when he encountered their double in lived experience.

> En somme, dans un cas comme dans l'autre, qu'il s'agît d'impressions comme celle que m'avait donnée la vue des clochers de Martinville, ou de réminiscences comme celle de l'inégalité des deux marches ou le goût de la madeleine, il fallait tâcher d'interpréter les sensations comme les signes d'autant de lois et d'idées, en essayant de penser, c'est à dire de faire sortir de la pénombre ce que j'avais senti, de le convertir en un équivalent spirituel ... qu'il s'agît de réminiscences dans le genre du bruit de la fourchette ou du goût de la madeleine, ou de ces vérités écrites à l'aide de figures dont j'essayais de chercher le sens dans ma tête où, clochers, herbes folles, elles composaient un grimoire compliqué et fleuri ...
> Quant au livre intérieur de signes inconnus (de signes en relief, semblait-il, que mon attention, explorant mon inconscient, allait chercher, heurtait, contournait, comme un plongeur qui sonde), pour la lecture desquels personne ne pouvait m'aider d'aucune règle, cette lecture consistait en un acte de création où nul ne peut nous suppléer ni même collaborer avec nous. (III, 878–9)

Like the past/present analogy engendered by an experience of involuntary memory, the obscure impressions signal a natural, metaphorical process.

The narrator perceives at this time a connection between the fashioning of a work of art from life experience and the rendering of an idea from an obscure impression: 'il fallait tâcher d'interpréter les sensations comme les signes d'autant de lois et d'idées, en essayant de penser, c'est à dire de faire sortir de la pénombre ce que j'avais senti, de le convertir en un équivalent spirituel. Or, ce moyen qui me paraissait le seul, qu'était-ce autre chose que faire une oeuvre d'art?' (III, 878–9). Just as he was not able to choose voluntarily the signs or impressions that life presented to him to decipher, so the narrator realizes that he is not free to decide how he shall create a work of art: the obscure impression intimates an idea because its shape duplicates that of a pre-existent idea outlined in the unknown book of symbols traced by life; similarly, his work of art is pre-existent in him and he is obliged to discover it:

Ainsi j'étais déjà arrivé à cette conclusion que nous ne sommes nullement libres devant l'oeuvre d'art, que nous ne la faisons pas à notre gré, mais que, pré-existant à nous, nous devons, à la fois parce qu'elle est nécessaire et cachée, et comme nous ferions pour une loi de la nature, la découvrir. Mais cette découverte que l'art pouvait nous faire faire, n'était-elle pas, au fond, celle de ce qui devrait nous être le plus précieux, et qui nous reste d'habitude à jamais inconnu, notre vrai vie, la réalité telle que nous l'avons sentie et qui diffère tellement de ce que nous croyons, que nous sommes emplis d'un tel bonheur quand un hasard nous apporte le souvenir véritable? (III, 881)

Before proceeding to tell us exactly how the work of art pre-existent in him may be drawn forth from life experience, the narrator describes one more experience of involuntary reminiscence: the resurrection of his younger self by his rediscovery, in the Guermantes' library, of *François le Champi* – a book by George Sand that he had read long ago in his childhood. As a result of his re-encounter with the novel, he comprehends that any object from the past re-encountered in the present brings with it multiple and different sensations: 'une chose que nous avons regardée autrefois, si nous la revoyons, nous rapporte, avec le regard que nous y avons posé, toutes les images qui le remplissaient alors' (III, 885). Because the reality of an object (in this case, the book) is not limited to the object itself, but includes the sights, sounds, and smells that are in any way associated with it, the narrator realizes the fallacy of 'realistic' literature: in its attempt to portray reality, it contents itself with describing a miserable abstract of lines and surfaces (III, 889), and takes for granted that the reality of the object is limited to the object itself. In fact, what constitutes reality is a certain connection between these immediate sensations and the memories that envelop us simultaneously with them: 'Une heure n'est pas qu'une heure, c'est un vase rempli de parfums, de sons, de projets et de climats. Ce que nous appelons la réalité est un certain rapport entre ces sensations et ces souvenirs qui nous entourent simultanément – rapport que supprime une simple vision cinématographique …' (III, 889). In order for a literary work to represent reality, therefore, it must reproduce the relationship between different objects that occurs naturally ('rapport unique que l'écrivain doit retrouver pour en enchaîner à jamais dans sa phrase les deux termes différents,' III, 889) and the only way a writer can duplicate that rapport in a work is through the use of metaphor – the illumination of a quality common to two sensations by linking them in an analogy, and thus extracting their common essence and reuniting them (III, 889).

After assuring us that the translation of 'reality' into a literary work is possible only through metaphor, the narrator investigates the materials or sources that give birth to a literary work, the methods by which these origins of writing are transformed into literature, and the relationship of art to life experience. He proclaims that the work of the artist and the function of art is to undo the heap of verbal concepts that form our 'false life' (the work of the spirit of imitation, our passions, our abstract intelligence) and to force us to travel back into the depths from which we originally came, where that which really existed lies unknown within us: 'c'est ce travail que l'art défera, c'est la marche en sens contraire, le retour aux profondeurs où ce qui a existé réellement gît inconnu de nous, qu'il nous fera suivre' (III, 896). We can perceive from this quotation that art has an affinity with the narrator's previously discussed experiences of involuntary memory – both effect a return to a previous reality. His experiences of involuntary memory allowed him to regain a moment of time in its pure state. Similarly, he now perceives that art catalyses the re-creation of one's true life, or rejuvenates one's true impressions of reality that were apparently irrevocably lost through their translation into the everyday language of habit and logic (III, 898).

The narrator realizes that the source materials for a work of art are his past life: 'Alors, moins éclatante sans doute que celle qui m'avait fait apercevoir que l'oeuvre d'art était le seul moyen de retrouver le Temps perdu, une nouvelle lumière se fit en moi. Et je compris que tous ces matériaux de l'oeuvre littéraire, c'était ma vie passée' (III, 899). Before reaching this conclusion, he discusses the means by which life experience is reduced and translated into literature. If we compare the metaphorical process as just experienced by the narrator to the process an artist employs to reduce life experience into general laws, we can see that the relationship between art and its source (life experience) is metaphorical in nature. Just as the 'obscure impressions' appeared to him to be signs of an idea, so he now realizes that the people and places in life are fragmentary reflections of a divinity or an idea. In order to restore to life (Albertine, Gilberte, Saint-Loup, Guermantes, Balbec, etc.) the true meaning stolen by the false life of habit, he realizes that he must detach himself from the individuals and translate them into generalities, which can then be expressed and conserved in a work of art: 'Il me fallait rendre aux moindres signes qui m'entouraient (Guermantes, Albertine, Gilberte, Saint-Loup, Balbec, etc.) leur sens que l'habitude leur avait fait perdre pour moi. Et quand nous aurons atteint la réalité, pour l'exprimer, pour la conserver nous écarterons ce qui est différent d'elle et que ne cesse de nous apporter la vitesse acquise de l'habitude' (III, 897).

The reduction of multiple life experiences into generalities is an essential step: in order to express and preserve reality, the artist must eliminate all the extraneous elements that continuously envelop everyday life:

> c'est le sentiment du général qui, dans l'écrivain futur, choisit lui-même ce qui est général et pourra entrer dans l'oeuvre d'art ... Il ne se souvient que du général. Par de tels accents, par de tels mouvements de physionomie, eussent-ils été vus dans sa plus lointaine enfance, la vie des autres était représentée en lui et, quand plus tard il écrirait, viendrait composer d'un mouvement d'épaules commun à beaucoup, vrai comme s'il était noté sur le cahier d'un anatomiste, mais ici pour exprimer une vérité psychologique, et emmanchant sur ses épaules un mouvement de cou fait par un autre, chacun ayant donné son instant de pose. (III, 900)

A writer's comparison of multiple characters and their consequent reduction into one general character that expresses one truth structurally resembles the narrator's previous comparison of all of his diverse experiences that engendered in him the same inexplicable happiness and their subsequent reduction into one revelation – the essence of things. By disengaging an internal essence common to externally different phenomena, both of these multiple-termed comparisons duplicate the metaphorical process.

During his analysis of his experiences of involuntary memory, the narrator suggested that such occurrences produced in him the same inexplicable happiness because they all disengaged a common essence, and they therefore all fed the 'being' in him which was only able to make itself known through its recognition of itself in its double – the essence of things. In a similar vein, he suggests that the reader and the text of a literary work are doubles whose reflective relationship allows their common truth to reveal itself: on reading the book, the reader reads himself, and by recognizing himself in the text, allows the truth of the text to reveal itself as such, and vice versa: 'chaque lecteur est, quand il lit, le propre lecteur de soi-même. L'ouvrage de l'écrivain n'est qu'une espèce d'instrument optique qu'il offre au lecteur afin de lui permettre de discerner ce que, sans ce livre, il n'eût peut-être pas vu en soi-même. La reconnaissance en soi-même, par le lecteur, de ce que dit le livre, est la preuve de la vérité de celui-ci, et vice versa ...' (III, 911).

Although the narrator does not draw a parallel between the translation of life into art and the reading of a book, their common binary structure and their similar effect (the revelation of a third reality which was not apparent except through the binary relationship) causes a macrometaphorical rapport to establish itself between these two processes which individually, are macrometaphorical in their own right. In the first case, the reduction of life experience into literary expression gives rise to a metaphor-like relationship between life and literature which allows us to perceive the true life of inexpressible impressions that elude the false life of thought, intellect, and habit. In the second case, the reader and the book disengage a common truth through the other's recognition of itself in its internal double.

Having reached the eighth level of the narrator's investigation, it is necessary to explore the common essential nature of the first and last link in the analytical chain which Marcel has just forged: involuntary memory experiences and the process of writing both give a second life to sentiments that had apparently ceased to exist (III, 905), but this second life is more than a moment of the past regained; it is a truth which transcends the component parts of the interaction that revealed it. In all eight links of the analytical chain of ideas expounded by the narrator – beginning with his examination of the nature of all of the experiences that produced in him the same inexplicable happiness, climaxing in his consequent discovery of the device of metaphor, and culminating in his realization of the means whereby life experience may translate itself into art – the narrator consistently employs a technique that reflects the metaphorical process. When considered as a whole unit, the eight succeeding levels of investigation constitute a serial superimposition of innately similar phenomena whose juxtaposition allows their common denominators to reveal themselves, even though the narrator does not articulate in all cases the exact nature of the resemblance. When examined individually, each link in the chain of ideas gives rise to a comparison of externally dissimilar terms whose innate similarity is clarified as a result of the comparison. Whether the comparison is conducted among several phenomena or in the context of a bipolar interaction, its effect is the same: it liberates the essential quality common to different sensations and re-establishes their innate relationship, in a connection that eludes expression through the language of logic.

Metaphor is not simply comparison, however. In order to understand the metaphorical process, we must also understand the conditions and forces which metaphor brings into play. All the comparisons made by Proust's narrator in the course of his investigation of the three 'intimations' and related experiences give rise to three interrelated conditions that are responsible for the revelation of the common essence shared by dissimilar phenomena: (1) the limitation of the field of observation through selection, (2) the ensuing self-recognition of reflected doubles in each other, and (3) the consequent play of repetition and difference. Paradoxically, it is the external differences not shared by internal reflected doubles which put into relief the essence common to them both. During an experience of involuntary memory, for example, the difference between the present scene and the distant scene engendered around the sensation common to the past and the present causes the present scene to shatter momentarily and to grapple with the past scene: 'Toujours, dans ces résurrections-là, le lieu lointain engendré autour de la sensation commune s'était accouplé un instant, comme un lutteur, au lieu actuel' (III, 874–5). The difference between the past moment experienced in its pure state in the present, and the past moment as remembered in the present and as experienced in the past causes the pure past moment to be a truly new experience. At first, the narrator thinks that he has regained a moment of past time, that he is repeating the same moment. Then he realizes that the resuscitated past moment is something common to the past and to the present; something more essential and therefore different from both of them (III, 874) that was not able to reveal itself until the past and present moments engaged themselves in a play of repetition and difference. Just as the past/present analogy extricated a pure moment of time which was truly extratemporal, the reader/book analogy disengages a truth that is common to, but also different from, the two phenomena whose relationship revealed it.

I have explored the common macrometaphorical structure of the past/present analogies experienced by the narrator, the translation of life experience into art, and the interaction of a reader with his book, and I have also investigated the metaphorical process and the forces to which it gives rise. I can now proceed to analyse *A la recherche du temps perdu* from a 'metaphorical' perspective, comparing structural devices which the novel employs with the mechanism of metaphor as described in *Le temps retrouvé*. The analysis will show that all aspects of the novel reflect one basic pattern – the metaphorical process – and will thus demonstrate that the structure of Proust's novel corresponds to the theory of art expounded by his narrator in *Le temps retrouvé* – that metaphor is the fundamental building block of a literary work.

PART TWO

A LA RECHERCHE DU TEMPS PERDU: THE TEXT AS MACROMETAPHOR

4 Structure as Macrometaphor

Proust's narrator tells us that the original idea behind everyday reality can be retrieved through the translation of life experience (the people, places, and ideas an author has encountered) into a work of art (III, 897). In order to reveal beneath the signs of life the innate reality of an idea which habit, passion, and intellect masked and distorted, a writer will reduce multiple life experiences into generalities and then translate them into a literary work, in which readers will see themselves because it is composed of general laws (see pp 24–5). The narrator realizes that a series of particular incidents in his own life – his love affairs – have naturally merged into one general law – the nature of love:

> Tous ces êtres qui m'avaient révélé des vérités et qui n'étaient plus, m'apparaissaient comme ayant vécu une vie qui n'avait profité qu'à moi, et comme s'ils étaient morts pour moi. Il était triste pour moi de penser que mon amour, auquel j'avais tant tenu, serait, dans mon livre, si dégagé d'un être que des lecteurs divers l'appliqueraient exactement à ce qu'ils avaient éprouvé pour d'autres femmes. Mais devais-je me scandaliser de cette infidélité posthume et que tel ou tel pût donner comme objet à mes sentiments des femmes inconnues, quand cette infidélité, cette division de l'amour entre plusieurs êtres, avait commencé de mon vivant et avant même que j'écrivisse? J'avais bien souffert successivement pour Gilberte, pour Mme de Guermantes, pour Alberteine. Successivement aussi je les avais oubliées, et seul mon amour dédié à des êtres différents avait été durable. (III, 902)

Following the method that he has suggested, we can complete the narrator's project and demonstrate how the multiple life experiences described by Marcel Proust in *A la recherche du temps perdu* merge into one basic pattern – metaphorical structure. When examining the 'natural' metaphorical processes[1] which led to the narrator's realization of the rule of metaphor and its intrinsic relationship to art and life, we saw that metaphor gives rise to a series of redoublings which build upon each other.[2] Explaining how Proust's novel illustrates the rule of metaphor as an existential figure at the heart of life, human reality, and art is an almost overwhelming task, as every word of the novel is metaphorical in nature insofar as it represents the displacement of sense between a signifier and its signified concept,[3] and the number of metaphorical relationships which the text engenders is thus infinite. Even when one limits the field of investigation to specific ideas, places, structures, and symbols which reflect the structure and effect of metaphor, one is still overwhelmed with material, as there is scarcely an incident, symbol, character, or idea introduced in Proust's novel that is not functionally metaphorical, either as a single unit or in combination with another phenomenon.

It is essential, therefore, that we select for analysis only the most prominent 'signposts' of the work (keeping in mind that the principles demonstrated by these predominant phenomena are reflected in the novel's subsidiary characters, ideas, imagery, and symbols), in order that we may perceive clearly the total symmetry of the novel, and not lose ourselves in the contemplation of composite elements, beautiful though they may be. Ideally, upon completion of our analysis, we would be able to schematize on a large sheet of paper the 'geometric metaphor'[4] traced by Proust's cross-referential images, characters, symbols, ideas, and structures, in order to illustrate how they structurally compose a geodesic labyrinth of repetitions of the same focal image – metaphorical structure.

Although metaphor may take the form of a comparison involving more than two terms, Proust's narrator equates the metaphorical process in its most basic form with the establishment of a binary opposition: ('la vérité ne commencera qu'au moment où l'écrivain prendra deux objets différents, posera leur rapport ...,' III, 889). In order to show, therefore, that the novel in its entirety constitutes a macrometaphor, we must look for binary oppositions built into the novel's architectonics, characterizations, symbols, ideas, and imagery.

After a cursory glance at the whole work, two poles of reference are paramount in the reader's mind: the narrator's assumption in the concluding pages of Book One of the novel (*Du côté de chez Swann*) that the past is irrevocably lost to him ('La réalité que j'avais connue n'existait plus ... le souvenir d'une certaine image n'est que le regret d'un certain instant; et les maisons, les routes, les avenues, sont fugitives, hélas! comme les années,' I, 427), and his jubilation in the last book (*Le temps retrouvé*) when he discovers that past time can be restored to him through the power of metaphor, or art: 'Alors, moins éclatante sans doute que celle qui m'avait fait apercevoir que l'oeuvre d'art était le seul moyen de retrouver le Temps perdu, une nouvelle lumière se fit en moi. Et je compris que tous ces matériaux de l'oeuvre littéraire, c'était ma vie passée' (III, 899). The title of the novel suggests that its subject of investigation is the search for lost time, while the title of the final volume of the novel intimates that the time which had previously been lost has now been found. Because 'time lost' and 'time regained' coincide with the beginning and the end of the novel, the structural placement of these concepts renders the totality of the novel a vast macrometaphor. The 'body' of the novel is thus comparable to the 'middle term' of a metaphorical phrase. The original manuscripts of *A la recherche du temps perdu* and some letters by Proust support this premise, as they provide evidence that the first and last volumes of the novel were written consecutively and the middle volumes were written later,[5] so that in the event of writing itself, the middle volumes were engendered from the polaric interaction of themes introduced in the first volume of the novel and consolidated in the last volume.[6]

The narrator's investigation of his 'intimation' experiences was conducted in *Le temps retrouvé* along two levels of comparison, which ultimately clarified each other. The primary level of his comparisons took the form of a spontaneous recall of all of the experiences that had produced in him a similar, inexplicable happiness. The recall of these experiences did not result from the work of his intelligence or any externally imposed criteria of selection that it could impose, but occurred spontaneously as these experiences summoned up each other through the intermediary of their common, essential quality – the inexplicable happiness which they all evoked:

> Mais c'est quelquefois au moment où tout nous semble perdu que l'avertissement arrive qui peut nous sauver; on a frappé à toutes les portes qui ne donnent sur rien, et la seule par où on peut entrer et qu'on aurait cherchée en vain pendant cent ans, on y heurte sans le savoir, et elle s'ouvre ... au moment où, me remettant d'aplomb, je posai mon pied sur un pavé qui était un peu moins élevé que le précédent, tout mon découragement s'évanouit devant la même félicité qu'à diverses époques de

ma vie m'avaient donnée la vue d'arbres que j'avais cru reconnaître dans une promenade en voiture autour de Balbec, la vue des clochers de Martinville, la saveur d'une madeleine trempée dans une infusion, tant d'autres sensations dont j'ai parlé et que les dernières oeuvres de Vinteuil m'avaient paru synthétiser ... Sans que j'eusse fait aucun raisonnement nouveau, trouvé aucun argument décisif, les difficultés, insolubles tout à l'heure, avaient perdu toute importance. (III, 866–7)

After the impression of inexplicable happiness had recalled to itself all experiences that engendered a similar effect, the narrator compared these experiences to each other in order to discern the nature of their similarity. His conscious comparison of one phenomenon to another, however, was only possible after these phenomena had spontaneously evoked each other through the intermediary of their common essential nature. In Chapters 2–3, we saw that the subterranean relationship of these different experiences is both the manifestation and the source of a 'natural' metaphorical process. Just as poetic metaphor consists of the combination of two terms in a single phrase (a comparison that is facilitated by the common essential quality which these terms share), a 'natural' metaphor results from the correspondence which links different phenomena whose common essential natures are analogous. Because these 'natural' metaphors may leap across vast distances in time and space, and dovetail symbols, ideas, and entities that are not necessarily connected causally, I described them as 'macrometaphors' (see pp 6, 11, 18).

The pattern traced by the introduction and development of characters, places, and ideas in Proust's novel reflects the order of introduction of material during the narrator's investigation of his 'natural' metaphorical experiences. Almost all of the main elements and the binary oppositions they bring into play are introduced to the reader in the first book of the novel, *Du côté de chez Swann*, in superimposed form. Although the narrator does not articulate immediately the internal connection that exists between the many characters, milieus, symbols, and ideas introduced at this time, their textual proximity intimates, as if through an unvoiced 'natural' metaphor, a common denominator which manifests itself more directly in succeeding books through a complex network of 'traditional' poetic analogies. This network takes form as the narrator compares diverse characters, symbols, places, and ideas. Through these cross-comparisons and the multilevelled play of reflected doubles that they engender, the common, internal essence of these diverse phenomena reveals itself. The intertwined analogies of Books Two–Seven thus reflect the inarticulate macrometaphors of Book One, which emerge from the textual superimposition of characters, symbols, and ideas, in the course of the text's unfolding.

In order to explicate successfully the macrometaphorical quality of the totality of *A la recherche du temps perdu*, our analysis must proceed through three distinct levels which duplicate those the narrator used in his analysis of the natural analogies he experienced. The first step of his inquiry into the nature of his past/present 'intimations' entailed the recognition of all the experiences in his life which had produced in him the same, inexplicable happiness. Similarly, the first step of this analysis of Proust's novelistic structure will be to enumerate the major elements introduced in *Du côté de chez Swann*, and to show how their close textual proximity intimates a common essence that is left unexpressed at this time. The second step of the narrator's investigation consisted of direct comparisons of different types of phenomena which produced in him the same feeling of inexplicable happiness. He first compared the three experiences of involuntary memory to each other, in order to discern clearly the nature of the common effect they gave rise to and the conditions which produced it. Next, he compared the experiences of involuntary memory to another group of phenomena – the obscure impressions – that also produced a feeling of inexplicable happiness in him, in order to clarify the nature of the common denominator which he intuitively felt that they possessed. Correspondingly, in the second step of this analysis of *A la recherche du temps perdu*, I shall examine the comparative cross-references the narrator establishes between different elements in Books Two–Seven, showing how the common denominator which is suggested through the textual superimposition of diverse phenomena in Book One (*Du côté de chez Swann*) is clarified through the establishment of analogies in succeeding books. The third and most essential step which led to the narrator's discovery of metaphor consisted of his recognition of a structure and effect common to all the various groups of natural analogies investigated, and to poetic metaphor. Thus, after examining the cross-references which the narrator establishes between the multiple elements introduced in the novel, the third step of this analysis will be to establish the common denominator which predominates after the multiple cross-references have reduced themselves into each other through their interplay. If the common denominator that reveals itself at the heart of all of the characters, symbols, places, and ideas examined in the novel is the metaphorical process, then the novel will illustrate that metaphor can function as the basic building block of a literary work.

BOOK ONE, PART I ('COMBRAY')

The first chapter of the first book of *A la recherche du temps perdu* consists primarily of an enumeration of many characters, experiences, and ideas which are not directly related to each other in any way except that they are all experienced by the narrator. Because of their close proximity in the text, however, the reader begins to perceive their unvoiced common structure and effect, which not only engenders a subliminal communication between these phenomena, but also clarifies the common, essential nature that gave rise to it.

In the first few pages of *Du côté de chez Swann*, Proust introduces in quick succession three events whose effect and basic structure all parallel metaphor, even though the narrator does not recognize their underlying relationship at this time: (1) the interaction of the narrator with the book that he is reading, (2) a description of the transformational effects induced by a sleep-like state, and (3) the transmutation of reality by the magic lantern. All the experiences examined entail a bipolar interaction, either in themselves or in their relationship to another entity.

The first paragraph describes the primary macrometaphor engendered by any literary work – the interaction of a reader with the text: 'je n'avais pas cessé en dormant de faire des réflexions sur ce que je venais de lire, mais ces réflexions avaient pris un tour un peu particulier; il me semblait que j'étais moi-même ce dont parlait l'ouvrage' (I, 3). The interaction of two realities – the narrator and his book – produces a fusion of these two realities; the narrator becomes the subject of his book, which is neither like the book nor its reader, but a new reality that transcends them both – a book about the reader. Similarly, the superimposition of his drifting memories onto the reality of the present moment – the room in which he has slept – causes that room to alter itself and become all the rooms in which he has ever slept in his life: 'Sa mémoire, la mémoire de ses côtes, de ses genoux, de ses épaules, lui présentait successivement plusieurs des chambres où il avait dormi, tandis qu'autour de lui les murs invisibles, changeant de place selon la forme de la pièce imaginée, tourbillonaient dans les ténèbres' (I, 6).

Shortly after presenting his reflections on the transformations induced by his semi-somnambulistic state, the narrator describes a physical device – the magic lantern – which produces a similar effect. The series of memory images conjured up in the narrator's mind erimposed themselves upon the reality of his room and successively transformed it into every room he had slept in. Similarly, the superimsition of the images projected by the magic lantern onto the curtains of his bedroom in Combray when he was young altered the reality of that room and rendered a new reality, which was a fusion of the pictorial coloured images of a distant Merovingian past with the objects of the present (I, 9–10).

The remainder of the characters, incidents, phenomena, and milieus introduced in the first chapter of Part I, Book One repeat over and over again the dual structure and transformational effect of the three experiences analysed above. When discussing his first encounter with the novel *François le Champi*, the narrator tells us that the work appeared to have the power of transforming the commonplace into the sublime. The mundane words and thoughts which comprise the story interacted to produce an intonation or strange, rhythmic utterance: 'Les procédés de narration destinés à exciter la curiosité ou l'attendrissement, certaines façons de dire qui éveillent l'inquiétude et la mélancolie, et qu'un lecteur un peu instruit reconnaît pour communs à beaucoup de romans, me paraissaient simplement ... une émanation troublante de l'essence particulière à François le Champi' (I, 41).

Although the narrator does not investigate at this time the structures that caused the commonplace words to transform themselves into a mysterious emanation, he does immediately describe – without articulating their common effect or establishing in any way a direct comparison – a series of other phenomena that also produce new realities. As an illustration of his conviction that past time may be restored to us through the intermediary of a physical object, for example, he recounts a Celtic myth which describes the liberation of dead souls through a person's chance encounter in the present with the object that houses the soul: 'Je trouve très raisonnable la croyance celtique que les âmes de ceux que nous avons perdus sont captives dans quelque être inférieur, dans une bête, un végétal, une chose inanimée, perdues en effet pour nous jusqu'au jour, qui pour beaucoup ne vient jamais, où nous nous trouvons passer près de l'arbre, entrer en possession de l'objet qui est leur prison. Alors elles tressaillent, nous appellent et sitôt que nous les avons reconnues, l'enchantement est brisé' (I, 44). Without the interaction between the two entities (the object containing the departed's soul, and the friend of the departed), the soul would not be released. Thus, the Celtic myth recounts a phenomenon that is purely metaphorical in nature.

The narrator recounts an incident of his own life – his involuntary memory of his past in Combray induced by the repetition in the present of an action first performed in the past – whose effect parallels the release of the soul of the departed through the chance encounter of the object which enclosed it. One cold day in winter, he accepts some tea from his mother, and she serves it with a 'madeleine.' Like a metaphorical phrase, the joining together of the tea and the madeleine gives rise to a third reality: 'D'où avait pu me venir cette puissante joie? Je sentais qu'elle était liée au goût du thé et du gâteau, mais qu'elle le dépassait infiniment, ne devait pas être de même nature' (I, 45). Although the narrator does not immediately define the source of the joy that the tea and the cake produces in him (ibid.), he finally identifies it with other cups of tea accompanied by madeleines that he used to take with his Aunt Léonie years earlier on Sunday mornings at Combray. He will not discover until the last volume of the novel the reason why the memory of Combray made him so happy; he does realize at this time that the repetition in the present of an action performed in the past resuscitates the memory of that past action and all the sights and sounds associated with it:

> Et comme dans ce jeu où les Japonais s'amusent à tremper dans un bol de procelaine rempli d'eau, de petits morceaux de papier jusque-là indistincts qui, à peine y sont-ils plongés, s'étirent, se contournent, se colorent, se différencient, deviennent des fleurs, des maisons, des personnages consistants et reconnaissables, de même maintenant toutes les fleurs de notre jardin et celles du parc de M. Swann, et les nymphéas de la Vivonne, et les bonnes gens du village et leurs petits logis et l'église et tout Combray et ses environs, tout cela qui prend forme et solidité, est sorti, ville et jardins, de ma tasse de thé. (I, 47–8)

This simile – utilized by Proust to illustrate the nature of the transcendental experience engendered by the tea and the madeleine – describes a phenomenon which is essentially metaphorical also: the paper used in the Japanese game exists in two states – a crumpled ball and an emergent, distinct form. Both states co-exist in one entity – the paper – just as two phenomena co-exist in the links of one poetic image (I, 47).

The imagery, phenomena and characters introduced in the second chapter of Part I ('Combray') reflect the structure and effect of the phenomena described in the first chapter. The lime blossoms of the tisane he shares with his Aunt Léonie recall in their nature the Japanese papers: the blossoms are a single entity that assumes two distinct appearances. In the process of drying, the leaves lost or altered their former appearance of green buds, and now suggest instead the most incongruous things: 'Les feuilles, ayant perdu ou changé leur aspect, avaient l'air des choses les plus disparates, d'une aile transparente de mouche, de l'envers blanc d'une étiquette, d'un pétale de rose, mais qui eussent été empilées, concassées ou tressées comme dans la confection d'un nid' (I, 51).

The lime blossoms – whose dual nature reflects the binary structure of metaphor – then become one part of a ceremony which unites two components (the taking of tea with madeleines) which recalled (in the narration of Chapter One) the whole of Combray to the narrator: 'Bientôt ma tante pouvait tremper dans l'infusion bouillante dont elle savourait le goût de feuille morte ou de fleur fanée une petite madeleine dont elle me tendait un morceau quand il était suffisamment amolli' (I, 52). One pole of the two-part ceremony is thus itself dual in nature, forming the structural pattern of the whole novel, which is primarily binary in nature and continually divides into smaller binary units.

Immediately following his description of the dual nature of the lime blossoms, the narrator sketches the portrait of the church of Combray – yet another entity whose component parts manifest the dual structure possessed by metaphor and all the other phenomena discussed above. As a result of the interaction of the light with their little panes of glass, the stained glass windows of the church transform themselves to represent multiple realities, in a manner that recalls the narrator's former description of the Japanese papers:

> Il y en avait un qui était un haut compartiment divisé en une centaine de petits vitraux rectangulaires où dominait le bleu, comme un grand jeu de cartes pareil à ceux qui devaient distraire le roi Charles VI; mais soit qu'un rayon eût brillé, soit que mon regard en bougeant eût promené à travers la verrière, tour à tour éteinte et rallumée, un mouvant et précieux incendie, l'instant d'après elle avait pris l'éclat changeant d'une traine de paon, puis elle tremblait et ondulait en une pluie flamboyante et fantastique qui dégouttait du haut de la voûte sombre et rocheuse, le long des parois humides. (I, 60)

Likewise, on the walls of the church, the colours of two tapestries have melted into one another, to add expression, light, and relief to the pictures: 'Deux tapisseries de haute lice représentaient le couronnement d'Esther ... auxquelles leurs couleurs, en fondant, avaient ajouté une expression, un relief, un éclairage' (I, 60–1). The apse of the church introduces into Proust's narrative an example of a lack of correspondence between external appearance and internal reality – a dichotomy which shall be one of the main subjects of investigation of the *Recherche:* 'L'abside de l'église de Combray peut-on vraiment en parler? ... le tout avait plus l'air d'un mur de prison que d'église' (I, 62). The church also produces in the narrator the same effect engendered by the tea and the madeleine: he tells us that the chance encounter in a three-cornered alley of a duplication of the same old crumbling wall with windows pierced in it like the apse of Combray causes the essence of the church – that of a dear, familiar friend – to be restored to him (I, 62–3). Bringing together two of the main cross-currents of Proust's investigation (past/present reminiscences, the dichotomy of appearance and reality), the church at Combray represents the common essential nature of these phenomena, which is recognized by the narrator years later, in *Le temps retrouvé*.

Like a metaphor, the Combray steeple is a bipartite structure whose components merge into each other. The steeple is characterized by the dual symmetry of pairs of windows which rise one above the other until they reach the spire itself, at which time the stony slopes draw together (I, 63–4). The effect engendered by the steeple also resembles the effect produced by metaphor: the narrator attributes to the spire some quality 'beyond the power of words' ('quelque chose d'ineffable,' I, 65).

After alluding to the artistic quality of the steeple of Saint-Hilaire and the common denominator that it shares with works of genius, the narrator explores more directly another parallel between life experience and art – the mirror resemblance of the pregnant kitchen girl in his Aunt Léonie's kitchen, and the allegorical figure of Charity in Giotto's frescoes. As a result of their similar appearances, the servant girl and the figure of Charity co-exist in a macrometaphorical relationship which gives rise to a total reversibility of their characteristics: the work of art, which is apparently an abstract entity, appears as much alive as the pregnant servant girl, while she herself seems to be an abstract personality who is scarcely less allegorical than the fresco (I, 82).

The narrator's observations on the mirror relationship of life and art as exemplified by the servant girl and Giotto's Charity is followed soon after by a comparison of novelistic time with actual time. His reflections once again assume the form of a bipolar comparison, similar to the structure of metaphor: the juxtaposition of dissimilars (in this case, the time of the novel versus the time of the real world) allows us to perceive new truths that would not be apparent without the opposition. The accelerated time of novels, for example, permits us to perceive things about real life that real life would not reveal to us, as the slow course of its development would prevent our perception of them (I, 85).

Although the narrator does not establish any connection between the life/novel dichotomy and the view from the top of the belfry in Combray (his next subject of investigation), there are structural parallels between the two occurrences which cause a metaphor-like correspondence to establish itself between them. He remarks that, from the top of the belfry, one can see places together that one is accustomed to seeing separately, with the result that the view from up there is like a fairy-tale (I, 106). Similarly, the life/novel parallel discussed above allows us to see in quick succession experiences that would take several years or even several lives to experience in reality. Thus, both experiences are like metaphors that bring together dissimilars not customarily associated with each other, and allow us to perceive new realities which transcend the components that engendered them.

The next few pages of Proust's text and my textual analysis are devoted largely to an exploration of the dichotomy of external appearance and internal reality – a key theme of the novel which was introduced through the narrator's description of the apse of Combray. In swift succession, superimposed upon one another in the text, Proust describes two characters – Legrandin and Vinteuil's daughter – and one natural phenomenon – the hawthorn blossoms – which are all characterized by a lack of correspondence between their external appearance and their internal reality. Mlle Vinteuil, the daughter of the composer whose music will later play a paramount role in revealing to the narrator the intrinsic relationship of metaphor and art – is a walking incarnation of metaphorical structure: she brings together in one entity (her own body) two dissimilar natures –her external self of a mannish, good-sort of woman, and her internal reality of a sensitive woman in tears. Both natures, we are told, occasionally reveal themselves simultaneously in the same face, as though one transparent picture was superimposed upon a different one: 'on voyait s'éclairer, se découper comme par transparence, sous la figure hommasse du 'bon diable,' les traits plus fins d'une jeune fille éplorée' (I, 113).

Immediately upon leaving the church where he has seen Mlle

Vinteuil, the narrator feels the bittersweet smell of almonds steal towards him from the hawthorn blossoms, and remarks that the colouring of this flower – which smells like something it is not – is dual, even though it first appears to be monochromatic. It consists of little spots of a creamier colour almost concealed beneath the dominant colour, like the sweetness of Mlle Vinteuil's cheeks beneath their freckles (I, 113).

Shortly after describing the dual nature of Mlle Vinteuil and the hawthorn blossoms, the narrator introduces us to two other dichotomous entities – the chicken prepared for dinner by Françoise, and Legrandin, an intellectual who is a friend of the family. The chicken, which is classified first as a 'filthy creature' (sale bête') in life, is transformed in death into a 'gold-embroidered chasuble' which is served up at dinner: 'au dîner du lendemain, par sa peau brodée d'or comme une chasuble et son jus précieux égoutté d'un ciboire' (I, 122). Like Mlle Vinteuil's internal, feminine nature which is hidden behind her boyish appearance, the other side of Legrandin's predominantly intellectual nature surfaces: while momentarily observing him being introduced to a woman, Marcel sees a base, sensual side of Legrandin he didn't know existed (I, 125).

Through a common disparity between external appearance and internal reality, a subterranean connection establishes itself between two dissimilar characters (Mlle Vinteuil and M. Legrandin) and two dissimilar phenomena (the apse of Combray and the hawthorn blossoms), even though the narrator articulates a link between only two of these – the hawthorn blossoms and Mlle Vinteuil's cheeks. The device that allows us to perceive this common denominator of dissimilars is macrometaphor, which, in this case, takes the form of a series of innately similar, externally different phenomena superimposed upon each other by means of their contiguous introduction in the text.

The dichotomous relationships of reader/text, past/present, art/life, exterior/interior that we have examined, and the binary structures which we have observed in characterizations and other phenomena introduced in 'Combray' all have as their macro-double the topographical and geographical bifurcation that characterizes Combray: in the neighbourhood are two ways or roads which the narrator and his parents take for their walks. These two ways are seemingly so diametrically opposed that members of the family actually have to leave the house by a different door according to the way they have chosen. The way towards Méséglise-la-Vineuse is called Swann's Way because it passes along the boundary of Swann's estate, and the other way is called the Guermantes' Way because it proceeds towards the Guermantes' estate (I, 134). Although the two ways are one of the primary macrometaphorical structures of the novel, it is difficult to establish immediately their essential metaphorical function, as the narrator stresses their total physical and spiritual separation: whereas the Méséglise Way comprises the finest view of a plain that one could see anywhere, the Guermantes' Way typifies river scenery (I, 134).

More important than the physical characteristics which separate them, however, is the distance which exists between the two ways in the narrator's mind: 'Mais surtout je mettais entre eux bien plus que leurs distances kilométriques, la distance qu'il y avait entre les deux parties de mon cerveau où je pensais à eux, une de ces distances dans l'esprit qui ne font pas qu'éloigner, qui séparent et mettent dans un autre plan' (I, 135). In spite of their apparently irrevocable separation, the narrator implies that the two ways are paradoxically united by their difference: 'je leur donnais, en les concevant ainsi comme deux entités, cette cohésion, cette unité qui n'appartiennent qu'aux créations de notre esprit' (I, 135). The narrator's concluding remarks about what the two ways did for him at the end of Chapter Two affirms their unity, and suggests their essential metaphorical nature: they make him feel several separate things at the same time, and invest his impressions with depth and foundation:

> Sans doute pour avoir à jamais indissolublement uni en moi des impressions différentes, rien que parce qu'ils me les avaient fait éprouver en même temps, le côté de Méséglise ou le côté de Guermantes m'ont exposé, pour l'avenir, à bien des déceptions et même à bien des fautes ... Mais par là même aussi, et en restant présents en celles de mes impressions d'aujourd'hui auxquelles ils peuvent se relier, ils leur donnent des assises, de la profondeur, une dimension de plus qu'aux autres. Ils leur ajoutent aussi un charme, une signification qui n'est que pour moi. (I, 185)

In the previous pages, I have analysed from a structural point of view an assortment of different phenomena, objects, characters, experiences, and places that are presented in Part I ('Combray') of the first book of the novel. Despite their externally dissimilar natures, all these phenomena manifest a common, dual structure and transformational effect, which resemble the structure and effect of metaphor as described by the narrator in the final volume of the novel – *Le temps retrouvé.* The superimposition of these diverse phenomena one upon the other in the text reveals their innate similitude, even though it is never voiced by the narrator, and consequently causes macrometaphorical correspondences to engender themselves between these entities and events.

BOOK ONE, PART II ('UN AMOUR DE SWANN')

The second part of *Du côté de chez Swann* ('Un amour de Swann') introduces themes and characters whose structures, effects, or essential natures internally reflect motifs introduced in Part I ('Combray'). The play of doubles which these two chapters engender cause them to function as the two terms of a macrometaphor.

The structure and effect of the Vinteuil Sonata, for example, closely resembles the structure of and the effect produced by the steeple of Combray and the madeleine dipped in tea. In 'Combray,' the narrator told us that the taste of the tea and the madeleine was an infinitely transcendental experience (I, 45), and that the steeple of Combray possessed some quality beyond the power of words (I, 65). Similarly, when Swann hears the Vinteuil Sonata for the second time, he remembers that it opened and expanded his soul (I, 209). Just as the tea and the madeleine produced in the narrator a feeling of inexplicable happiness (I, 45), so the Vinteuil Sonata leads Swann towards a state of happiness that is noble, unintelligible, but yet clearly indicated: 'D'un rythme lent elle le dirigeait ici d'abord, puis là, puis ailleurs, vers un bonheur noble, inintelligible et précis' (I, 210).

We saw previously that the steeple and the experience of the madeleine dipped in tea are both dual structures whose binary components and the effect to which they give rise reflect the structure and effect of metaphor. While paraphrasing some thoughts of Swann's about the Vinteuil Sonata, the narrator tells us that it is essentially a dialogue: 'Le beau dialogue que Swann entendit entre le piano et le violon au commencement du dernier morceau ... D'abord le piano solitaire se plaignit, comme un oiseau abandonné de sa compagne; le violon l'entendit, lui répondit comme d'un arbre voisin' (I, 351). This dialogue is compared to the original duality which existed at the beginning of the world: 'C'était comme au commencement du monde, comme s'il n'y avait encore eu qu'eux deux sur la terre, ou plutôt dans ce monde fermé à tout le reste, construit par la logique d'un créateur et où il ne serait jamais que tous les deux: cette sonate' (I, 352). The combination of two unlike entities in a metaphorical phrase gives rise to a movement of signification that brings into play all of the sights, sounds, and phenomena previously associated with each phenomenon. Similarly, the dialogue of violin and piano in the Vinteuil Sonata divides into multiple colours: 'Tel un arc-en-ciel, dont l'éclat faiblit, s'abaisse, puis se relève et, avant de s'éteindre, s'exalte un moment comme il n'avait pas encore fait: aux deux couleurs qu'elle avait jusque-là laissé paraître, elle ajouta d'autres cordes diaprées, toutes celles du prisme, et les fit chanter' (I, 352).

In 'Combray,' the narrator told us that the sight of steeples resembling the steeples of Combray caused memories of his past to surge up in him (I, 67). The repetition of the ceremony of the madeleine dipped in tea also caused memories of his childhood to be restored to him (I, 47–8). Correspondingly, in 'Un amour de Swann,' Swann discovers that hearing the Vinteuil Sonata causes his past to be reawakened in him and the essence of his former happiness with Odette to be recalled to him (I, 345).

The lack of correspondence between internal reality and external appearance – a theme previously explored in the narrator's descriptions of the apse of the church of Combray, the hawthorn blossoms, Vinteuil's daughter, and Legrandin – is reintroduced and further developed in 'Un amour de Swann,' through the depiction of Odette's apartment, the catleyas blossoms, and love. Swann discovers that the loneliness, coldness, and barren emptiness that characterize the external appearance of the neighbourhood where Odette lives contrast sharply with, and serve to add an air of mystery to, the warmth, flowers, and luxury which characterize the interior of her apartment (I, 219).

Just as the tea which was part of a dual-natured ceremony – the taking of the tea with a madeleine – was itself dual in nature, so the orchids that Odette keeps in her apartment further reflect the dichotomy of external appearance and internal reality which the physical aspects of the apartment brought into play. The catleyas – her favourite orchid – do not look like flowers at all, but rather like scraps of silk or satin (I, 221).

Love – the main subject of investigation of 'Un amour de Swann' – brings into play the dichotomy of external appearances and internal reality also. After his love affair has ended, Swann becomes aware that the circumstances of his love were not what they appeared to be. Swann's comparison of Odette's confessions about her casual, bisexual activities to the past that he thought that he alone shared with her causes him to perceive that the essential nature of their love was deception and falsehood, rather than the deep, unspeakable truth which he felt that it intimated to him (I, 372, 382).

The narrator's discussion of the physical resemblance of the pregnant servant girl to Giotto's 'Charity' indicated in 'Combray' that life and art may co-exist in a relationship of reflected doubles. This theme is repeated in 'Un amour de Swann' when Swann recognizes Odette's physical resemblance to the figure of Zipporah, Jethro's daughter, which is seen in one of the Sistine frescoes: 'elle frappa Swann par sa ressemblance avec cette figure de Zéphora, la fille de Jethro, qu'on voit dans une fresque de la chapelle Sixtine' (I, 222). We saw that the work of art (Giotto's Charity) – which is, by its very nature, an abstract entity – appeared to be as much alive as the pregnant servant girl, while she herself seemed to be an abstract personality who was scarcely less allegorical than the fresco (I, 82). In the comparison of Odette to Botticelli's figure 'Zipporah,' the metaphor-like relationship which exists between art and life is explored more extensively than in the first example. Whereas Giotto's 'Charity' and the pregnant servant girl illustrated the reflective rapport shared by life and art, Swann's comparison of Odette to a work of art illustrates the effect engendered by the bond which establishes itself between life and art through their common features. In *Le temps retrouvé*, the narrator tells us that metaphor allows us to perceive a new reality – an internal essence common to two externally dissimilar phenomena – which transcends the two terms whose superimposition allowed it to reveal itself. Similarly, Swann finds great pleasure in comparing the features of real-life people to those portrayed in historical portraits, as the comparison allows these individual features (of both the historic portrait and the modern real-life model) to take on a more general significance when uprooted and disembodied through the similarity between art and life (I, 223). Like a metaphor, the resemblance shared by a work of art and its real-life double gives rise to a transcendent effect: as a result of the common feature she shares with the Florentine painting, for example, the image of Odette is able to enter into a world of dreams (I, 224).

Although the motif of the 'two ways' (le Côté de Méséglise [de chez Swann] and le Côté de Guermantes) does not appear as such in 'Un amour de Swann,' the narrator introduces another bifurcation of milieus which recalls structurally the previous one. We were introduced previously to two distinct geographical locations which converged on the town of Combray; now we make the acquaintance of two rival social salons in Paris – the Guermantes' and the Verdurins' – frequented by Swann. Although Madame Verdurin likes to think that her salon totally avoids the pretentiousness and snobbish elitism that she equates with the salons of the old nobility, the narrator – through juxtaposed portraits of the two salons – allows the reader to perceive the unvoiced common denominators which transcend the external differences of the two social sets: the conversation at both salons is common, petty, and backbiting, the main topic of conversation being destructive portraits of members of the salon who are either absent or out of range of hearing. While Madame Verdurin slanders Swann in his absence, calling him a filthy creature ('sale bête,' I, 285), several of the guests of the Guermantes' social sphere (during the concert at St Euvertes) amuse themselves by speculating on the propriety of the activities of young Madame de Cambremer (I, 337). Swann views the guests at the concert at St Euvertes as 'stupid and absurd' (I, 344). Similarly, he condemns the guests of the Verdurin salon as 'the worst form of life' and 'the most degraded class of society' (I, 287). Like the 'two ways' discussed in 'Combray,' therefore, the two apparently distinct social salons converge as a result of their innate common natures.

Some of the main characters introduced in 'Un amour de Swann' reflect – in their responses and their natures – other characters previously introduced in 'Combray.' I have already mentioned that Swann reacts to the Vinteuil Sonata in the same manner that the narrator responds to the steeples and to the perfume of the madeleine dipped in tea. In this respect, the narrator and Swann are internal doubles whose common reaction not only establishes a rapport between them, but also engenders a subliminal communication between the experiences that produced the common reaction. We saw that Legrandin and Vinteuil's daughter possessed dual natures which occasionally manifested themselves simultaneously. Similarly, Swann discovers that Odette is capable of being two people at once: she shows one face to him while the other face – the one that is possibly unfaithful to him – rises up and momentarily peers through the first face (I, 302). Through her dual nature, Odette enters into a macrometaphorical relationship with the previously sketched characters of Vinteuil's daughter and Legrandin.

Because the major themes introduced in Part II ('Un amour de Swann') manifest an innate similarity to the themes and characters introduced in Part I ('Combray'), Parts I and II of Book One collectively function as a macrometaphor. When considered together, the diametrically opposed tone of the conclusions of Parts I and II reflect on a macro-scale the many binary oppositions introduced in Book One. Whereas the conclusion of 'Combray' is retrospectively positive – the narrator asserts that all the beautiful memories he has just narrated were restored to him by the perfume of a cup of tea (I, 186 – the conlusion of 'Un amour de Swann' is retrospectively negative: Swann realizes that he has wasted years of his life for, and experienced the greatest love of his life with, a woman who did not please him (I, 382).

BOOK ONE, PART III ('NOMS DE PAYS: LE NOM')

The three-part structure of *Du côté de chez Swann* resembles the structure and ensuing movement of signification of metaphor. Metaphor is essentially a three-part process: the joining together of two dissimilar phenomena in the links of one poetic phrase gives rise to a third reality that is born from the interaction of the two original components. Although Part III, 'Noms de Pays: le Nom,' does not categorically present itself as the 'essence' revealed by the juxtaposition of the themes of Parts I and II onto each other, it does develop two motifs – one of which was introduced in Part I and another which was introduced in Part II – that synopsize the main currents introduced in both chapters. In my analysis of 'Combray' (Part I), we saw that the majority of the phenomena described by the narrator gave rise to a transformational effect: sleep and the subconscious musings of memory, the magic lantern, the arrangement of words in novelistic form in *François le Champi*, the changing appearance of the lime blossoms in the tisane, the resuscitation of memories of Combray through the repetition in the present of an action associated with the past from which the memories sprang. Correspondingly, the first few pages of Part III describe the transformational effect produced by names: the narrator tells us that the names of places conjure up an imaginary aura that transforms the place itself and makes it different from anything that it could in reality be (I, 387). The transformational effect engendered by the place names themselves – independent of the geographical location they designate – repeats the mysterious effect produced by the name *François le Champi* in Part I, mirrors the transformational effect arising from all of the other phenomena discussed in 'Combray,' and also duplicates the transformatory effect engendered by love, which was the primary theme of part II ('Un amour de Swann'): Swann, when in love, began to realize that he was no longer the same person, that love transformed him into a being other than his usual self (I, 228). During the second half of the third chapter, the narrator falls in love with Gilberte and repeats actions and feelings exhibited by Swann in Part II, when he fell in love with Odette. Just as Swann previously embellished the image of Odette by comparing her to a Botticelli painting, so the narrator now associates Gilberte with a page by Bergotte upon the beauty of old myths from which Racine drew inspiration (I, 410).

The main theme of Part I (transformational effects produced by a series of diverse but structurally related phenomena) and the primary topic of Part II (the effect of love) converge, therefore, in one short chapter of fifty pages. It is necessary to stress at this time that this convergence of themes is never voiced by the narrator, and is apparent only through the textual contiguity of Parts I, II, and III. Neither is there any resolution arising from the interaction of these three chapters with each other: Part III closes on a strong negative note – time is irrevocably lost – which is diametrically opposed to the equally strong positive conclusion of Part I – that time has been restored to him through a cup of tea. This binary opposition ('time regained/time lost') functions as one pole of the primary macrometaphor of the *Recherche*, which embraces all previously mentioned, internally related dichotomies introduced in Book One, gives rise to new reflections upon these themes in Books Two–Seven, and ultimately finds its mirror reversal ('time lost/time regained') in *Le temps retrouvé*.

5 Repetition and Cross-Referentiality as Macrometaphor

In the course of the recognition and expansion of the primary themes in Books Two–Seven, Proust frequently compares one motif to another one, and thereby reaffirms through analogy the internal similarities that were intimated macrometaphorically through textual contiguity in Book One. I shall trace the repetition, expansion, and cross-referentiality of some of the major landmarks, milieus, characters, works of art, symbols, ideas, and natural phenomena that recur in the *Recherche*, in order to achieve a better understanding of the overall structure of the novel as a labyrinth of multiple reflections of a common structure: internal repetitions with external differences which, through textual contiguity and cross-referentiality, reveal their common essential nature – the metaphorical process.

READER/TEXT/METAPHOR

During the analysis of Part 1, Book One ('Combray'), we saw that the first paragraph of *A la recherche du temps perdu* describes a relationship between the narrator and the book he is reading, which is essentially metaphorical in its structure and effect (see p 36). Proust introduces the dichotomy of 'book/reader' one more time during *Du côté de chez Swann*: while reading in his hideaway in the garden, the young narrator first admires the setting depicted by a novel, then imagines himself with an imaginary woman whom he loves, and lastly, envisions himself and the woman transposed into the setting of the novel (1, 86, 90). Like the first incident alluded to, the narrator's experience consists primarily of a fusion of himself with his book that engenders a new perception of reality which is different from, but common to, the two primary phenomena that engendered it.

Although the investigation of the reader/book alliance would appear to be a primary consideration of the novel, Proust does not mention it again until the concluding pages of *Le temps retrouvé*, wherein his narrator describes the book as a sort of optical instrument that permits a reader to read himself (III, 911) by virtue of a common essence shared with the book which causes them to engage in a play of reflected doubles. Like the first reader/book interaction discussed, the reader/book relationship described in *le temps retrouvé* constitutes a macrometaphor (see pp 25–6).

As a result of their placement in the book – the first mention of the reader/book duality occurring on the first page of the novel with the second allusion occurring in the concluding pages – the narrator's discussions of this fundamental relationship correspond structurally to the macrometaphorical signification that spans the totality of the novel – time lost/time regained. The duality of reader/text presented in the book also forms a macrometaphorical relationship with its reflection outside the book – the union of the reader of *A la recherche du temps perdu* with the novel itself.

During the analysis of 'Combray,' we saw that unvoiced, subterranean connections (macrometaphors) arise between the reader/book dichotomy and all other binary relationships explored in the text, through their common bipolar architectonics and their ensuing transcendent effect. One description of the process of reading establishes a connection between the act of reading and the duality of interior/exterior: reading is associated with an incessant movement from the 'outside' to the 'inside' towards the discovery of truth: 'Après cette croyance centrale qui, pendant ma lecture, exécutait d'incessants mouvements du dedans au dehors, vers la découverte de la vérité, venaient les émotions que me donnait l'action à laquelle je prenais part, car ces après-midi-là était plus remplis d'événements dramatiques que ne l'est souvent toute une vie' (I, 84). This implied relationship between reading and an exterior/interior movement is sufficient to catalyse a macrometaphorical link between the act of reading and the many phenomena, characters, and symbols in which external appearance and internal reality differ.

EXTERIOR/INTERIOR/METAPHOR

The difference between external appearance and internal reality is explored extensively in all seven books of the novel in relation to several milieus (Odette's apartment, Book One; the Hôtel de Maineville, Book Four; Jupien's establishment, Book Seven), in relation to the majority of the characterizations (Vinteuil's daughter, Legrandin,

Saint-Loup, Jupien, Octave, Françoise, Gilberte, Odette, the Verdurins, Elstir, Mme de Villeparisis, Charlus, Rachel, Albertine, Morel, Andrée, Mme de Guermantes), as well as in the recurring images linking flowers and homosexuality: the condition underlying the disparity between the external and internal reality of most of the characters. Above all, the contrast of external appearance and internal reality is at the heart of the narrator's discovery and investigation of the metaphorical process. Through the 'natural' metaphors that life presented to him (the three intimations, the obscure impressions, the resuscitation of his past self through the re-encounter in the present of a book from his past) the narrator realizes that the reality of an object is not its external appearance, but a certain internal rapport which exists between itself and other phenomena (III, 889). He comprehends that a rapport can exist between externally dissimilar objects because of an internal similarity that is able to reveal itself as such through a metaphor-like superimposition or contiguity of these phenomena. The bipolarity of exterior/interior, therefore, is at the heart of the metaphorical process.

If the bipolarity of exterior/interior is the common denominator shared by many diverse characters, milieus, and other phenomena described in the novel, then this internal connection between dissimilars will cause them to enter into a multilevelled, macrometaphorical rapport with each other, and with the metaphorical process. During the course of his novel, Proust introduces the reader to three different houses – separated from each other in novelistic time and space – which are all characterized by a disparity between their external appearance and internal reality: Odette's apartment (Book One), the Hôtel de Maineville (Book Four), and Jupien's establishment (Book Seven). We saw previously, during the analysis of 'Un amour de Swann,' that the neighbourhood where Odette's apartment is located is dark, sinister, and bleak, in contrast to the interior of the apartment itself, which is warm, sensuous, and luxurious (I, 219–20). This disparity repeats itself in the external appearance and internal reality of the Hôtel de Maineville, which is the subject of a little scenario the narrator witnesses during one of his rides along the 'transatlantique' – the railway to La Raspellière: a stranger – who is looking for a hotel of impeccable taste to which he can invite his guests – sees a 'palace' (the Hôtel de Maineville) and never suspects that it is a house of prostitution. Instead, he comically insists that Mme Cottard must show him through it, for he thinks that she must have visited it often, as it is the perfect setting for her (II, 1075–6).

In *Le temps retrouvé*, the narrator commits a similar error when he comes upon a busy, prosperous-looking hotel in the midst of a quarter characterized by poverty, dereliction, and fear. From the assortment of military people entering and leaving the hotel, the narrator first assumes that it must be a meeting place for spies. After overhearing a conversation conducted between two patrons, he next decides that the hotel is soon to be the scene of a bloody murder and he must contact the police. After meeting Jupien and occultly seeing M. de Charlus being beaten by two 'ruffians,' however, the narrator finally understands the true nature of the establishment: it is a brothel offering special services to homosexuals.

The lack of correspondence between the external appearance and internal reality of these three establishments would not be especially remarkable were it not for the fact that the duality manifested by the buildings is reflected in the natures of the characters associated with them. Swann discovers that Odette, like her residence, has two distinct personalities: the one that she shows to him, and her other side, which he learns of through her confessions to him (I, 362–3, 370–1). Similarly, the Hôtel de Maineville is introduced to the reader towards the end of *Sodome et Gomorrhe*, whose primary theme is homosexuality, and in which the existence of that condition in M. de Charlus and some of the other characters is revealed. The second hotel mentioned above – Jupien's establishment – is frequented by homosexuals also. In both cases, the hotel's internal reality is different from the image it projects externally, just as the external appearance of a homosexual and the sexual signals which this appearance transmits differs from his internal reality as revealed by his sexual preferences.

The majority of the characters depicted in the novel manifest a similar lack of correspondence between their external appearance and their internal reality. In the course of the structural analysis of 'Combray,' we saw that an exterior/interior duality characterizes Vinteuil's daughter, who is a mannish sort of woman on the outside and a woman in tears on the inside, and Legrandin, whose intellectual, external shell occasionally breaks to reveal another contradictory nature of base sensuality (see pp 41–2). I subsequently noted that the dual nature manifested by Vinteuil's daughter and Legrandin repeats itself in Odette, in 'Un amour de Swann.'

Saint-Loup, who is first introduced to us in *A l'ombre des jeunes filles en fleurs*, is characterized at first by a cold manner diametrically opposed to the warm, sensitive, inquisitive nature he displays to the narrator the day after his introduction (I, 732). In the course of the

novel, Saint-Loup's duality shows itself in other facets of his personality. In *La fugitive*, for example, the narrator inadvertently overhears a conversation that Saint-Loup is having with a servant, in which he counsels the other man how to cause the dismissal of a fellow servant. The narrator cannot believe that advice so cruel and Machiavellian came from the mouth of a person he regarded as so good and so tenderhearted (III, 470–1). The disparity between Saint-Loup's external appearance and internal reality reflects itself in his sexual life also: whereas Saint-Loup's affair with Rachel and his marriage with Gilberte led the narrator to believe that Saint-Loup was heterosexual, he later discovers – through some love letters found by Gilberte – that Saint-Loup has had an affair with Morel, his uncle's former 'friend' (III, 678).

Odette, Gilberte, Albertine, Andrée, Jupien, and Charlus (to name only a few!) manifest a similar hidden, homosexual tendency. Odette, whose dual personality I have already commented upon, is also occasionally a lesbian: she admits to Swann that she may have indulged in lesbian activities three or four times without realizing what she was doing (I, 363). In the case of Gilberte, her homosexuality is implied, rather than directly stated: after being plagued by doubts about Gilberte's faithfulness to him, the narrator discovers the apparent truth from her maid – that she is seeing another man. Years later, he discovers the real truth: the man he had seen her walking with down the Champs Elysées was Lea in male attire (III, 695). This implied bisexual nature which the narrator does not discover in Gilberte until late in his life (the last volume of the novel) reflects the aura of duplicity she communicated to him the first time that he met her when they were children. Years later, he wonders whether or not the 'indecent gesture' which Gilberte first addressed to him did not express her real self, even though this gesture – both at the time and even presently – appeared to be totally incongruous with everything that he supposed her reality to be (I, 141).

Correspondingly, when he first meets Albertine in person, he is struck by the disparity between her reality and what he imagined her to be when he saw her from a distance. After he gets to know her, he is even more confused, because her appearance and personality change constantly as his point of perspective changes. In turn, the series of contradictory images that her appearance presents to him reflect the series of contradictory verbal statements that she makes as their relationship unfolds (III, 146). Evidence is given many times over that Albertine is one of those people with many hidden surfaces: ('N'avais-

je pas deviné en Albertine une de ces filles sous l'enveloppe charnelle desquelles palpitent plus d'êtres cachés, je ne dis pas que dans un jeu de cartes encore dans sa boîte, que dans une cathédrale fermée ou un théâtre avant qu'on n'y entre, mais que dans la foule immense et renouvelée? Non pas seulement tant d'êtres, mais le désir, le souvenir voluptueux, l'inquiète recherche de tant d'êtres,' (III, 94). Thus, it appears not all out of character for Albertine that he should discover after her death that she was in fact guilty of the homosexual tendencies of which he had always suspected her. When he compares Aimé's written reports about Albertine's lesbian adventures with the previous doubts he had formulated about her behaviour through his own observation, he discovers a girl different from the one he thought he knew when he was living with her (III, 525).

Perhaps the most clearly defined and best-developed example of the dual-natured characters that the novel presents to us is the Baron de Charlus. Almost from the time that we are introduced to him, we are made aware of a lack of correspondence between the extra-masculine, exterior nature that he attempts to project, and his innately feminine nature which Madame de Guermantes laughingly terms his 'female heart' ('C'est un coeur de femme, Mémé,' II, 508). The disparity between Charlus' interior and exterior (which is sensed by some of his associates and strongly denied by others – M. de Guermantes, for example, protests that his wife's opinion of Charlus is absurd, that there is no one more virile than he is, II, 508) is irrevocably affirmed when the narrator secretly observes M. de Charlus engaged in a homosexual act with Jupien (II, 604). This incongruity between Charlus' external and internal reality is reflected in the diverse, conflicting opinions that his friends and associates express about him. Wheras he is prized and honoured for his sharp intellect and social finesse at the Guermantes' salon, he is regarded as stupid, interfering, and intolerable at the Verdurins' (II, 1090).

In the final volumes of the novel, Charlus is not only remarkable for the bipolar nature of his personality, but for the profound change that his duality has produced in his external appearance: his previously hidden nature manifests itself on the surface. In *La prisonnière*, the narrator remarks that M. de Charlus' constant attempts to conceal his homosexuality have had quite the opposite effect, and it now overflows in all of his speech (III, 207); in *Le temps retrouvé*, he re-encounters M. de Charlus and realizes that his previous mask has become his reality (III, 763). The inversion of exterior appearance and internal reality that M. de Charlus represents has a profound affinity with the effect produced by metaphor: in both cases, a combination of dissimilar phenomena (man/woman; the two terms of a metaphor) in one entity (Charlus; metaphor) causes the essential nature of the bipolar terms to reveal itself.

The duality of external appearance and internal reality manifested by all of the major characters of the novel – Odette, Charlus, Saint-Loup, Albertine, Gilberte, Vinteuil's daughter – is reflected in several minor characters, and also in the body/spirit, male/female polarities that characterize all human beings.

Octave, the protégé of the Verdurin salon who is introduced to us in *Albertine disparue*, is described as a coarse brute on the outside who must in reality be a sensitive man of genius on the inside, as the best-qualified critics regard his work as of capital importance (III, 606). His patrons – the Verdurins – are not of one cloth either. We usually see them portrayed as totally egocentric (they demand absolute fidelity from their friends) and coldly devoid of any true human feelings: although the Princess Sherbatoff was apparently one of their 'dear' friends, news of her death is regarded by the Verdurins as a bothersome disturbance that could ruin their party, which must go on (III, 227–8). On the other hand, they do have a good, generous side: learning that Saniette has lost all of his money and is now penniless, the Verdurins decide to support him anonymously with 10,000 francs a year. This discovery teaches Marcel that he ought never to judge people solely on the grounds of an unkind action, for one does not know all the good that at other moments they may have done (III, 326).

Through Jupien, the life-long friend of Charlus, the narrator realized very early in his life that reality may be different from appearance: Jupien gave the narrator information allowing him to perceive that his relationship with Françoise was different from what he thought it was. Whereas he always felt that Françoise adored him, he learns that she once told Jupien that he was not worth the piece of rope that it would take to hang him (II, 66). It is doubly significant that Jupien should be the one to reveal this basic truth about the disparity between appearance and reality to the narrator, as Jupien is another walking incarnation of this bipolarity: in the first pages of *Sodome et Gomorrhe*, we learn that Charlus and Jupien are, as Françoise ironically tells us later, 'the same sort of people' ('Il y a beau avoir des riches et des pauvres misérables, ça ne fait rien pour la nature. Le baron et Jupien, c'est bien le même genre de personnes,' II, 630).

Andrée, Albertine's closest female friend, has homosexual inclinations also: during her confessions to the narrator after Albertine's death, she tells him that she had spent many happy hours with Albertine, who was 'si caressante, si passionnée' (III, 599). As with most of the other characters discussed above, Andrée's sexual duality reflects the nature of her entire personality. The narrator tells us that he had become aware of Andrée's dual nature years earlier, when he heard her maliciously slander a young man of his acquaintance, in order to cause the narrator displeasure: 'Ainsi, telle qu'elle était devenue (et même sans ses haines courtes et folles), je n'aurais pas désiré la voir, ne fût-ce qu'à cause de cette malveillante susceptibilité qui entourait d'une ceinture aigre et glaciale sa vraie nature plus chaleureuse et meilleure' (III, 60).

Morel, Charlus' protégé, manifests a similar contradictory nature. Even the social insult he has suffered from Morel, coupled with reports he has heard about Morel's venal relations with M. de Charlus (II, 1032), do not permit the narrator to judge him as a totally base character because, although frequently conveying the impression of 'une méchanceté absolue,' Morel is sometimes capable of 'une gentillesse véritable' (II, 1031). Thus, the narrator compares Morel's character to an old book of the Middle Ages: 'mais ce caractère n'était pas si uniformément laid, et était plein de contradictions. Il ressemblait à un vieux livre du moyen âge, plein d'erreurs, de traditions absurdes, d'obscenités, il était extraordinairement composite' (II, 1032). Rachel is another 'dichotomous' personality: her present reality as Saint-Loup's mistress contradicts her previous reality as a common prostitute in a brothel (II, 157–8).

As well as describing the dual natures of specific individuals, the narrator alludes twice in the novel to what he perceives as the dichotomous nature of any personality, arising from the body/spirit duality that characterizes our 'being,' and from the mixture of sexual characteristics that even the most normal people demonstrate. In *Le côté de Guermantes*, his grandmother's illness makes the narrator realize that we live not alone but chained to a creature of a different kingdom – our body: 'C'est dans la maladie que nous rendons compte que nous ne vivons pas seuls, mais enchaînés à un être d'un regne différent, dont les abîmes nous séparent, qui ne nous connaît pas et duquel il est impossible de nous faire connaître: notre corps' (II, 298). In *Sodome et Gomorrhe,* he briefly comments on the exchange of male and female characteristics which can occur within a male-female sexual union, and observes that a woman married to a latent homosexual will frequently allow the masculine side of her nature to surface in order to please her husband. He stresses, however, that even the most normal couples end up resembling each other through an exchange of qualities (II, 646).

In the preceding pages, I have examined the dual personalities of thirteen distinct characters and three milieus in which external appearance and internal reality differ. Even if Proust did not compare any of these diverse milieus and personalities to each other, the common nature that they share would be sufficient to establish macrometaphorical relationships between them. Because almost every character in the novel possesses a dual nature, the superimposition of one character's nature upon the other in the text tends to disengage a general law about all of them: the disparity between external appearance and internal reality. The bipolarities of body/spirit and male/female that characterize the reality of any human being as Proust sees it, reflect the exterior/interior dissonance manifested by the characters presented in the novel, and encourage the reader to conclude that the inherent primary reality of any human being is a duality, like the structure of metaphor.[1]

For some of the characters, the common essential nature that they possess is also revealed to the reader through intertwined, cross-referential analogies: by comparing one character to another, and then that character to another one, the narrator occasionally accomplishes directly what the textual superimposition of one character's nature upon the other accomplished macrometaphorically through the diachronic unfolding of the text: he reduces multiple characters to one essential model. In *Sodome et Gomorrhe*, for example, the narrator notices a marked resemblance between the speech and actions of Morel, and the mannerisms and words spoken previously by Rachel, Saint-Loup's mistress: 'Non seulement il me parlait exactement comme autrefois Rachel, la maîtresse de Saint-Loup, mais encore, d'après ce que me répétait M. de Charlus, lui disait de moi, en mon absence, les mêmes choses que Rachel disait de moi à Robert. Enfin M. de Charlus me disait: "Il vous aime beaucoup," comme Robert: "Elle t'aime beaucoup"' (II, 1060). In *Le temps retrouvé*, Saint-Loup notices a physical resemblance between Rachel and Gilberte: '"Ne trouves-tu pas qu'elle a quelque chose de Rachel?" me disait-il. Et en effet j'avais été frappé d'une vague ressemblance qu'on pouvait à la rigueur trouver maintenant entre elles' (III, 702). The narrator compares Gilberte to Albertine: he realizes that the internal reality of both women revealed itself to him in the first impression he had of them: 'Et tout d'un coup, je me dis que la vraie Gilberte, la vraie Albertine, c'était peut-être celles qui s'étaient au premier instant livrées dans leur regard, l'une devant la haie d'épines roses, l'autre sur la plage' (III, 694). Albertine is also compared to Odette: upon hearing Albertine's confirmation that she has never indulged in any lesbian affairs, the narrator remembers a similar affirmation once offered to Swann by Odette, which later proved to be false: 'Aussi la douceur apportée par les affirmations d'Albertine faillit-elle en être compromise un moment parce que je me rappelai l'histoire d'Odette' (II, 834).

We are also told that Saint-Loup resembles his uncle, the Baron de Charlus. In the first books of the novel, M. de Charlus is portrayed as a man who disdains the company of other men and associates only with women at social gatherings: 'M. de Charlus fut bientôt assis à côté de Mme Swann. Dans toutes les réunions où il se trouvait, dédaigneux avec les hommes, courtisé par les femmes, il avait vite fait d'aller faire corps avec la plus élégante, de la toilette de laquelle il se sentait empanaché' (II, 267). His behaviour is revealed as poignantly ironic when we discover shortly after in *Sodome et Gomorrhe* that he is a homosexual. Years later, in *La Fugitive*, Saint-Loup repeats his uncle's behaviour patterns. After his marriage to Gilberte, he goes about openly with women whom everyone suspects are his mistresses, but in fact, he is having an affair with Morel, his uncle's former friend (III, 678). These direct comparisons between characters involving only one or two facets of the personalities in question reinforce the sense of common realities disengaged by the juxtaposition of one character upon another in the text.

HOMOSEXUALITY/FLOWERS/WRITING/METAPHOR

During the investigation of the exterior/interior duality, we saw that all characters of the novel manifested a bipolar nature, and that in the majority of cases, their personality traits mirrored a corresponding duality in their sexual habits, as most of them were homosexuals. I concluded that the superimposition of these externally dissimilar, innately similar natures one upon the other in the text tended – through a macrometaphorical process – to disengage a general law about them: that a bipolar nature or duality was their common essential nature. Although the narrator of the *Recherche* never directly makes the connection for us, the structure of the human personality, as depicted in *A la recherche du temps perdu*, resembles the structure of metaphor because the inherent primary reality of both of them is bipolar.

In 'Exterior/Interior/Metaphor' I alluded to the duality that homosexuality implied, but did not investigate in depth the nature of homosexuality as depicted in the novel or the correspondences between homosexuality, writing, art, and metaphor in the text. The narrator never categorically establishes a parallel between the nature of homosexuality and the structure of metaphor, but he does tell us in *La prisonnière* that two of the homosexual unions depicted in the novel function as transversals which allow one work of art – the Vinteuil Septet – to become famous (III, 264). As the last works of Vinteuil are a 'synthesis' of the sensations (III, 866) that lead the narrator to an understanding of the power of art – its ability to transcend everyday reality and to restore 'lost time' to us – the two homosexual unions referred to are integral links in the chain of resemblances leading the narrator to perceive that power. The homosexual relationship of Mlle Vinteuil and her girlfriend resulted in the translation of M. Vinteuil's illegible hieroglyphic manuscripts into a legible form. In turn, the muscial masterpiece brought to light through the diligence of Mlle de Vinteuil's female lover is played and presented to foremost members of the art public by Morel, who has a relationship with Charlus which 'parallels' that which existed between Mlle Vinteuil and her friend (III, 264), and who is given the opportunity to play to this elite audience because his relationship with the Baron made the latter anxious to ensure the artistic triumphs of his friend (III, 264).

Before commencing the discussion of the transversal effect that Mlle Vinteuil's friend and Morel had on the realization of a great work of art (the Vinteuil Septet), the narrator alluded to the profound union that seems to exist between genius and homosexuality: 'Au reste, ce contraste apparent, cette union profonde entre le génie (le talent aussi, et même la vertu) et la gaine des vices où, comme il était arrivé pour Vinteuil, il est si fréquemment contenu, conservé, étaient lisibles, comme en une vulgaire allégorie, dans la réunion même des invités au milieu desquels je me retrouvai quand la musique fut finie' (III, 264). Instrumental as the two homosexual relationships may have been as agents allowing the narrator to perceive the transcendent power of art, they do not in themselves establish any innate rapport between the nature of homosexuality and the nature of art. However, a series of allegorical comparisons involving the fertilization of flowers as one term of the analogy suggest, through their common denominator, structural similarities shared by homosexuality, writing, the translation of life experience into art, and metaphor.

In *Sodome et Gomorrhe*, the chance fertilization of a flower by a honeybee is compared to a casual homosexual encounter. While waiting at the staircase window in order to watch the arrival of the Duc and Duchesse of Guermantes, the narrator notices a plant growing in the courtyard awaiting the unlikely visit of an insect to fertilize it. He doesn't get to see the fertilization, but he does witness another union whose consummation he feels to be equally as miraculous and comparable in every way to the contingent meeting of a bee with the pistil of a flower: the meeting of two homosexuals (Charlus and Jupien) who recognize each other as such and proceed immediately to mate. Jupien is compared to a plant and Charlus is likened to the bee who – through the miracle of a chance occurrence – meets the right, expectant flower: 'Or, Jupien, perdant aussitôt l'air humble et bon que je lui avais toujours connu, avait – en symétrie parfaite avec le baron – redressé la tête, donnait à sa taille un port avantageux, posait avec une impertinence grotesque son poing sur la hanche, faisait saillir son derrière, prenait des poses avec la coquetterie qu'aurait pu avoir l'orchidée pour le bourdon providentiellement survenu' (II, 604).

Having established his comparison between a homosexual union and the fertilization of an expectant flower, the narrator concludes his discussion with the statement that the exceptional creatures (homosexuals) with whom he has just commiserated are a vast crowd, for a reason to be disclosed at the end of the book: 'contrairement à ce que je croyais dans la cour où je venais de voir Jupien tourner autour de M. de Charlus comme l'orchidée faire des avances au bourdon, ces êtres d'exception que l'on plaint sont une foule, ainsi qu'on le verra au cours de cet ouvrage, pour une raison qui ne sera dévoilée qu'à la fin, et se plaignent eux-mêmes d'être plutôt trop nombreux que trop peu' (II, 631). Arriving at the end of the work, some readers may be disappointed to discover that the narrator never discloses directly what he promised to reveal earlier in the work: there is no paragraph that explains why the 'orchids' and the 'bees' are such a vast crowd. What we do find strewn along the course of the work, however, are several reiterations of the 'plant metaphor' applied to a series of different phenomena – Bergotte's writings, Albertine, Morel's writings, inverse and normal sexual behaviour, the narrator's life and its translation into a work of art – which are subterraneously connected one to the other through the common metaphor applied to all of them. We surmise, therefore, that the narrator's promised response articulates itself through the macrometaphorical process engendered by the repeated image, and by distilling the common essence uniting all of these diverse phenomena, we should be able to discover the relationship of homosexuality in the novel to art, writing, metaphor, and 'the two ways.'

In *La prisonnière*, we are told that Albertine, when sleeping, assumes the appearance of a plant: 'Etendue de la tête aux pieds sur mon lit, dans une attitude d'un naturel qu'on n'aurait pu inventer, je lui trouvais l'air d'une longue tige en fleur qu'on aurait disposée là; et c'était ainsi en effet: le pouvoir de rêver que je n'avais qu'en son absence, je le retrouvais à ces instants auprès d'elle, comme si, en dormant, elle était devenue une plante' (III, 69–70). Even if we had not been made aware previously of the latent homosexual tendencies that Albertine might possess, this comparison would establish a subterranean connection between Albertine and the homosexual act with which the plant was previously associated.

Through the image of a plant, a subterranean relationship is also established between homosexuality and the act of writing. In *Le temps retrouvé*, the narrator describes Morel's style of writing as 'oral fertilization' which produces only sterile flowers (III, 768). After likening Morel's writing to oral fertilization, the narrator tells us of Morel's recent change in sexual habits (he has abandoned M. de Charlus and has become totally faithful to a woman) and compares the law about humanity that this reversal of behaviour illustrates to the law governing the fertilization of flowers: 'Ainsi le jeu des différentes lois psychologiques s'arrange à compenser dans la floraison de l'espèce humaine tout ce qui, dans un sens ou dans l'autre, amènerait par la pléthore ou la raréfaction son anéantissement. Ainsi, en est-il chez les fleurs où une même sagesse, mise en evidence par Darwin, règle les modes de fécondation en les opposant successivement les uns aux autres' (III, 781). The 'flowers' theme, previously compared to homosexuality alone, is now applied to the 'flowering of humanity' as a whole; thus suggesting an innate resemblance between a homosexual union and a normal heterosexual relationship.

Somewhat later in the final volume of the novel, after he has recognized the power of art and understood how to translate life into art, the narrator compares his own life to the albumen of a germ cell, and the writing that his life shall translate itself into is likened to a plant:

> Elle l'aurait pu en ce que cette vie, les souvenirs de ses tristesses, de ses joies, formaient une réserve pareille à cet albumen qui est logé dans l'ovule des plantes et dans lequel celui-ci puise sa nourriture pour se transformer en graine, en ce temps où on ignore encore que l'embryon d'une plante se développe, lequel est pourtant le lieu de phénomènes chimiques et respiratoires

secrets mais très actifs. Ainsi ma vie était-elle en rapport avec ce qu'amènerait sa maturation. (III, 899)

No mention is made of homosexuality in this comparison, but a subliminal connection is nevertheless established between the nature of a homosexual union and the conditions giving birth to writing through a common denominator: both processes are compared to the procreation of flowers. In the first volume of the novel, the narrator had previously compared a profane act which occurred in the context of a homosexual union (Mlle Vinteuil and her friend spit on her father's portrait before making love) to the underlying sadism that is the foundation of the aesthetic of melodrama; which, if not a genre typifying all writing, is at least an example of a popular writing whose origins intermingle with the origin of the novelistic form (I, 163). Viewed collectively, the three comparisons (the culmination of a homosexual union/the fertilization of flowers, writing/the fertilization of flowers, and homosexuality/melodrama) function as a macrometaphor that suggests the existence of a quality shared by homosexuality and writing. In order to perceive clearly the essential quality common to a homosexual union and the process of writing (wherein life experience is translated into art), it is necessary to compare the two phenomena and look for structural components common to them both. The narrator's description of the initial meeting of Charlus and Jupien allows us to perceive that any two men (Charlus/Jupien, Charlus/Morel, Sait-Loup/Morel) who enter into a homosexual relationship are doubles of each other (insofar as they are both men and they both enjoy the same sexual preference) who recognize each other as such (II, 604-5). A writer's past life and his future writing co-exist in a 'doubles' relationship also: the narrator realizes that the source of his literary work is his past life (III, 899). After witnessing the courtship ritual of Jupien and Charlus, the narrator comprehends that their coupling allowed him to perceive a truth about M. de Charlus that was not previously apparent – that he is actually a woman. Correspondingly, the narrator realizes that the writing of a life into literature allows us to perceive truths about life that cannot be apprehended through life experience: 'En somme, cet art si compliqué est justement le seul art vivant. Seul il exprime pour les autres et nous fait voir à nous-même notre propre vie, cette vie qui ne peut pas s'"observer," dont les apparences qu'on observe ont besoin d'être traduites et souvent lues à rebours et péniblement déchiffrées' (III, 896). In accordance with the parallel that I am establishing in Proust's text between homosexuality and writing, the narrator compares the transformation of M. de Charlus into a woman, to the rearrangement of letters scattered at random upon the table into a meaningful sentence, that expresses a thought which can never be forgotten afterwards:

> Maintenant l'abstrait s'était matérialisé, l'être enfin compris avait aussitôt perdu son pouvoir de rester invisible, et la transmutation de M. de Charlus en une personne nouvelle était si complète que non seulement les contrastes de son visage, de sa voix, mais rétrospectivement les hauts et les bas eux-mêmes de ses relations avec moi, tout ce qui avait paru jusque-là incohérent à mon esprit, devenait intelligible, se montrait évident, comme une phrase, n'offrant aucun sens tant qu'elle reste décomposée en lettres disposées au hasard, exprime, si les caractères se trouvent replacés dans l'ordre qu'il faut, une pensée qu'on ne pourra plus oublier. (II, 614)

Like the combination of dissimilar phenomena in a metaphorical phrase, a homosexual union and the writing/reading of a literary work entail an interaction of internal doubles whose coupling reveals their common truth, which is different from their external appearance. The coupling of externally dissimilar entities which a metaphorical phrase, a homosexual union and a reader/book/author relationship all represent also reflects itself in the 'law of life' and the 'law of fecundation' that are both described by the narrator, in *La prisonnière,* as the coupling of contrary elements: 'D'autre part, l'accouplement des éléments contraires est la loi de la vie, le principe de la fécondation et, comme on verra, la cause de bien des malheurs' (III, 108). Through the labyrinth of cross-references joined by the 'plant' analogies, Proust thus suggests that the mechanism of metaphor is the structural double of the 'law of life.'

SLEEP/DREAMS/ART/LIFE/METAPHOR

In *Le temps retrouvé*, the narrator describes dreams as one of the major elements leading to his realization of the discrepancy between appearance and reality: 'Le rêve était encore un de ces faits de ma vie, qui m'avait toujours le plus frappé, qui avait dû le plus servir à me convaincre du caractère purement mental de la réalité, et dont je ne dédaignerais pas l'aide dans la composition de mon oeuvre' (III, 914). Only after he perceived the discrepancy between reality and appearance was the narrator able to recognize metaphor as the mechanism allowing the internal reality of things to suggest itself through art (III, 889). In the following pages, I will examine nine passages discussing sleep and dreams in the *Recherche* in order to clarify the common denominators of dreams and metaphor.

The narrator's analyses of dreams/sleep occur in seven books of the novel, are introduced in the context of six different milieus (Combray, Balbec, Paris, La Raspelière, the Parisian apartment which he shares with Albertine, the Guermantes' salon), and are compared to or analysed in connection with fifteen different phenomena: reader/text interaction, the magic lantern, Mme de Germantes, writing, flowers, the recapture of past years, an oriental fairy-tale, a great work of art, the Vinteuil Sonata, the mirror relationship of art and nature, androgynous beings, accelerated time, the reflective relationship of art and life experience, the resolution of contradictions, and the purely mental character of reality. Subliminal relationships establish themselves among these diverse realities through the intermediary of the common term to which they are all linked.

In view of the parallels that the narrator establishes between dreams and internal reality in *Le temps retrouvé*, it appears to be more than coincidence that the novel – whose ultimate revelation is a recognition of metaphor's power to suggest the internal reality of things through a literary work – should begin with the famous discourse on sleep, which is coupled with reflections on the transformational effects produced by the reader's interaction with his book (I, 3). The passage describes an apparent total reversibility of the asleep and the awake state ('mes yeux se fermaient si vite que je n'avais pas le temps de me dire: 'je m'endors.' Et, une demi-heure après, la pensée qu'il était temps de chercher le sommeil m'éveillait') and of the reader and his book ('il me semblait que j'étais moi-même ce dont parlait l'ouvrage,' I, 3) – a dual play of doubles that will find its counterpart in the reflective relationships of art and life, the reader and his book, in *Le temps retrouvé*. As the *Recherche* progresses, we discover that the subjects through which the young narrator establishes an equivalence between his 'dream' book and himself ('une église, un quatuor, la rivalité de François Ier et de Charles-Quint' (I, 3) have, in fact, their mirror counterparts in his own life experience (the church of Combray, the Vinteuil Sonata, the two ways), which will translate itself into his own literary work years later, in *Le temps retrouvé*.[2]

In *Du côté de chez Swann*, the narrator describes the transformational effects induced by sleep to illustrate his contention that the apparent immobility of things around us is imposed by our own mind, and is not an essential characteristic of the things themselves. Through the combined effect of memory and his somnambulistic state, for example, the room in which the narrator is presently resting transforms itself to become all of the rooms he has ever slept in (I, 6). His half-awake, half-asleep, dream-like musings culminate in an activity which reflects the subject of the novel itself: 'le branle était donné à ma mémoire, généralement je ne cherchais pas à me rendormir tout de suite; je passais la plus grande partie de la nuit à me rappeler notre vie d'autrefois à Combray chez ma grand'tante, à Balbec, à Paris, à Doncières, à Venise, ailleurs encore, à me rappeler les lieux, les personnes que j'y avais connues, ce que j'avais vu d'elles, ce qu'on m'en avait raconté (I, 8–9). These memories induced by sleep also find their counterpart – in *Le temps retrouvé* – in the narrator's discussions about the possibility of an author's resuscitation of his past through his translation of it into a literary work (III, 899, 905).

Considerably later in *Du côté de chez Swann*, during one of his walks along the Guermantes' way, the narrator describes a daydream which brings together in one image Madame de Guermantes, flowers, and the narrator's future work of art: 'Je rêvais que Mme de Guermantes m'y faisait venir, éprise pour moi d'un soudain caprice; tout le jour elle y pêchait la truite avec moi. Et le soir, me tenant par la main, en passant devant les petits jardins de ses vassaux, elle me montrait, le long des murs bas, les fleurs qui y appuient leurs quenouilles violettes et rouges et m'apprenait leurs noms. Elle me faisait lui dire le sujet des poèmes que j'avais l'intention de composer. Et ces rêves m'avertissaient que, puisque je voulais un jour être un écrivain, il était temps de savoir ce que je comptais écrire' (I, 172). Although there is no analogical connection or structural affinity established between flowers, Mme de Guermantes, and writing at this time, it is significant that they are all combined in the same dream, as these elements are compared to each other and to dreams in subsequent discussions about dreams in the novel. Both discourses on dreams in the first volume of the novel are either preceded or followed by allusions to the 'magic lantern.' In the first case, a discussion of the magic lantern immediately follows the narrator's examination of sleep/dreams, and in the second case, an allusion to the magic lantern immediately precedes the description of his dream (I, 171–2). During my analysis of 'Combray' in Chapter 2, I proposed that the textual contiguity of diverse phenomena such as the magic lantern and dreams allows their common characteristics to be revealed, despite the lack of any articulated comparison.

During his introductory discussion of the effects produced by sleep, the narrator emphasized the altered perception of time that sleep induces (I, 5). Similarly, in his third discussion of dreams which occurs in *A l'ombre des jeunes filles en fleurs,* he compares the journey induced by a deep sleep to a return to childhood, the recapture of past years and lost feelings: 'Tout à coup je m'endormais, je tombais dans ce sommeil lourd où se dévoilent pour nous le retour à la jeunesse, la reprise des années passées, des sentiments perdus, la désincarnation, la transmigration des âmes, l'évocation des morts, les illusions de la folie, la régression vers les règnes les plus élémentaires de la nature (I, 819–20). The narrator's comparison suggests a correspondence between the nature of sleep and one of his past/present reminiscences – the experience engendered by the taking of the tea with the madeleine, which recalled his childhood to him. By effecting a regression towards 'the most elementary of the natural kingdoms,' the deep sleep also resembles the function of a work of art, as described by the narrator in *Le temps retrouvé*: 'C'est ce travail que l'art défera, c'est la marche en sens contraire, le retour aux profondeurs où ce qui a existé réellement gît inconnu de nous, qu'il nous fera suivre' (III, 896).

The effects produced by a dream are also compared in *A l'ombre des jeunes filles en fleurs* to the mechanical function of a magic lantern. This analogy consolidates the subliminal connection between the two entities which established itself macrometaphorically through their common effect, and which revealed itself as a result of the contiguity of the narrator's discussion of dreams and his subsequent depiction of the effect of the magic lantern in *Du côté de chez Swann:* 'car on dit que nous voyons souvent des animaux en rêve, mais on oublie que presque toujours nous y sommes nous-même un animal, privé de cette raison qui projette sur les choses une clarté de certitude; nous n'y offrons au contraire au spectacle de la vie qu'une vision douteuse et à chaque minute anéantie par l'oubli, la réalité précédente s'évanouissant devant celle qui lui succède comme une projection de lanterne magique devant la suivante quand on a changé le verre ... ' (I, 820).

In his dream, the narrator sees himself cast for a part in an oriental fairy-tale, in which he is being punished for a crime he doesn't know the nature of: 'Celui où je tenais alors mon rôle était dans le goût des contes orientaux, je n'y savais rien de mon passé ni de moi-même, à cause de cet extrême rapprochement d'un décor interposé; je n'étais qu'un personnage qui recevais la bastonnade et subissais des châtiments variés pour une faute que je n'apercevais pas, mais qui était d'avoir bu trop de porto' (I, 820). Through the intermediary of this analogy, a subterranean correspondence engenders itself between the narrator's dream and M. de Charlus' experience with 'ruffians' in Jupien's brothel in *Le temps retrouvé*; both events involve a beating and both are compared to an Oriental fairy-tale: 'En attendant, dis-je à Jupien, cette maison est tout autre chose, plus qu'une maison de fous, puisque la folie des aliénés qui y habitent est mise en scène, reconstituée, visible, c'est un vrai pandemonium. J'avais cru comme le caliphe des *Mille et une Nuits* arriver à point au secours d'un homme qu'on frappait, et c'est un autre conte des *Mille et une Nuits* que j'ai vu réalisé devant moi, celui où une femme, transformée en chienne, se fait frapper volontairement pour retrouver sa forme première' (III, 832).

The narrator's fourth discussion of dreams occurs in *Le côté de Guermantes I*, in the setting of Paris. At this time, his dream brings together several phenomena that were previously connected to dreams in the text: Mme de Guermantes, the mirror relationship of art and nature, dual components, an oriental scene, and a return to past time. In the second dream which the narrator presented in *Du côté de chez Swann*, Mme de Guermantes was part of that dream. Just before the narrator begins his discussion of the fourth dream, he sees Mme de Guermantes on the boulevard, remarks that she appears to be dreaming (II, 145), and compares her to a work of art: 'admirant que ... la duchesse de Guermantes mêlât à la vie publique des moments de sa vie secrète, se montrant ainsi à chacun, mystérieuse, coudoyée de tous, avec la splendide gratuité des grands chefs-d'oeuvres' (II, 145). Before commencing his analysis of the dream, the narrator remarks that it appeared to him as if he had seen it many times before (II, 146). The 'déjà-vu' character of his dream recalls to itself the three intimations and the 'obscure impressions' later analyzed in *Le temps retrouvé*, as he discovers that they are also 'déjà-vu' (III, 867). Although the narrator does not classify his dream as a metaphor, it resembles the latter in its structure and its effect. Just as metaphor represents a synthesis of two realities, the dream is a combination of two phenomena that the narrator had tried to imagine while awake: 'Un de mes rêves était le synthèse de ce que mon imagination avait souvent cherché à se représenter, pendant la veille, d'un certain paysage marin et de son passé médiéval' (II, 146). The bisymmetrical urban scene depicted in the dream also resembles the dual structure of metaphor: 'Dans mon sommeil je voyais une cité gothique au milieu d'une mer aux flots immobilisés comme sur un vitrail. Un bras de mer divisait en deux la ville ...' (II, 146). In *Le temps retrouvé*, the narrator discovers that metaphor is a structure common to nature and to art. Correspondingly, the narrator's dream is a mingling of both artistic and natural elements: 'Ce rêve où la nature avait appris l'art, où la mer était devenue gothique, ce rêve où je désirais, où je croyais aborder à l'impossible, il me semblait l'avoir déjà fait souvent' (II, 146).

Moreover, the dream represents previously established pictorial analogies. I mentioned that, in *A l'ombre des jeunes filles en fleurs*, the narrator likens his dream to being in an Oriental fairy-tale, and compares the effect induced by the dream to a return to childhood, a recapture of past years. The Orient is represented in the dream under discussion in the form of an oriental-style church, and the narrator's previous return to a past time is suggested in the form of a fourteenth-century house: 'l'eau verte s'étendait à mes pieds; elle baignait sur la rive opposée une église orientale, puis des maisons qui existaient encore dans le XIV siècle, si bien qu'aller vers elle, c'eût été remonter le cours des âges' (II, 146).

The narrator suggests that the recapture of past time may be produced through dream-like reflection on a name, which suspends the perpetual motion of life experience and allows us to see the successive tints that, in the course of our existence, it has presented to us (II, 12). Because it can undo the masking imposed upon reality by habit, dream-like reflection resembles the active work of the intelligence described by the narrator in *Le temps retrouvé* that, drawing forth impressions from obscurity, culminates in the creation of a work of art (III, 878–9).

The narrator's fifth examination of dreams occurs in *Sodome et Gomorrhe*, during an evening when he returns late from visiting the Verdurins at La Raspelière. In this passage, the narrator's depiction of the nature of dreams establishes an affinity between dreams and another idea presented extensively in the novel – the reversibility of male/female characteristics (discussed in connection with the homosexual tendencies exhibited by many of the major characters of the work). He asserts that the race which inhabits dreams is androgynous: 'La race qui l'habite, comme celle des premiers humains, est androgyne. Un homme y apparaît au bout d'un instant sous l'aspect d'une femme' (II, 981). Thus, the homosexual personalities of the novel are aligned macrometaphorically with the nature of dreams and with the common affinities that the narrator later establishes between the nature of dreams, art, and metaphor.

The narrator also remarks that the time in dreams is frequently accelerated in relation to the time of reality: 'Le temps qui s'écoule pour le dormeur, durant ces sommeils-là, est absolument différent du temps

dans lequel s'accomplit la vie de l'homme réveillé. Tantôt son cours est beaucoup plus rapide, un quart d'heure semble une journée; quelquefois beaucoup plus long, on croit n'avoir fait qu'un léger somme, on a dormi tout le jour' (II, 981). This speeded-up quality attributed to time in dreams is the same tempo ascribed to novelistic time in *Du côté de chez Swann:* 'Et une fois que le romancier nous a mis dans cet état, où comme tous les états purement intérieurs toute émotion est décuplée, où son livre va nous troubler à la façon d'un rêve mais d'un rêve plus clair que ceux que nous avons en dormant ... voici qu'il déchaîne en nous pendant une heure tous les bonheurs et tous les malheurs possibles dont nous mettrions dans la vie des années à connaître quelques uns ...' (I, 85).

Just as metaphor creates or reveals realities that transcend normal discourse, so sleep creates sounds which do not exist in reality: 'Mais là, le sommeil avait fabriqué des sons. Plus matériels et plus simples, ils duraient davantage' (II, 986). Like a metaphor, the narrator's dream brings together people and events which are separate in life and thus intimates the existence of their common essence. Madame Verdurin, for example, assumes the role of Charlus' mother: 'Or j'avais rêvé que M. de Charlus avait cent dix ans et venait de donner une paire de claques à sa propre mère, Mme Verdurin, parce qu'elle avait acheté cinq milliards un bouquet de violettes' (II, 986). Although the kinship of Mme Verdurin and M. de Charlus as represented in the dream appears, in *Sodome et Gomorrhe,* to be ludicrous, events described in *Le temps retrouvé* indicate that the young narrator's dream had in fact revealed an internal reality – the innate similitude of the two rival social salons (the Verdurins/the Guermantes) – which manifests itself in visible reality years later, when Mme Verdurin marries the Prince de Guermantes, and becomes M. de Charlus' sister-in-law (III, 955).

In 'Homosexuality/Flowers/Writing/Metaphor,' I mentioned that Albertine is compared to a plant when asleep (III, 70). The analogy reinforces the subterranean relationship established between the homosexual characters depicted in the *Recherche* and the androgynous creatures that people the narrator's dream in *Sodome et Gomorrhe*. Also, the changes in Albertine's appearance wrought by sleep parallel the effects attributed to a work of art in *Le temps retrouvé*. Albertine, when asleep, is stripped of the many different masks that she assumes when awake: 'En fermant les yeux, en perdant la conscience, Albertine avait dépouillé, l'un après l'autre, ces différents caractères d'humanité qui m'avaient déçu depuis le jour où j'avais fait sa connaissance' (III, 70). Similarly, the function of art is to uncover the internal reality that lies

hidden beneath the masks created by the passions, the intellect, and the habits of everyday life (III, 895–6). Through Albertine, the narrator also implies that the unconscious world of sleep is a world more real than the waking world: 'Elle n'était plus animée que de la vie inconsciente des végétaux, des arbres, vie plus différente de la mienne, plus étrange, et qui cependant m'appartenait davantage' (III, 70). Correspondingly, in *Le temps retrouvé*, he tells us that the 'true life' – the life more real than lived experience – is literature: 'La vraie vie, la vie enfin découverte et éclaircie, la seule vie par conséquent réellement vécue, c'est la littérature; cette vie qui, en un sens, habite à chaque instant chez tous les hommes aussi bien que chez l'artiste. Mais ils ne la voient pas, parce qu'ils ne cherchent pas à l'éclaircir' (III, 895).

The narrator conducts a second study of the nature of sleep in *La prisonnière* that consolidates the macrometaphorical relationship between sleep and art engendered by Albertine. The ability of a dream to suggest a more human view of things is likened to the impression produced by a work of art – the 'Pietà' of the Renaissance (III, 125). He also compares scenes evoked by the Vinteuil Sonata to the inexpressible, almost forbidden visions one experiences at the moment of falling asleep (III, 374). Although he previously implied that sleep (like art) is a world more real than the waking world, the narrator now cautions us that sleep is not *more* real, but *as* real as the waking world (III, 122).

During his final discussions of sleep/dreams in *Le temps retrouvé*, the narrator employs a similar contradictory strategy: on the one hand he continues to note structures or effects shared by dreams and art, but on the other hand, he affirms the unique capacity that allows a work of art to recover past time – an effect that sleep and other phenomena may imitate or intimate, but cannot realize: 'Et c'était peut-être aussi par le jeu formidable qu'il fait avec le Temps que le Rêve m'avait fasciné ... jusqu'à nous faire croire, à tort d'ailleurs, qu'il était un des modes pour retrouver le Temps perdu' (iii, 912).

Perhaps the narrator does not realize that it is the reflective relationship which this 'false double' entered into with art and metaphor during the course of his life that clarified for him the common structures and effects shared by life, dreams, art, and metaphor. Immediately before launching into his first examination of dreams in *Le temps retrouvé*, the narrator describes the book as an optical instrument allowing the reader to read himself, because the general truths written into a book allow its reader to perceive things about himself that are not expressible or apparent until seen in their double in the book (III, 911). Similarly, dreams act as a 'double' of art whose

outlines and mechanisms allow the narrator and his reader to perceive truths about the structural principles which allow art to suggest the internal reality of things. Because of its ability to speed up time and bring together experiences which would be separated for years in actual life, the narrator acknowledges that the dream has taught him lessons about the subjective quality of reality (its purely mental character) that he will not forget when he composes his work (III, 914).

Lived experience and dream experience are also doubles of each other: the people in the narrator's life, like the people in a dream, have woven themselves together no matter how diverse the circumstances (III, 972). Seen from a perspective of several years, the lives of people of his acquaintance form patterns which resemble the mechanism of a dream: contradictions resolve themselves – people who used to hate each other have become good friends:

> Ce n'était pas que l'aspect de ces personnes qui donnait l'idée de personnes de songe. Pour elles-mêmes la vie, déjà ensommeillée dans la jeunesse et l'amour, était de plus en plus devenue un songe. Elles avaient oublié jusqu'à leurs rancunes, leurs haines, et pour être certaines que c'était à la personne qui était là qu'elles n'addressaient plus la parole il y a deux ans, il eût fallu qu'elles se reportassent à un registre, mais qui était aussi vague qu'un rêve où on a été insulté on ne sait plus par qui. Tous ces songes formaient les apparences contrastées de la vie politique, où on voyait dans un même ministère des gens qui s'étaient accusés de meurtre ou de trahison. (III, 973)

The quality that allows the narrator to establish a comparison between life experience and dream experience – the ability to resolve external differences or apparent contradictions in each other – is also the quality which causes life experience and dream experience to enter into a macrometaphorical, reflective relationship with metaphor, which can also resolve the apparent incompatibility of externally dissimilar objects by uniting them in such a way that their common internal essence is revealed (III, 889).

THE MAGIC LANTERN/ART/METAPHOR

In the introductory pages of *Du côté de chez Swann*, the narrator compares the impression effected by the magic lantern to that created by the works of the master builders and glass painters of gothic days:

the lantern substitutes for the opaqueness of his walls a new reality: 'On avait bien inventé, pour me distraire les soirs où on me trouvait l'air trop malheureux, de me donner une lanterne magique dont, en attendant l'heure du dîner, on coiffait ma lampe; et, à l'instar des premiers architects et maîtres verriers de l'âge gothique, elle substituait à l'opacité des murs d'impalpables irrisations, de surnaturelles apparitions multicolores, où des légendes étaient dépeintes comme dans un vitrail vacillant et momentané' (I, 9). In the course of the seven books of *A la recherche du temps perdu*, analogies involving the magic lantern appear nine times[3] and frequently have as their other term of comparison various art forms: legends, tapestries, stained glass windows, Elstir's paintings, the Vinteuil Sonata, all the other music that Albertine plays on the pianola, great works of art in general and the novel *François le Champi*. The magic lantern is also linked in the text with names/presences, sleep and dreams, the church of Combray, the Guermantes family, Albertine, the resuscitation of the past through the repetition in the present of an action from the past, the effects of memory, and Combray.

We saw in Chapter 2 that for Proust the essential nature of art is metaphor. The many comparisons which Proust establishes between the magic lantern and various art forms imply, therefore, that the mechanism of the magic lantern reflects the metaphorical process. The narrator's descriptions of the magic lantern support this hypothesis: he emphasizes the transcendental effect of the magic lantern projection[4] resulting from one reality (the projected scene) being substituted for another (the wall of his room): 'elle substituait à l'opacité des murs d'impalpables irrisations, de surnaturelles apparitions multicolores' (I, 9). Like metaphor, the magic lantern projection is essentially a superimposition of two dissimilar realities (the coloured picture is overlaid upon the existent reality of the room) which gives a rise to an intermingling of the two realities: the transparent body of Golo overcomes all material obstacles by taking each – the doorknob, for example – as a skeleton and embodying it in itself. Like metaphor, the superimposition of these two realities one upon the other has the effect of vanquishing material reality (the room as it originally appeared) and producing a new transcendent vision:

> Le corps de Golo lui-même, d'une essence aussi surnaturelle que celui de sa monture, s'arrangeait de tout obstacle matériel, de tout objet gênant qu'il rencontrait en le prenant comme ossature et en se le rendant intérieur, fût-ce le bouton de la porte sur

> lequel s'adaptait aussitôt et surnageait invinciblement sa robe rouge ou sa figure pâle toujours aussi noble et aussi mélancolique, mais qui ne laissait paraître aucun trouble de cette transvertébration. (I, 10)

As well as giving rise (like a work of art) to a metaphor-like process, the magic lantern duplicates the external function of a work of literature: it depicts 'legends' (narratives).

In *Le temps retrouvé*, the narrator proclaims that literature (art) is the only means through which past time may be recovered (III, 905). The projections of the magic lantern achieve a similar effect: they seem to bring to life a Merovingian past that merges with the present reality of the room: 'Certes je leur trouvais du charme à ces brillantes projections qui semblaient émaner d'un passé mérovingien et promenaient autour de moi des reflets d'histoire si anciens' (I, 10). By bringing images of the past into the present, the magic lantern (when viewed from the perspective of the totality of the novel) also recalls the effect produced by the narrator's many experiences of involuntary memory (the resuscitation of his past in Combray through the taste of the madeleine dipped in tea; the recall of his grandmother through his repetition of an identical action performed in the same circumstances when she was alive; the three 'intimations' experienced when invited to the Guermantes' new residence) which are integrally linked in *Le temps retrouvé* to the nature of metaphor – its structure, effect, and the unique power it has for intimating the internal reality of things that eludes expression through habitual discourse.

The narrator's anticipatory response to the slide show introduces a theme to be explored extensively in *Le côté de Guermantes* and reiterated repeatedly in all ensuing volumes of the novel: the signification of a proper name independent of the presence it represents. The narrator tells us that, before he could see the moor and the castle depicted in the slide show, he knew that their colour was yellow because the name Brabant had given him a clue: 'Le château et la lande étaient jaunes, et je n'avais pas attendu de les voir pour connaître leur couleur, car, avant les verres du chassis, la sonorité mordorée du nom de Brabant me l'avait montrée avec évidence' (I, 9). Similarly, the sound of the name 'Guermantes' later evokes entire landscapes in his imagination (II, 12–14). It is not only the effect that their name produces which establishes a rapport between the Guermantes and the characters depicted by the magic lantern, however, as the Merovingian past depicted in the slide show is the past reality of the Guermantes family:

in this same volume of the *Recherche*, the narrator tells us that Geneviève de Brabant – the heroine of the 'magic lantern' legend – was an ancestor of the Guermantes (I, 171). Correspondingly, in *Le temps retrouvé*, members of the Guermantes family are aptly described as personages of the magic lantern (III, 884).

In *Du côté de chez Swann*, the narrator also compares the projections of a magic lantern to his memories of Combray. Because their colours and physical aspect are so different from his present reality, his memories of Combray seem unreal and fictional to him – more insubstantial than the projections of his magic lantern: 'ces rues de Combray existent dans une partie de ma mémoire si reculée, peinte de couleurs si différentes de celles qui maintenant revêtent pour moi le monde, qu'en vérité elles me paraissent toutes, et l'église qui les dominait sur la Place, plus irréelles encore que les projections de la lanterne magique ...' (I, 48).

The third 'magic lantern' comparison that the narrator presents to us establishes a relationship among four phenomena which are all enveloped in a similar air of mystery: (1) his reminiscences about the unknown life of the Guermantes; (2) the changing colours of a stained glass window in the church of Combray; (3) a tapestry in the same church depicting a former countess of Guermantes; and (4) the image of the magic lantern portraying Geneviève de Brabant, an ancestor of the Guermantes:

> Je savais que là résidaient des châtelains, le duc et la duchesse de Guermantes, je savais qu'ils étaient des personnages réels et actuellement existants, mais chaque fois que je pensais à eux, je me les représentais tantôt en tapisserie, comme était la comtesse de Guermantes dans le Couronnement d'Esther de notre église, tantôt de nuances changeantes, comme était Gilbert le Mauvais dans le vitrail où il passait du vert chou au bleu prune, selon que j'étais encore à prendre de l'eau bénite ou que j'arrivais à nos chaises, tantôt tout à fait impalpables comme l'image de Geneviève de Brabant, ancêtre de la famille de Germantes, que la lanterne magique promenait sur les rideaux de ma chambre ou faisait monter au plafond, – enfin toujours enveloppés du mystère des temps mérovingiens et baignant, comme dans un coucher de soleil, dans la lumière orangée qui émane de cette syllabe: 'antes.' (I, 171)

Each of the four phenomena involved in the comparison with the

magic lantern is remarkable for the transformational effect engendered by it. During his description of the interior of the church of Combray, for example (I, 59–60), which occurs shortly after his second allusion to the magic lantern in *Du côté de chez Swann* (I, 48), the narrator emphasizes a stained glass window and a tapestry of Esther which, as observed previously, both give rise to metaphor-like metamorphoses (see pp 39–40): the predominantly blue-toned stained glass window engenders a rare and transient fire which shakes and wavers in a flaming fantastic shower, each time that a ray of sunlight passes through it (I, 60), and the tapestry's colours have melted into one another to add expression, light, and relief to the pictures (I, 60–1). It is more than coincidence, therefore, that this same stained glass window and the same tapestry depicting Esther are compared to a magic lantern (whose metaphorical character is described above) and to his imaginary musings about the Guermantes (whose family name also gives rise to a metaphor-like effect).

In *Le côté de Guermantes II*, the narrator provides us with an analogy that suggests a basis for all previous comparisons established between the magic lantern and art. While examining M. de Guermantes' collection of Elstir's paintings displayed on the walls of the drawing room, the narrator remarks that the series of paintings resembles a sequence of magic lantern projections; the magic lantern being, in this case, the brain of the artist, who, when seen without his paintings, would resemble the iron box of the magic lantern without its slides (II, 419).

The above comparison is immediately succeeded by a discussion of the nature of the natural optical illusions which are re-created in several of the paintings: 'Parmi ces tableaux, quelques-uns de ceux qui semblaient les plus ridicules aux gens du monde m'intéressaient plus que les autres en ce qu'ils recréaient ces illusions d'optique qui nous prouvent que nous n'identifierions pas les objets si nous ne faisions pas intervenir le raisonnement' (II, 419). The lesson that the painted optical illusions teach recalls the lesson which his sleep vision taught him in *Du côté de chez Swann* (I, 6) and anticipates the illumination about metaphor and the true nature of reality which his analysis of the three 'intimations' leads him to in *Le temps retrouvé:* after studying the paintings, he realizes that the reality of an object is not confined to its external appearance, the name imposed upon it, or our perception of it; that surfaces and volumes are in reality independent of the names of objects which our memory imposes on them after we have recognized them. In order to reproduce in his paintings the reality inherent in his first impression of a scene, Elstir represented one thing by the other for

which in the flash of a first impression, he first mistook it. By doing so, the narrator thinks that Elstir attempted – through his art – to break up that aggregate of impressions commonly called visions, and to intimate instead an internal reality – the root of the impression:

> Dès lors n'est-il pas logique, non par artifice de symbolisme mais par retour sincère à la racine même de l'impression, de représenter une chose par cette autre que dans l'éclair d'une illusion première nous avons prise pour elle? Les surfaces et les volumes sont en réalité indépendants des noms d'objets que notre mémoire leur impose quand nous les avons reconnus. Elstir tâchait d'arracher à ce qu'il venait de sentir ce qu'il savait; son effort avait souvent été de dissoudre cet agrégat de raisonnements que nous appelons vision. (II, 419)

If we examine the above passage from the perspective of the totality of the novel, we immediately discern – through the intermediary of their common natures – that the method used by Elstir – the representation of one object in another to create a work of art – is essentially the metaphorical process, as defined by the narrator in *Le temps retrouvé*.

Analytical observations about the structure and effect of Elstir's paintings are immediately followed by a discussion of the similarities shared by Elstir's 'bizarre horrors' (the commonly held view of Elstir's paintings at the time of the narrator's observation of them) and traditional 'great works' such as those by Chardin and Perroneau. The narrator realizes that, in striving to reproduce reality, Elstir had to make the same effort as Chardin or Perroneau, and he consequently admired in them attempts of the same order as his own, which were like fragments anticipatory of his own work:

> Les gens qui détestaient ces 'horreurs' s'étonnaient qu'Elstir admirât Chardin, Perroneau, tant de peintres qu'eux, les gens du monde, aimaient. Ils ne se rendaient pas compte qu'Elstir avait pour son compte refait devant le réel (avec l'indice particulier de son goût pour certaines recherches) le même effort qu'un Chardin ou un Perroneau, et qu'en conséquence, quand il cessait de travailler pour lui-même, il admirait en eux des tentatives du même genre, des sortes de fragments anticipés d'oeuvres de lui. (II, 419–20)

Elstir's work, therefore, represents both a repetition and a transforma-

tion of existing art forms: the repetition of elements from previous works of art in a new work of art enables the observer to perceive structures which are possibly common to all works of art, and it is this common structure which allows the unbridgeable gulf between two canvases as apparently different as Manet's 'Olympia' and a masterpiece by Ingres to be spanned:

> Mais les gens du monde n'ajoutaient pas par la pensée à l'oeuvre d'Elstir cette perspective du Temps qui leur permettait d'aimer ou tout au moins de regarder sans gêne la peinture de Chardin. Pourtant les plus vieux auraient pu se dire qu'au cours de leur vie ils avaient vu, au fur et à mesure que les années les en éloignaient, la distance infranchissable entre ce qu'ils jugeaient un chef d'oeuvre d'Ingres et ce qu'ils croyaient devoir rester à jamais une horreur (par exemple l'*Olympia* de Manet) diminuer jusqu'à ce que les deux toiles eussent l'air jumelles. (II, 420)

The reflective rapport which links a painting by Elstir and a Chardin masterpiece (or any two works of art from different time periods) constitutes a macrometaphor which transcends time and space. Like two phenomena joined in a metaphorical phrase, the works invite comparison with each other because of the common element they share; and just as the common essence revealed by a metaphor transcends the components whose union allowed it to reveal itself, the common nature of the two works of art from apparently incompatible periods transcends their external differences to such an extent that they appear as doubles.

During his visit to Elstir's studio at Balbec (an incident related in *A l'ombre des jeunes filles en fleurs*), the narrator described Elstir's paintings as 'metaphors.'[5] During his examination of the Guermantes' collection of Elstir's works, he does not mention metaphor in connection with the paintings, but he does describe their technique and subject matter in such a way that we can perceive their metaphorical character. He tells us, for example, that Elstir's paintings taught him that value is subjective: by combining apparently incompatible subjects in the same painting and giving them the same value in tone and light (he refers to a painting of a waterside carnival, in which a beautiful sailboat and the dress of a vulgar lady are given equal emphasis), he demonstrates that there are no degrees of beauty; that the commonplace dress and the sail are 'deux miroirs du même reflet' (II, 421). The narrator does not proclaim in any part of the *Recherche* that the magic lantern engenders a metaphor-like process, but he does depict Elstir's paintings as metaphors. In turn, the metaphorical quality of Elstir's paintings reaffirms – through analogical transference – the innate metaphorical quality of the magic lantern projection.

The magic lantern is compared not only to the graphic arts, but also to music. In *La prisonnière*, the narrator describes the pianola that Albertine plays as a scientific magic lantern. By playing music from different periods, she causes images of different times and places to be projected into his room in Paris (III, 382). The slide which is being projected on the 'magic lantern' (the pianola) at the time of the reminiscence we are discussing is the Vinteuil Sonata, which the narrator (immediately before the comparison above) describes as the expression of certain states of the soul analogous to that which he experienced when he tasted the madeleine that had been dipped in tea: 'si les phrases de Vinteuil semblaient l'expression de certains états de l'âme analogues à celui que j'avais éprouvé en goûtant la madeleine trempée dans la tasse de thé, rien ne m'assurait que le vague de tels états fût une marque de leur profondeur ... Pourtant ce bonheur, ce sentiment de certitude dans le bonheur, pendant que je buvais la tasse de thé, que je respirais aux Champs-Elysées une odeur de vieux bois, ce n'était pas une illusion ... le charme de certaines phrases de Vinteuil fait penser à eux parce qu'il est lui aussi inanalysable' (III, 381). No direct connection is established at this time between his experience of the madeleine dipped in tea and the magic lantern, but their mutual comparison to the Vinteuil Sonata within the space of one page establishes a subterranean, macrometaphorical link between them which illuminates a second common effect: both cause images of another reality to be brought into the context of the narrator's present reality.

Albertine – the player of the 'scientific magic lantern' – is like the magic lantern herself. Her constantly changing nature (I, 857) resembles the constantly changing slides of a magic lantern show. This subterranean connection between Albertine and the magic lantern is consolidated in *Albertine disparue*. After Albertine's death, the narrator realizes that he is prevented from consummating a meeting with her in his dreams because of an abrupt, intervening blackness, which obliterates his vision like the shadow of the magic lantern or of its operator inadvertently falling across the image being projected (III, 539).

Le temps retrouvé contains two 'magic lantern analogies' whose secondary terms of comparison suggest two references to the magic lantern that occurred in the first volume of the novel. The second 'magic lantern' analogy in *Du côté de chez Swann* compared the narrator's memories of Combray to the projections of a magic lantern (I, 48). In *Le temps retrouvé*, the penultimate 'magic lantern analogy' likens the 'lights-out' regulation imposed on Paris during the First World War to the mysterious half-darkness of a room in which slides are being shown on a magic lantern; 'Puis à 9 h.½, alors que personne n'avait encore eu le temps de finir de dîner, à cause des ordonnances de police on éteignait brusquement toutes les lumières, et la nouvelle bousculade des embusqués arrachant leurs pardessus aux chasseurs du restaurant où j'avais dîné avec Saint-Loup un soir de perme, avait lieu à 9 h. 35 dans une mystérieuse pénombre de chambre où l'on montre la lanterne magique ...' (III, 735). Although this comparison does not mention Combray, it is immediately followed by a second image likening the darkness of the 'lights-out' regulation in Paris to the darkness of the Combray he knew in his childhood: 'Mais après cette heure-là, pour ceux qui, comme moi, le soir dont je parle, étaient restés à dîner chez eux, et sortaient pour aller voir des amis, Paris était, au moins dans certains quartiers, encore plus noir que n'était le Combray de mon enfance ...' (III, 735). Through the common denominator of 'darkness' which both comparisons share, a macrometaphorical correspondence establishes itself between the other terms in the two comparisons – the magic lantern and Combray – that recall to us the poetic simile of the first volume of the novel, in which memories of Combray were compared to the projections of a magic lantern.

I mentioned previously that a cousin of Mme de Guermantes is described in *Le temps retrouvé* as a personage of the magic lantern – an analogy that consolidates the macrometaphorical correspondences between the Guermantes and the magic lantern in *Du côté de chez Swann* (I, 10, 171). More important, however, this final 'magic lantern' analogy establishes a rapport between the aura of mystery surrounding the Guermantes family, and the air of mystery engendered by a work of literature (in this case, the novel *François le Champi*): 'A ce moment-là, l'idée que telle personne dont j'avais fait la connaissance dans le monde était cousine de Mme de Guermantes, c'est-à-dire d'un personnage de lanterne magique, me semblait incompréhensible, et tout autant, que les plus beaux livres que j'avais lus fussent – je ne dis pas même supérieurs, ce qu'ils étaient pourtant – mais égaux à cet extraordinaire *François le Champi*' (III, 884).

I can conclude my remarks on the magic lantern, therefore, with the observation that this little network of metaphorical references not only suggests the presence of a common essential nature shared by many of the recurring phenomena in Proust's novel (dreams, Elstir's paintings, the Vinteuil Sonata, Albertine, the church of Combray, the Guermantes, works of art in general, metaphor), but also causes the work to fold over on itself through the cross-references repeated at the beginning and the end of the novel, and thus illuminates the common denominator linking projections of the magic lantern to the structure of the novel – a metaphor-like superimposition of dissimilar realities, that produces a transcendent effect.

NAMES/ART/PRESENCE/METAPHOR

During his theoretical discussion about names in the first pages of *Le côté de Guermantes*, the narrator compares them to an allegorical painting: 'ce n'est pas seulement aux villes et aux fleuves qu'ils donnent une individualité, comme le font les peintures allégoriques ...' (II, 10–11). Later, after he has had the opportunity of listening to M. de Guermantes discuss at length the intertwined genealogies of some of France's old families, he compares the order assumed by the names in his mind to a finished work of art: 'Ainsi les espaces de ma mémoire se couvraient peu à peu de noms qui, en s'ordonnant, en se composant les uns relativement aux autres, en nouant entre eux des rapports de plus en plus nombreux, imitaient ces oeuvres d'art achevées où il n'y a pas une seule touche qui soit isolée, où chaque partie tour à tour reçoit des autres sa raison d'être comme elle leur impose la sienne' (II, 537). Despite the comparisons that he draws between names and art, the narrator never provides in any part of *A la recherche du temps perdu* a categorical explanation of why names resemble a work of art. On the other hand, he does present to us a detailed analysis supported by concrete examples from his life experience of (1) the nature of the signification to which a name itself gives rise, (2) the relationship that exists between a name and its referent, and (3) the consequences arising from the superimposition of a name onto its referent. The narrator's discoveries about the relationship of a proper name to its referent result from his comparison of the different effects a name provokes in him before and after he establishes personal contact with the name's referent. In the following pages, I will explore all passages of the novel in which the narrator describes the effect engendered in him by a name and/or its referent, in order to determine what the essential qualities of the name itself or the name/presence relationship are, that allow the narrator to compare the name to a work of art.

The pattern arising from the order and manner of presentation of the narrator's investigation of the name/presence relationship in successive volumes of *A la recherche du temps perdu* reflects metaphorical structure. Books One and Two of the *Recherche* are joined by the cross-referentiality of two chapters that correspond to each other because of the sequential relationship of their subject-matter – names. The third part of *Du côté de chez Swann* – 'Noms de pays: le nom' – introduces the narrator's investigation of the signification engendered by a name independent of its referent, through a brief discussion of the visions that the name of the town of Balbec evoked in his imagination (I, 384–7). The second chapter of *A l'ombre des jeunes filles en fleurs* – 'Noms de pays: le pays' – completes the investigation that the narrator began in 'Noms de pays: le nom' by describing the lack of correspondence between the visions evoked by the name of Balbec and the reality of the town itself. In the same way that metaphorical superimposition brings into play all of the sights, sounds, and characteristics associated with each term of the comparison, the direct link forged between Books One and Two of the *Recherche* by the two chapters dealing with names not only establishes a metaphor-like rapport between the name of Balbec and its referent – the city itself – but also causes all of the subject-matter of Book One (*Du côté de chez Swann*) to align itself with all of the characters, themes, places, events, and phenomena described in Book Two (*A l'ombre des jeunes filles en fleurs*), facilitating the establishment of macrometaphorical relationships among externally dissimilar but innately similar phenomena and characters introduced in the first two volumes.

The bipolar movement of name/presence introduced in 'Noms de pays: le nom' and 'Noms de pays: le pays' repeats itself in *Le côté de Guermantes I* and *II*, when the narrator explores the lack of correspondence between the imaginary visions which the names of the Guermantes and other old noble families evoked in his imagination before he personally made their acquaintance, and the vulgar impressions produced in reality by the nobles' physical presences and conversation. Just as the repetition of internal doubles in a metaphorical phrase disengages a common essence which transcends the superimposed phenomena, so the 'common' disparity between the names and presences of Balbec and the noble families not only establishes an internal correspondence between a city and human beings, but also suggests a general law about the incongruous relationship of a name and its referent. In subsequent volumes of *A la recherche du temps perdu*, the problem of the relationship of a name to its presence continues to be reintroduced in the text, with reference to a variety of new characters and situations, and thus functions as a common denominator linking diverse characters, milieus, and situations to each other. In order to understand fully how and why the drama of names/presences as explored in all volumes of *A la recherche du temps perdu* resembles the metaphorical structure of a work of art, we must trace the development of this theme from its earliest introduction as a sub-theme associated with the magic lantern in *Du côté de chez Swann*, to its culmination as a representation of the essence of things in *Le temps retrouvé*.

We saw that the narrator's first observations about the power of name occur almost surreptitiously within the context of his preliminary description of the magic lantern given to him by his parents: he knew that the castle and the moor depicted in the magic lantern projection were going to be yellow in colour, for the sound of the name 'Brabant' had given him a clue (I, 9). Subsequent events provide us with evidence that the magic lantern and the bipolarity of names/presences produce innately similar effects as a result of their common metaphor-like structure: the imaginary signification of a name (like the immaterial projection of a Magic Lantern) superimposes itself upon the reality of the presence that is its referent (in the same way that the magic lantern projection superimposes itself upon the existing reality of the room) and gives rise to a third field of signification that does not arise from the name or its referent, but from their interaction (just as the magic lantern's superimposition of one reality upon another has the effect of vanquishing material reality – the room as it originally appeared – and producing a new transcendent vision). The narrator never elucidates the common metaphorical structure and effect of the magic lantern and the duality of name/presences but he does describe a cousin of Mme de Guermantes as a personage of the magic lantern (III, 884). As the Guermantes are the primary subjects of the narrator's investigation of the correspondence between a name and its referent, his analogy suggests a relationship between the effect of the magic lantern and of the name/presence dichotomy.

The name of the novel *François le Champi* gives rise to an impression similar to that previously engendered by the sound of the name of Brabant:

> L'action s'engagea; elle me parut d'autant plus obscure que dans ce temps-là, quand je lisais, je rêvassais souvent pendant des pages entières à tout autre chose. Et aux lacunes que cette distraction

> laissait dans le récit, s'ajoutait, quand c'était maman qui me lisait
> à haute voix, qu'elle passait toutes les scènes d'amour. Aussi
> tous les changements bizarres qui se produisent dans l'attitude
> respective de la meunière et de l'enfant et qui ne trouvent leur
> explication que dans les progrès d'un amour naissant me parais-
> saient empreints d'un profond mystère dont je me figurais volon-
> tiers que le source devait être dans ce nom inconnu et si doux de
> 'Champi' qui mettait sur l'enfant qui le portait sans que je susse
> pourquoi, sa couleur vive, empourprée et charmante. (I, 42)

The aura of mystery engendered collectively by daydreams, omitted love scenes, and the name 'Champi' suggests that a common nature is shared by these three externally different phenomena. Future events in the novel support this intimation. In *Le côté de Guermantes*, for example, we discover that a name has the ability to transform material reality into the immaterial: Mme de Guermantes' residence is metamorphosized through its association with the name of Guermantes into 'un donjon sans épaisseur qui n'était qu'une bande de lumière orangée' (II, 13). Similarly, in *Sodome et Gomorrhe*, we see that a dream has the power to transform reality also – changing masculine beings into feminine form, or causing that which is ugly in reality to appear to be beautiful (II, 981). Love – the third phenomenon mentioned above – is also an agent of transformation. In *Du côté de chez Swann*, we are told that love transforms Swann, creating a new person who is totally different from his former self (I, 228). The aura of mystery engendered collectively from the name Champi, the narrator's daydreaming, and the omitted love scenes are also integrally linked in the narrator's mind (when a young boy) to the strange, rhythmic utterance emanating from the narration of the text itself, which paradoxically consists of everyday incidents, commonplace thoughts, and hackneyed words (I, 41). Through their similar mysterious effect, a macrometaphorical relationship is engendered between love, dreams, the movement of signification of a name, and the movement of signification of a literary work.

In 'Noms de pays: le nom,' the narrator tells us that the name of exotic towns foreign to his own environment such as Balbec, Florence, or Venice conjure up imaginary scenes and vistas:

> Même au printemps, trouver dans un livre le nom de Balbec
> suffisait à réveiller en moi le désir des tempêtes et du gothique
> normand; même par un jour de tempête, le nom de Florence ou

> de Venise me donnait le désir du soleil, des lys, du palais des Doges, et de Sainte-Marie-des-Fleurs.
>
> Mais si ces noms absorbèrent à tout jamais l'image que j'avais de ces villes, ce ne fut qu'en la transformant, qu'en soumettant sa réapparition en moi à leurs lois propres; ils eurent ainsi pour conséquence de la rendre plus belle, mais aussi plus différente de ce que les villes de Normandie ou de Toscane pouvaient être en réalité. (I, 387)

Despite the specificity of its title, the chapter is not devoted entirely to an investigation of the movement of signification produced by a name, but also discusses, in some depth, the narrator's desire to find the counterpart of books in reality, describes his first real encounters with Gilberte, comments on the lack of correspondence between reality and memory, and closes by affirming the apparently irrevocable difference between the past and the present, because of which the past may never be recovered. Although the narrator does not establish any direct parallels between the duality of names/presences and the other phenomena discussed in this chapter, the contiguity of these themes in the text allows us to perceive that subjects which are apparently unrelated to the study of names (Gilberte/the narrator, memory/reality, past/present) all have an innate similarity to the names/referents duality. The narrator realizes that his imaginary musings about Balbec transform the town into something different from what it could ever be in reality, thus indicating that, paradoxically, the characteristic common to a name and its referent is their lack of correspondence. Similarly, when he begins to meet Gilberte regularly on the Champs Elysées (the girl whose reality he previously imagined so frequently, I, 141-2), he attempts to relate the image of her in his memory and imagination to the reality of her being, and discovers over and over again that her reality and the visions she inspires are different (I, 401). Correspondingly, the narrator's attempts – by revisiting old familiar spots – to relive his memories of past years only serve to demonstrate the disparity between memory and reality. The final pages of *Du côté de chez Swann* describe the narrator's impressions of the Champs-Elysées when he revisits it in his later years, in an era when motor cars have replaced the carriage and pair, ladies have lost the art of dressing elegantly, and men no longer wear hats (I, 425-6). He consequently realizes that he can never rediscover in the reality of the present the pictures of the past that are stored in his memory, because the charm he associates with past memories comes to them from memory itself and not from their being apprehended by the senses (I, 427). Present reality and past memories are as incongruous as a name and its referent.

In the second part ('Noms de pays: le pays') of Book Two, the narrator completes his discussion of the lack of correspondence between a name and its referent begun in Chapter Three of Book One ('Noms de pays: le nom'). He assumed previously that his imaginary musings about Balbec transformed the town into something different from what it could ever be in reality. His visit to Balbec confirms his previous assumptions: the church and statue which are Balbec's main attractions are far less impressive than his expectations: 'c'était elle enfin, l'oeuvre d'art immortelle et si longtemps désirée, que je trouvais métamorphosée, ainsi que l'église elle-même, en une petite vieille de pierre dont je pouvais mesurer la hauteur et compter les rides' (I, 660). It appears at this point in the novel that, despite a similar binary structure, the interaction of a name with its referent produces a totally opposite effect to the combination of dissimilar entities in a metaphorical phrase. Metaphor reveals an internal reality common to the externally dissimilar phenomena that it joins together, while the comparison of names to their presences discloses their dissimilarities:

> pour Balbec, dès que j'y étais entré, ç'avait été comme si j'avais entr'ouvert un nom qu'il eût fallu tenir hermétiquement clos et où, profitant de l'issue que je leur avais imprudemment offerte, en chassant toutes les images qui y vivaient jusque-là, un tramway, un café, les gens qui passaient sur la place, la succursale du Comptoir d'Escompte, irrésistiblement poussés par une pression externe et une force pneumatique, s'étaient engouffrés à l'intérieur des syllabes qui, refermées sur eux, les laissaient maintenant encadrer le porche de l'église persane et ne cesseraient plus de les contenir. (I, 660–1)

In the first pages of *Le côté de Guermantes*, the narrator clarifies, in more general terms, some indirect observations concerning the name/presence duality presented in the first two books of the novel. He compares the movement of signification of a name independent of its presence to a fairy who dies when we come into contact with it:

> chaque château, chaque hôtel ou palais fameux a sa dame ou sa fée, comme les forêts leurs génies et leurs divinités les eaux ...
> Cependant, la fée dépérit si nous nous approchons de la per-

> sonne réelle à laquelle correspond son nom, car, cette personne, le nom alors commence à la refléter et elle ne contient rien de la fée; la fée peut renaître si nous nous éloignons de la personne; mais si nous restons auprès d'elle, la fée meurt définitivement et avec elle le nom ... (II, 11)

Like a metaphor, a name brings into play two distinctly different movements of signification: an image of the unknowable that originates in the observer's imagination, and a 'realistic' vision which corresponds to an existing place or person. However, whereas metaphor allows us to see the common essence of things, the superimposition of dissimilars engendered by a name makes clear their difference: 'A l'âge où les Noms, nous offrant l'image de l'inconnaissable que nous avons versé en eux, dans le même moment où ils désignent aussi pour nous un lieu réel, nous forcent par là à identifier l'un à l'autre, au point que nous partons chercher dans une cité une âme qu'elle ne peut contenir mais que nous n'avons plus le pouvoir d'expulser de son nom ...' (II, 10).

It is necessary to point out that the narrator's investigation of names/presences in *A la recherche du temps perdu* progresses through four distinct levels: in level one, the narrator investigates the movement of signification that the name itself gives rise to; in level two, the narrator encounters the presence (cities, people) to whom the name refers and discovers that it has the effect of nullifying the movement of signification that the name itself engendered. In the third stage, we begin to see the development of a reflective relationship between names and their referents, as the narrator perceives individual traits in his subjects of study which transcend the vulgarity that first characterized their presences. Names and presences begin to interact like two dissimilar objects linked together in a metaphorical phrase, as the name begins to act as a mirror that allows the internal reality of the presence to reveal itself. In level four of his investigation, the narrator realizes that names signify the essence of a person or an object. Names therefore become the symbol of the internal reality of things that is revealed through the metaphorical process, and intimated by a work of art.

As mentioned above, the narrator discovers in the second stage of his investigation of the 'name/presence' relationship that the signification evoked by the names of noble families is incongruous with their physical presences. The narrator expects Mme de Guermantes' appearance and conversation to reflect the unknown element of her name: 'j'avais peine à retrouver dans le beau visage, trop humain, de

Mme de Guermantes, l'inconnu de son nom, je pensais du moins que, quand elle parlerait, sa causerie, profonde, mystérieuse, aurait une étrangeté de tapisserie médiévale, de vitrail gothique' (II, 209). On the contrary, he finds her face to be altogether too human; and instead of the fine, beautiful, profound words he expected to hear coming from her mouth, he is subjected to the most common sort of slanderous gossip as she compares an overweight woman to a frog who has swollen to the size of an ox (II, 210). The disparity between the effects of the name and the presence of Mme de Guermantes (and all the other characters analysed by the narrator) recalls to mind the lack of correspondence between the internal and external reality of the many homosexual characters of the novel, and also reflects the incongruity between the body and spirit of any human being (II, 298).

I observed previously in 'Interior/Exterior/Metaphor' and in 'Homosexuality/Flowers/Writing/Metaphor' that the superimposition of all of the novel's characters one upon the other in the text disengages a general law about all of them: that a lack of correspondence between their internal and external realities is their common essential nature. Similarly, the incongruity produced by the name and presence of Mme de Guermantes is converted to a generality through the textual superimposition of multiple personalities one upon the other in *Le côté de Guermantes*. A similar disparity between name and presence is demonstrated, for example, by the Prince von Faffenheim and the Prince d'Agrigente. The speech of the Prince von Faffenheim totally destroys the effect evoked by his name: 'Le nom du prince gardait, dans la franchise avec laquelle ses premières syllabes étaient – comme on dit en musique – attaquées, et dans la bégayante répétition qui les scandait, l'élan, la naïveté maniérée, les lourdes "délicatesses" germaniques projetées comme des branchages verdâtres sur le "Heim," d'émail bleu sombre qui déployait la mysticité d'un vitrail rhénan derrière les dorures pâles et finement ciselées du xviiie siècle allemand (II, 256) ... Ma profonde désillusion eut lieu quand il parla' (II, 263). Similarly, the name of the Prince d'Agrigente conjures up in the narrator's mind visions of a transparent glass through which he could see a rose marble city on the shore of a violet sea. However, the vulgar drone whom the name designates is as independent of his name as any work of art he might have owned (II, 432–3).

In the course of his reflections on the signification of a name, the narrator also realizes that a name assumes seven or eight different shapes: 'Mais plus tard je trouve successivement, dans la durée en moi de ce nom, sept ou huit figures différentes ...' (II, 13). In *A l'ombre des jeunes filles en fleurs,* the narrator had described the appearance of the human face in similar terms, likening it to a many-faced god whose appearance fluctuates from day to day (I, 916). In *Le côté de Guermantes II*, he specifically applied this image to Albertine, comparing her fluctuating appearance (the changes in its aspect wrought by variations in the distance from which he perceived her) to that of a goddess with many heads (II, 365). The many levels of signification arising from both names and human presences suggests that they may not be as opposed as the narrator's previous observations about them would indicate.

Correspondingly, the third level of the narrator's investigation of names and their referents is characterized by the development of a mirror relationship between names and presences, despite their former apparent incongruity. As in his previous experiences of Balbec and Florence, the narrator discovers that, upon getting to know them better, the Guermantes begin to appeal to his intellect because of certain distinctive characteristics they possess, such as their bodily structure, the peculiar pink colour of their skin, a certain brilliance of intellect, and their distinctive comportment (II, 438). The historical pedigrees of the nobility that the Duc de Guermantes and the General discuss in the presence of the narrator also restore to the friends of M. and Mme de Guermantes some of their vanished poetry:

> Chacun des convives du dîner, affublant le nom mystérieux sous lequel je l'avais seulement connu et rêvé à distance, d'un corps et d'une intelligence pareils ou inférieurs à ceux de toutes les personnes que je connaissais, m'avait donné l'impression de plate vulgarité que peut donner l'entrée dans le port danois d'Elseneur à tout lecteur enfievré d'*Hamlet*. Sans doute ces régions géographiques et ce passé ancien qui mettaient des futaies et des clochers gothiques dans leur nom, avaient, dans une certaine mesure, formé leur visage, leur esprit et leurs préjugés, mais n'y subsistaient que comme la cause dans l'effet, c'est-à-dire peut-être possibles à dégager pour l'intelligence, mais nullement sensibles à l'imagination.
>
> Et ces préjugés d'autrefois rendirent tout à coup aux amis de M. et Mme de Guermantes leur poésie perdue. (II, 532)

In view of the labyrinth of metaphorical cross-references that I am in the process of unravelling, it is significant that the historical accounts of the noble families put 'clochers gothiques' into their names; as the allusion reinforces the common transcendent reality suggested by names and by the steeples of Combray and Martinville.

After hearing the genealogies of the nobility, the narrator realizes that the names take order in his memory – relate themselves to one another – and collectively resemble those finished works of art in which there is not one isolated element (II, 537). His analogy not only reinforces the metaphorical parallels that he has drawn between a work of art and a name on previous occasions, but also evokes his description of the Vinteuil Septet, which he categorizes in *La prisonnière* as a triumphal work of art combining different elements into one harmonious whole (III, 252). In turn, the finished work of art realized by the intertwined labyrinth of names and the complete masterpiece of Vinteuil both reflect the structure of *A la Recherche du temps perdu*, in which diverse themes reveal their essential unity through a complex network of metaphorical cross-references.

While commenting on the lack of correspondence between the name and presence of the Prince d'Agrigente, the narrator suggests that the vision evoked by the name of Agrigente is so different from the actual vulgar man that the name is liberated from the person it designates and assumes an independent existence as 'les syllabes enchantées' (II, 433). He also discovers that the names cited in the genealogies narrated at the party have the effect of disincarnating the guests of the duchess and delivering them from the face and speech that prevented one from recognizing them (II, 542). In both cases, the interaction of a name with its presence gives rise to a transcendental reality which can only reveal itself through the disparity of two engaged terms. The relationship of a name to its presence is like the interaction of a reader with his text. Both are metaphorical processes in which the interaction of two dissimilar phenomena clarifies an essential nature: 'L'ouvrage de l'écrivain n'est qu'une espèce d'instrument optique qu'il offre au lecteur afin de lui permettre de discerner ce que, sans ce livre, il n'eût peut-être pas vu en soi-même' (III, 911).

In the discussion of 'Noms de pays: le nom,' we saw that, despite the apparent specificity of its title, the chapter was not entirely devoted to names but also discussed three other subjects (his first meetings with Gilberte, the discrepancy between memory and reality, and the apparently irrevocable difference between past and present) which manifested an innate similarity to the duality of 'name/presence.' *Le côté de Guermantes I* and *II* display a similar pattern. Although both these books are more specifically devoted to the study of the relationship between names and presences than any of the other volumes of the novel, they also include investigations of other phenomena that bring into play forces and mechanisms paralleling those produced by the interaction of names and presences. The various kinds of sleep described by Marcel and the visions induced by them, for example, recall the multiple levels of signification evoked by the proper name (II, 86–8).

Similarly, the forces provoking the aura of mystery caused by the presence of Rachel (Saint-Loup's mistress) are analogous to those that give rise to the enchanted world the narrator associates with the name of Guermantes. Her name connotes a realm of dreams for the narrator because the real life of Mme de Guermantes is unimaginable to him. Likewise, Rachel represents every possible delight in life for Saint-Loup, precisely because her secret self is unknown to him, and his imagination must supplement this lack of knowledge (II, 157–8). The disparity between the name and its referent is reflected in the incongruity of the body and the psyche that pertains to it (II, 298), and in the dissimilitude between the external interpretation and internal motivation of human conduct: the origin of signification of human conduct is indefinable (like a name without its presence) because the external interpretation of a social gesture is based on the absence of any true knowledge about its intended purpose (II, 272).

In the resurgence of the investigation of names in the remaining volumes of *A la recherche du temps perdu*, a reverse bipolaric movement occurs. Just as metaphor gives rise to a play of reflected doubles in which the internal essence of one object is identified by its mirror reflection in the second object, so the basic movement of signification of 'name-referring-to-presence' that was explored in the first three books is succeeded by its mirror reversal of 'presence-referring-to-name' in *Sodome et Gomorrhe*. During another party held at the Guermantes, for example, a lady who apparently knows the narrator greets him, but he cannot recall her name, although he can remember her face and previous conversation. Previously, proper names did not correspond to the presences to which they referred; now presences do not connote their names (II, 650). Although the narrator cannot recall the woman's name when he consciously applies his active intelligence to it, the name is restored to him in a flash just after he considers himself beaten: 'D'ailleurs ce travail de l'esprit passant du néant à la réalité est si mystérieux, qu'il est possible, après tout, que ces consonnes fausses soient des perches préalables, maladroitement tendues pour nous aider à nous accrocher au nom exact' (II, 651). The unconscious process that culminates in the emergence of the woman's name from the obscurity of his memory strongly suggests the drawing forth of impressions from the shadow, which he describes as the creation of a work of art in *Le temps retrouvé* (III, 879). The narrator does not draw a parallel between the two experiences for us, but their enclosure in the totality of Proust's text allows their similarities to reveal themselves through a 'natural' metaphorical process.

The disparity between the presence and the name of Mme d'Arpajon is repeated when the Princess Sherbatoff's presence fails to suggest the true nature of her being. During one of his train trips to La Raspelière, the narrator shares a compartment with a woman whom, to judge by her appearance, he assumes to be the keeper of a brothel. Two days later, he meets her at the Verdurins' and discovers that she is Princess Sherbatoff. We saw previously in *Le côté de Guermantes* that the names cited in the genealogies of the noble guests had the effect of restoring to them their true natures obscured by their vulgar faces and speech (II, 542). Similarly, the name of Princess Sherbatoff allows the narrator to pierce the obscurity created by her appearance, and perceive clearly the true personality of the woman: 'c'était la dame que, dans le même train, j'avais cru, l'avant-veille, pouvoir être la tenancière d'une maison publique. Sa personnalité sociale, si incertaine, me devint claire aussitôt quand je sus son nom, comme quand, après avoir peiné sur une devinette, on apprend enfin le mot qui rend clair tout ce qui était resté obscur et qui, pour les personnes, est le nom' (II, 892). Once again, the name functions like a literary work which allows the reader to perceive his true self (III, 911).

Life experience has previously taught the narrator that a name does not necessarily correspond to its referent; that the signification of a name does not originate in any definable presence. He discovers that the information revealed through the study of the origin of names is equally as illusory, deceptive, and disappointing. In the case of place names, there may be conflicting etymological studies concerning the origin and true meaning of words. There is confusion, for example, as to whether or not the origin of the word 'Bricq' – which is found in a number of place names in the neighbourhood of La Raspelière – is the Celtic word 'Briga', meaning height, or the Old Norse word 'bricg,' meaning a bridge (II, 888). Like the presence to which a proper name refers, a clearly definable etymological origin for a word frequently destroys the signification which the sound of the name evoked, as the name in reality may mean something totally different from what he had thought: 'J'avais trouvé charmant la fleur qui terminait certains noms, comme Fiquefleur, Honfleur, Flers, Barfleur, Harfleur, etc.; et amusant le bœuf qu'il y a à la fin de Bricqueboeuf. Mais la fleur disparut, et aussi le boeuf, quand Brichot (et cela, il me l'avait dit le premier jour dans le train) nous apprit que "fleur" veut dire "port" (comme "fiord") et que "bœuf," in normand budh, signifie "cabane"'(II, 1098).

In *Le temps retrouvé*, the narrator tells us that the true nature of things is obscured by daily habit (III, 896). His experience of the places designated by names supports this contention. The name of St Pierre des Ifs, for example, was previously shrouded for him in the mists of a historical past, but his repeated exposure to it as a name on a train station platform and the life experience now associated with that name cause it to lose all of its previous mystery, until it simply signifies the place where M. de Cambremer lives (II, 1108).

Just as the imaginary movement of signification evoked by a name becomes lost and buried under familiarity like the true nature of things about which the narrator speaks in *Le temps retrouvé*, so the narrator's subsequent experiences with names support the parallels previously established among names, and the function of a work of art. A work of art, according to the narrator, allows us to perceive the essential quality of reality (III, 896). In a similar vein, the narrator finishes his investigation of 'names/presences' by equating a 'name' with the 'essence' of its referent. In death, Saint-Loup becomes nothing more than his name, which is his essence (III, 851). Similarly, after re-encountering the novel *François le Champi* in the Guermantes' library, the narrator realizes that the name of the novel signifies the essence of what the book meant for him in the past: 'Le souvenir de ce qui m'avait semblé inexplicable dans le sujet de *François le Champi* tandis que maman me lisait le livre de George Sand, était réveillé par ce titre (aussi bien que le nom de Guermantes, quand je n'avais pas vu les Guermantes depuis longtemps, contenait pour moi tant de féodalité – comme François le Champi l'essence du roman –), et se substituait pour un instant à l'idée fort commune de ce que sont les romans berrichons de George Sand' (III, 883).

The name of the novel also functions as an object from the past re-encountered in the present that catalyses an experience of involuntary memory: 'si je reprends, même par la pensée, dans la bibliothèque, *François le Champi*, immédiatement en moi un enfant se lève qui prend ma place, qui seul a le droit de ce titre: *François le Champi*, et qui le lit comme il le lut alors, avec la même impression du temps qu'il faisait dans le jardin ...' (III, 885). By acting as a catalyst which resuscitates past time for the narrator, the name 'François le Champi' recalls all other experiences in the narrator's life that have produced the same effect (the taste of a madeleine dipped in tea, stepping on an uneven paving stone, etc.), and thus constructs a macrometaphorical bridge between two of the narrator's main subjects of investigation: names/presences and past/present reminiscences.[6]

In the course of the narrator's investigation of the relationship of the name of "Guermantes" to the presences it represents, three stages of signification were traced and these collectively interacted in a way resembling the metaphorical process. First of all, the name signified something mysterious. Then, after the narrator made the acquaintance of the Guermantes, the name came to signify something common and familiar. Finally, while reading an invitation from the Guermantes in *Le temps retrouvé*, the narrator sees the letters divorce themselves from anything that they have ever been before, and become something totally new and independent: 'j'avais continué à relire l'invitation jusqu'au moment où, révoltées, les lettres qui composaient ce nom si familier et si mystérieux, comme celui même de Combray, eussent repris leur indépendance et eussent dessiné devant mes yeux fatigués comme un nom que je ne connaissais pas' (III, 857). Like metaphor, the combination of two dissimilar 'names' (the name as something mysterious, and the name as something familiar) gives rise to a new reality (their essential nature) which is neither one nor the other. Thus, we are able to perceive the metaphorical process as the essential common denominator of a work of art and the signification of a name which permitted the narrator to compare them to one another in a poetic simile.

STEEPLES/ART/METAPHOR

The first time that the narrator mentions the steeple of Combray in *Du côté de chez Swann*, he describes it as a sign of art and of humanity sketched upon the sky by the fingernail of a painter:

> Et dans une des plus grandes promenades que nous faisions de Combray, il y avait un endroit où la route resserrée débouchait tout à coup sur un immense plateau fermé à l'horizon par des forêts déchiquetées que dépassait seule la fine pointe du clocher de Sainte-Hilaire, mais si mince, si rose, qu'elle semblait seulement rayée sur le ciel par un ongle qui aurait voulu donner à ce passage, à ce tableau rien que de nature, cette petite marque d'art, cette unique indication humaine. (I, 63)

In *Le temps retrouvé*, immediately after having experienced the first of the three 'intimations' that lead him to his discovery of the nature of art and metaphor, the narrator lists all the other experiences in his life which have produced in him a similar inexplicable happiness. Included in this list are the sight of the twin steeples of Martinville and the view of three trees on a road near Balbec (III, 866). Because the narrator's analysis of these experiences culminates in his realization of the metaphorical structure that must undergird a work of art if it is to intimate the internal reality of things, all of the experiences which engendered in him the same 'inexplicable happiness' are 'signs of art.' However, experiences such as his past/present reminiscences and his 'obscure impressions' constitute 'natural' metaphors bringing together circumstances far removed in time and space, whereas the steeple of Combray, the twin steeples of Martinville, and the three trees on a road near Balbec graphically represent the metaphorical process.

In addition to being linked analogically to the nature of art, the steeples and/or the three trees are also compared to, or share a common denominator in the text with nature, music, birds, flowers, maidens, a page in a book, a pattern, obscure impressions, a preliminary sketch, hieroglyphic characters, a dream, the movement of signification engendered by a proper name, and experiences of involuntary memory.

Metaphor commences with the joining together of two externally dissimilar phenomena. Similarly, the steeple of Combray and its adjoining tower constitute a binary structure with dissimilar component parts: the tall, slim steeple is flanked by a shorter square tower half in ruins: 'Quand on se rapprochait et qu'on pouvait apercevoir le reste de la tour carrée et à demi détruite qui, moins haute, substistait à côté de lui ...' (I, 63). Its windows, placed two and two – one above the other – give the steeple tower a bisymmetrical appearance: 'Des fenêtres de sa tour, placées deux par deux les unes au-dessus des autres, avec cette juste et originale proportion dans les distances qui ne donne pas de la beauté et de la dignité qu'aux visages humains ...' (I, 63). The binary superimposition inherent in a metaphorical phrase causes the signification of individual phenomena to merge and give rise to a new reality or a third field of signification which transcends its binary origins. Correspondingly, the tower (distinguished by its binary symmetry) discharges from its windows, at regular intervals, flights of ravens: 'il lâchait, laissait tomber à intervalles réguliers des volées de corbeaux qui, pendant un moment, tournoyaient en criant, comme si les vieilles pierres qui les laissaient s'ébattre sans paraître les voir, devenues tout d'un coup inhabitables et dégageant un principe d'agitation infinie, les avaient frappés et repoussés' (I, 63). From the perspective of their function as symbols of transcendence in Western culture,[7] the birds expelled from the bisymmetrical tower are like the transcendental quality arising from the interaction of two elements in a metaphorical phrase.

We are told that the structural lines of the steeple suggest the architectonics of a great work of art: the narrator's grandmother perceives in the steeple of Sainte-Hilaire that same absence of vulgarity, pretention, and meanness which makes her love nature and works of genius: 'Sans trop savoir pourquoi, ma grandmère trouvait au clocher de Saint-Hilaire, cette absence de vulgarité, de prétention, de mesquinerie, qui lui faisait aimer et croire riches d'une influence bienfaisante la nature quand la main de l'homme ne l'avait pas, comme faisait le jardinier de ma grand'tante, rapetissée, et les oeuvres de génie' (I, 64).

I mentioned above that the tower is characterized by its bisymmetrical appearance. The grandmother's comparison thus implies that art and nature may also manifest a similar, simple binary structure. In this way, the steeple not only reflects in itself the nature of metaphor, but also the correspondence established by the narrator among nature, metaphor, and art in *Le temps retrouvé* (III, 889.) If we compare the two analogies (the metaphor/art/nature analogy from *Le temps retrouvé* and the steeples/art/nature analogy from *Du côté de chez Swann*), we can see that, through the macrometaphorical correspondence which the common terms of the comparisons establish between them, 'metaphor' and 'steeples' become interchangeable:

    art = steeples = nature,
    art = metaphor = nature,
    therefore, steeples = metaphor.

As well as structurally evoking metaphor, nature, and art, the steeple of Combray also gives rise to a macrometaphorical link between these three subjects of investigation and the human personality. I mentioned above that, when we first encounter the steeple in *Du côté de chez Swann*, it is described not only as a sign of art ('cette petite marque d'art' (I, 63)), but also as a sign of humanity ('cette unique indication humaine' (I, 63). Subsequent descriptions of the steeple consolidate its 'human' qualities; the symmetry of its windows is compared to the proportions of human face: 'Des fenêtres de sa tour, placées deux par deux les unes au-dessus des autres, avec cette juste et originale proportion dans les distances qui ne donne pas de la beauté et de la dignité qu'aux visages humains' (I, 63); its natural, distinguished air inspires the narrator's grandmother to compare it to a gifted pianist ('sa vieille figure bizarre me plaît. Je suis sûre que s'il jouait du piano, il ne jouerait pas sec' (I, 64)). The latter comparison summons to mind another 'gifted pianist' mentioned in the *Recherche* – Morel, Charlus' protégé – who is frequently linked (through implication)[8] with another phenomenon associated by Proust with art and writing – homosexuality (see p 63).

The metaphorical process reveals an internal rapport transcending external reality. Similarly, the narrator tells us that, through its steeple, the church seems to display a consciousness of itself: 'c'était dans son clocher qu'elle semblait prendre conscience d'elle-même, affirmer une existence individuelle et responsable. C'était lui qui parlait pour elle' (I, 64). In metaphor, two dissimilar phenomena merge to reveal a common, internal essence that transcends its binary components. Similarly, the parallel lines of the body of the tower slope together as they reach the steeple, until they join at the tip of the pinnacle. The topmost pinnacle of the steeple seems to transcend its material reality, becoming suddenly far higher, like a song whose singer breaks into falsetto, an octave above the accompanying air:

> Et en le regardant, en suivant des yeux la douce tension, l'inclinaison fervente de ses pentes de pierre qui se rapprochaient en s'élevant comme des mains jointes qui prient, elle s'unissait si bien à l'effusion de la flèche, que son regard semblait s'élancer avec elle; et en même temps elle souriait amicalement
> aux vieilles pierres usées dont le couchant n'éclairait plus que le faîte et qui, à partir du moment où elles entraient dans cette zone ensoleillée, adoucies par la lumière, paraissaient tout d'un coup montées bien plus haut, lointaines, comme un chant repris 'en voix-de-tête' une octave au-dessus. (I, 64).

The most notable piece of music introduced over and over again in the *Recherche* being the Vinteuil Sonata, the transcendental effect attributed to both the steeple and music in the comparison engenders a macrometaphorical rapport between the steeples and the sonata. This implied link between the two phenomena is later consolidated in *La prisonnière* through an analogy: the narrator compares the transcendental impression evoked by the Vinteuil Sonata to a similar feeling produced by the twin steeples of Martinville and the three trees of Balbec, whose reflective relationship with the steeple of Saint-Hilaire shall soon be examined (III, 374).

The steeple of Combray is also described as the central focal point of the village: 'c'était toujours à lui qu'il faillait revenir, toujours lui qui dominait tout, sommant les maisons d'un pinnacle inattendu, levé devant moi comme le doigt de Dieu dont le corps eût été caché dans la foule des humains sans que je le confondisse pour cela avec elle' (I, 66). As the steeple is to the village, so metaphor is to the novel *A la recherche du temps perdu*: its structure is inherent in all aspects of the text, and its essential nature transcends its collective manifestations.

The narrator describes a second experience with steeples which, when viewed in conjunction with his first experience, constitutes both a doubling and a continuation of the metaphorical model presented to us through the steeple of Combray. On his way home in a carriage, after an exceptionally long walk along the Guermantes' Way, the narrator inadvertently sees the twin steeples of Martinville and discovers that they produce in him the same special pleasure as that given previously by the steeples of Combray. The basic outline of the twin steeples repeats the basic shape of the steeple of Combray flanked by the ruined tower, but introduces a difference: whereas in Combray, the superstructure consisted of one well-defined shape (the steeple tower) and one less-defined shape (the ruined tower beside the steeple tower), the twin steeples of Martinville constitute two clearly defined outlines that are mirror reflections of each other. If the steeple of Combray and the old ruined tower are like two dissimilar phenomena joined together in a metaphorical phrase, then the twin steeples of Martinville are a macromodel of the second stage of the metaphorical process. Just as the superimposition of dissimilar phenomena in a metaphorical phrase reveals an essence common to them both which renders them internal doubles of each other, so the twin steeples are 'doubles.'

When viewed from the perspective of the constantly moving carriage and the twisting road, the twin steeples of Martinville appear to be joined by a third steeple – the steeple of Vieuxvicq – although they are separated in reality by a hill and a valley: 'Au tournant d'un chemin j'éprouvai tout à coup ce plaisir spécial qui ne ressemblait à aucun autre, à apercevoir les deux clochers de Martinville, sur lesquels donnait le soleil couchant et que le mouvement de notre voiture et les lacets du chemin avaient l'air de faire changer de place, puis celui de

Vieuxvicq qui, séparé d'eux par une colline et une vallée, et situé sur un plateau plus élevé dans le lointain, semblait pourtant tout voisin d'eux' (I, 180). This third steeple structurally resembles the new reality or the common essence born from the interaction of two terms in a metaphorical phrase. Just as the essence revealed through metaphorical superimposition transcends the two terms that revealed it, so the third steeple is on 'higher ground' than the twin steeples of Martinville.

The narrator previously described the steeple of Combray as a sign of art (I, 63), and suggested that its simple structure is the same as that which manifests itself in nature and in works of genius. He never compares the twin steeples of Martinville to a work of art, but they inspire him to translate into words the impression they evoke. After viewing the steeples, he felt that 'something more' was concealed behind their luminosity. In order to uncover their hidden meaning, he tried to keep in mind their converging lines: 'je sentais que je n'allais pas au bout de mon impression, que quelque chose était derrière ce mouvement, derrière cette clarté, quelque chose qu'ils semblaient contenir et dérober à la fois' (I, 180). Could he have kept those converging lines of the steeples in his mind, he realizes that they would have been engulfed in a great medley of sights, scents, and sounds which had previously given him the same obscure sense of pleasure (I, 180). The narrator's initial reaction to the twin steeples closely resembles his response – years later – to the first 'intimation' experienced in the Guermantes' courtyard in *Le temps retrouvé*: at that time also, he recalls all of the other experiences which produced in him a similar inexplicable happiness. Just as he later resolves, after his first 'intimation' in *Le temps retrouvé* (III, 867), to analyse his experience in order to determine the cause of the inexplicable happiness just given him, so the young narrator attempts to recapture the vision of the steeples in his mind; and presently, as a result of his reflection, their outlines break apart to reveal a little of what they concealed. An idea which had not existed previously forms itself in his mind, and frames itself in words which enhance the pleasure that the sight of the steeples had first produced in him (I, 180–1). The narrator describes the unknown element that lay behind the outlines of the steeples as 'quelque chose d'analogue à une jolie phrase' (I, 181), commits to paper the words suggested by his mental apprehension of the steeples, and thus creates in rough draft a literary work: 'demandant un crayon et du papier au docteur, je composai malgré les cahots de la voiture, pour soulager ma conscience et obéir à mon enthousiasme, le petit morceau suivant que j'ai retrouvai depuis et auquel je n'ai eu à faire subir que peu de changements' (I, 181). The three-step process which the narrator follows in his effort to grasp what lay behind the steeples – apprehension of the impression by his mind, the revelation of an idea behind the impression, the conversion of that idea into words – parallels the procedure the narrator describes as 'the creation of a work of art' in *Le temps retrouvé* (III, 879). In this way, the twin steeples of Martinville not only reflect graphically metaphorical structure, but also illustrate how a metaphor-like impression may be translated into a work of art.

In the written work that is born from his reflections on the steeples, the narrator compares the three steeples to three birds, three maidens in a legend, and three flowers. Like the ravens issuing from the steeple of Combray, the comparison of the steeples to birds establishes a correspondence between the steeples and the transcendent reality revealed through metaphor. The bird/steeple analogy also establishes a macrometaphorical relationship between the steeples and two principal characters: Mme de Guermantes – the central subject of the narrator's investigation of the names/presences duality – is compared to a bird ('Une fois ce ne fut pas seulement une femme à bec d'oiseau que je vis, mais comme un oiseau même ...,' II, 62), and Swann, also of the 'two ways,' has a name that sounds like an English word designating a kind of bird (a swan). In 'Homosexuality/Flowers/Writing/Metaphor,' we saw that a series of somewhat allegorical comparisons involving flowers as one term of the analogy establishes a relationship between the nature of homosexuality, flowers and writing. As the steeples are also compared to flowers, an underlying correspondence is established among the steeples, homosexuality, writing, and all other phenomena compared to flowers (such as the Vinteuil Sonata, I, 208–9; III, 250, 375). The comparison of the steeples to three maidens suggests an internal rapport between the nature of the steeples and the nature of the three women in the narrator's life – Mme de Guermantes, Gilberte, and Albertine – who in turn reveal to him the contradictory relationship of a name to its presence, the disparity between the external appearance and the internal reality of a human being, and the transformational nature of love.

In his written commentary on the three steeples, the narrator observes that from a distance, the steeples slip one behind the other until they become a single form: 'je les vis timidement chercher leur chemin et, après quelques gauches trébuchements de leurs nobles silhouettes, se serrer les uns contre les autres, glisser l'un derrière l'autre, ne plus faire sur le ciel encore rose qu'une seule forme, noire, charmante et résignée, et s'effacer dans la nuit' (I, 182). The merging of the three steeples into one entity symbolizes graphically the ultimate merging of the multiple recurring themes of *A la recherche du temps perdu* into one structure – metaphor.

While out on a drive on a road near Balbec (an event recounted in *A l'ombre des jeunes filles en fleurs*), the narrator sees three trees whose appearance overwhelms him with a happiness analogous to that given him by the steeples of Martinville and other phenomena. The three trees form a pattern that is not new to him, but he cannot remember where he has seen the pattern before:

> Nous descendîmes sur Hudimesnil, tout d'un coup je fus rempli de ce bonheur profond que je n'avais pas souvent ressenti depuis Combray, un bonheur analogue à celui que m'avaient donné, entre autres, les clochers de Martinville. Mais, cette fois, il resta incomplet. Je venais d'apercevoir, en retrait de la route en dos d'âne que nous suivions, trois arbres qui devaient servir d'entrée à une allée couverte et formaient un dessin que je ne voyais pas pour la première fois, je ne pouvais arriver à reconnaître le lieu dont ils étaient comme détachés, mais je sentais qu'il m'avait été familier autrefois ... (I, 717)

Just as he tried to recapture in his mind the view of the twin steeples of Martinville, so the narrator attempts to apprehend the image summoned by the three trees, but to no avail. He suggests that his inability to recollect where he previously saw the three trees may arise from the probability that the past of which they are a part is so distant that it is already obliterated from his memory: 'Fallait-il croire qu'ils venaient d'années déjà si lointaines de ma vie que le paysage qui les entourait avait été entièrement aboli dans ma mémoire et que, comme ces pages qu'on est tout d'un coup ému de retrouver dans un ouvrage qu'on s'imaginait n'avoir jamais lu, ils surnageaient seuls du livre oublié de ma première enfance? N'appartenaient-ils au contraire qu'à ces paysages du rêve ...' (I, 718). Although the trees are not compared to a book or to a dream, the narrator's suggestion that their origin is in a book or in a dream implies that dreams, a book, and the pattern of the three trees may have something in common. He also wonders if the three trees are not simply 'obscure impressions': 'Ou bien ne les avais-je jamais vus et cachaient-ils derrière eux, comme tels arbres, telle touffe d'herbe que j'avais vus du côté de Guermantes, un sens aussi obscur, aussi difficile à saisir qu'un passé lointain, de sorte que, sollicité par eux d'approfondir une pensée, je croyais avoir à reconnaître un souvenir' (I, 719). Because the origin of signification of the three trees may be either in a distant memory or in an obscure impression, the three trees function as an intermediary linking these two sorts of phenomena together – a correspondence which foreshadows the narrator's discoveries in *Le temps retrouvé* about the common metaphorical quality of both sorts of experiences. In any case, the narrator does emphasize that he sees the trees 'double in time' – simultaneously in the present and in an indefinable past moment. Through this quality of dual time which the trees engender, they recall the narrator's many experiences of involuntary memory (past/present 'intimations'): 'Or cette cause, je la devinais en comparant ces diverses impressions bienheureuses et qui avaient entre elles ceci de commun que je les éprouvais à la fois dans le moment actuel et dans un moment éloigné, jusqu'à faire empiéter le passé sur le présent' (III, 871).

Although the narrator emphasizes that he cannot remember where he has seen their pattern before, the reader is in a better position to perceive the common structural patterns shared by the three trees and some other phenomena investigated in the *Recherche*. The narrator told us that the three trees engender in him a happiness analogous to that which had been given him by the twin steeples of Martinville. This common effect invites us to investigate their structural affinities. We saw previously that, when seen from a distance, the twin steeples of Martinville are joined by a third steeple to form a triadic pattern of three vertical shapes standing one beside the other. The three trees on the road near Balbec repeat this triadic pattern, and the triadic structure of a metaphorical comparison. They also macrometaphorically summon up all other triadic structures in the novel: the three intimations the narrator experiences in *Le temps retrouvé* (III, 866–7), the 'third' terms engendered by the interaction of a reader with his book, a name with its presence, the tea with the madeleine, to name only a few examples.

In *La prisonnière*, the narrator compares the feeling evoked by the Vinteuil Septet to the effect created by the twin steeples of Martinville, the three trees on the road near Balbec, and the drinking of the tea with the madeleine. In an effort to explain the common nature of these experiences, he suggests that they all originate in an impression like the fragrance of a geranium: 'les sensations vagues données par Vinteuil, venant non d'un souvenir, mais d'une impression (comme celle des clochers de Martinville), il aurait fallu trouver, de la fragrance de géranium de sa musique, non une explication matérielle, mais l'équivalent profond ...' (III, 375). The narrator reiterates this analogy in *Le temps retrouvé* immediately after he steps on the recessed paving stone in the Guermantes' courtyard: 'Mais au moment où, me remettant d'aplomb, je posai mon pied sur un pavé qui était un peu moins élevé que le précédent, tout mon découragement s'évanouit devant la même félicité qu'à diverses époques de ma vie m'avaient donnée la vue d'arbres que j'avais cru reconnaître dans une promenade en voiture autour de Balbec, la vue des clochers de Martinville, la saveur d'une madeleine trempée dans une infusion, tant d'autres sensations dont j'ai parlé et que les dernières œuvres de Vinteuil m'avaient paru synthétiser' (III, 866). The twin steeples of Martinville and the three trees near Balbec being structural macro-models of metaphor, their parallel association with Vinteuil's last works and the experience of the madeleine dipped in tea suggests that those experiences may be metaphorical also.

In the course of analysing all of the obscure impressions which produced in him the same feeling of inexplicable happiness, the narrator realizes that images such as a church spire have functioned like hieroglyphic characters: 'déjà à Combray je fixais avec attention devant mon esprit quelque image qui m'avait forcé à la regarder, un nuage, un triangle, un clocher, une fleur, un caillou, en sentant qu'il y avait peut-être sous ces signes quelque chose de tout autre que je devais tâcher de découvrir, une pensée qu'ils traduisaient à la façon de ces caractères hiéroglyphiques qu'on croirait représenter seulement des objets matériels' (VIII, 878). In view of the parallels that I have established between the graphic structure of the steeples and the pattern traced by the structure of metaphor and its ensuing movement of signification, it appears that the steeples are the key hieroglyphic figure of *A la recherche du temps perdu*, whose shape, when superimposed upon the other hieroglyphs that the narrator has encountered in his life, reveals a common metaphorical nature.

The narrator likens to the creation of a work of art his previous attempts to interpret given sensations such as the steeples:

> En somme, dans un cas comme dans l'autre, qu'il s'agît d'impressions comme celle que m'avait donnée la vue des clochers de Martinville ou de reminiscences comme celle de l'inégalité des deux marches ou le goût de la madeleine, il fallait tâcher d'interpréter les sensations comme les signes d'autant de lois et d'idées, en essayant de penser, c'est-à-dire de faire sortir de la pénombre ce que j'avais senti, de le convertir en un équiva-

> lent spirituel. Or, ce moyen qui me paraissait le seul, qu'était-ce autre chose que faire une œuvre d'art? (III, 878–9)

Immediately upon his return to Combray after many years' absence (an event described in the first few pages of *Le temps retrouvé*), the narrator saw the steeple of Combray through his window, and remarked then that it appeared to be a 'preliminary sketch' engraved upon his window pane:

> je reconnus, peint lui au contraire en bleu sombre, simplement parce qu'il était plus loin, le clocher de l'église de Combray. Non pas une figuration de ce clocher, ce clocher lui-même, qui mettant ainsi sous mes yeux la distance des lieux et des années, était venu, au milieu de la lumineuse verdure et d'un tout autre ton, si sombre qu'il paraissait presque seulement dessiné, s'inscrire dans le carreau de ma fenêtre. (III, 698)

Because its outlines are a graphic representation of the metaphorical process that is the basic building block of art (III, 889), the steeple of Combray truly is the preliminary sketch of any work of art. More specifically, the steeple is also the sign of a work of art's unique ability to recover past time: the narrator does not see a representation ('une figuration') of the steeple, but the steeple itself which, by its very intrusion into his 'present' reality, causes past time – 'la distance des lieux et des années' – to reveal itself in 'visible form.' Although the narrator does not explicitly state the exact link between his past/present 'intimation' experiences and work of art (apart from describing at separate times their ability to recover past time for him) (III, 899), his vision of the steeples as a 'preliminary sketch' that makes time 'visible' acts as a connecting link which clarifies, through the macrometaphorical parallel it establishes between them, the common essential nature of art and the past/present reminiscences. Just as he realized that he did not see a representation of the steeple of Combray sketched upon his window pane but the steeple itself, so the narrator later comprehends that, during a past/present reminiscence, he does not experience a replica of a past sensation, but the past sensation itself: 'Ce n'était d'ailleurs même pas seulement un écho, un double d'une sensation passée que venait de me faire éprouver le bruit de la conduite d'eau, mais cette sensation elle-même' (III, 874). Subsequently, the narrator perceives that, when a writer translates his past life into a work of literature, past sensations are resuscitated and re-experienced (III,

904–5). More than that, these sensations resuscitated through literature are truer than past or present life experience, as they allow the writer and the reader to perceive the true nature of reality (the internal relationship between dissimilar phenomena) usually hidden or obscured by passion, intellect, and habit: 'La vraie vie, la vie enfin découverte et éclaircie, la seule vie par conséquent réellement vécue, c'est la littérature' (III, 895).

Just as a steeple signifies a church, so the steeple of Combray is the 'sign' of the literary work that the narrator resolves to write.[9] When he considers how to construct the literary work that will recover lost time, the narrator compares the work to a 'church' in which his readers might be able to learn some truths and discover some harmonies. He also considers the possibility that this 'church' might remain unvisited, like an abandoned Druid monument. His comparison macrometaphorically recalls to itself the Celtic myth he recounted in *Du côté de chez Swann*, which describes how the chance encounter in the present of an object retaining the departed soul of a beloved could resuscitate that person for us. At the time that he described the Celtic myth, the narrator compared the soul trapped in a material object to his own past: 'Il en est ainsi de notre passé. C'est peine perdue que nous cherchions à l'évoquer, tous les efforts de notre intelligence sont inutiles. Il est caché hors de son domaine et de sa portée, en quelque objet matériel ...' (I, 44). The common denominator shared by these two comparisons so widely separated in the time and space of *A la recherche du temps perdu* causes the distant 'past' time of the novel (*Du côté de chez Swann*) to telescopically converge upon its present (the 'time' that the reader is living with the narrator in *Le temps retrouvé*), illuminating the essential quality common to a past/present reminiscence and to a literary work – the ability to recover past time.

THE TWO WAYS/ART/METAPHOR

In *Du côté de chez Swann*, the narrator describes two 'ways' that he used to take for his walks: 'Car il y avait autour de Combray deux "côtés" pour les promenades, et si opposés qu'on ne sortait pas en effet de chez nous par la même porte, quand on voulait aller d'un côté ou de d'autre: le côté de Méséglise-la-Vineuse, qu'on appelait aussi le côté chez Swann par ce qu'on passait devant la propriété de M. Swann pour aller par là, et le côté de Guermantes' (I, 134). Immediately after remarking on their irréconcilability, the narrator paradoxically proceeds to describe the two ways in terms of their unity: 'je leur donnais, en les concevant ainsi comme deux entités, cette cohésion, cette unité qui n'appartiennent qu'aux créations de notre esprit' (I, 134). Being conceptually linked, the two ways fulfil the first condition of the metaphorical process. The narrator's preliminary description of the two ways is apparently intended to emphasize their differences rather than their similarities ('S'il était assez simple d'aller du côté de Méséglise, c'était une autre affaire d'aller du côté de Guermantes' I, 165), but the textual superimposition of the two descriptions in *Du côté de chez Swann* accomplishes the opposite effect: like a metaphor, it allows the reader to perceive the many physical characteristics shared by both ways, even though the narrator himself does not perceive their common factors at this time. Thus, the 'two ways' are the perfect illustration of a 'macrometaphor.'[10]

During this investigation of the *Recherche*, we have seen that one phenomenon – for example, flowers – is frequently compared to another recurring theme, such as the Vinteuil Sonata, with the result that the text weaves a labyrinth of metaphorical cross-references which ultimately merge into one basic figure – the metaphorical process. Although neither the Guermantes' Way nor Swann's Way is compared to other recurring themes such as flowers, the steeples, or the Vinteuil Sonata, the 'two ways' function as the background against which all of the other recurring themes, characters, ideas, and symbols are introduced: whereas the concept of homosexuality introduces itself through Mlle Vinteuil along Swann's Way, for example, so the narrator's reflections about the twin steeples of Martinville result from a walk along the Guermantes' Way. Thus, just as a metaphor gives rise to a chain of new metaphorical processes engendered by the self-recognition of reflected doubles (see p 18), so the 'two ways' introduce into the text multiple reflections of themselves – characters, themes, symbols, and ideas which are all characterized by a common binary nature.

In *Le temps retrouvé*, the narrator remarks on a conversation that described as 'tout un roman' (III, 962) the social merger of the two ways brought about by the marriage of Gilberte de Forcheville née Swann to the Marquis de Saint-Loup. The following pages will elucidate why the merger of the two ways does in fact constitute an 'entire' novel – the totality of *A la recherche du temps perdu*.

In his preliminary descriptions of the two ways, the narrator stresses that they are distinctly different entities not only because of their physical characteristics and the distance in kilometres separating them, but more especially because of the distance that there is between the two parts of his brain to which he allocates the respective ideas associated with each of the two ways (I, 135). However, even while enumerating the factors that render the two ways so distinctly different, the narrator inadvertently describes them in terms which suggest to us their internal similarities: 'si Méséglise était pour moi quelque chose d'inaccessible comme l'horizon, dérobé à la vue, si loin qu'on allât, par les plis d'un terrain qui ne ressemblait déjà plus à celui de Combray, Guermantes, lui, ne m'est apparu que comme le terme, plutôt idéal que réel, de son propre "côté," une sorte d'expression géographique abstraite comme la ligne de l'équateur, comme le pôle, comme l'orient' (I, 134). 'Méséglise' signified for him something as inaccessible as a horizon hidden from sight. 'Guermantes,' on the other hand, meant the ultimate goal, ideal rather than real. Although the tone of the commentary suggests that the 'unknowable' and the 'ideal' are quite different qualities, are they not, in fact, reflections of each other? Is not the 'ideal' generally regarded as unreachable and unknowable?

The characteristics attributed by the narrator to the two ways (the unknowable, the ideal) are the same characteristics that he attributes to a literary work – when his mother read *François le Champi* to him, for example, he was especially impressed by its indefinable, mysterious quality: 'Maman s'assit à côté de mon lit; elle avait pris *François le Champi* à qui sa couverture rougeâtre et son titre incompréhensible donnaient pour moi une personalité distincte et un atttrait mystérieux' (I, 41). Just as the narrator perceives the two ways as distinct entities with that cohesion and unity belonging only to creations of the mind (I, 134), so a work of art is also a creation of the mind. In *Du côté chez Swann*, the narrator briefly summarizes what the two ways collectively did for him: they made him feel separate things at the same time, and they invested his impressions with depth and foundation (I, 186), (see p 43). In *Le temps retrouvé*, he describes the effects produced by metaphor and a work of art in quite similar terms: a work of art is able to 'draw forth from the shadow' and intimate the true nature of reality to us through the metaphorical process, which, like the 'two ways' is a binary combination of dissimilar entities (III, 878–9, 889, 896).

I suggested that the two ways are the primary architectural structure of the novel into which all of the other characters, ideas, symbols and phenomena are introduced. In order to see how the two ways bring all of the diverse themes of the novel together, it is essential to enumerate and compare the phenomena associated in the narrator's mind with each way. Flowers characterize the Méséglise (Swann's) Way.

The narrator is especially impressed with the lilacs (I, 135) and the hawthorns (I, 138) bordering the Swann estate. He compares the hawthorn hedge to a series of chapels ('La haie formait comme une suite de chapelles qui disparaissaient sous la jonchée de leurs fleurs amoncelées en reposoir' (I, 138). As the church of Combray is the 'chapel' with which the narrator is most closely associated, a subliminal link establishes itself between the church (and its steeple) and the flowers. The narrator also tells us that the hawthorns have a rhythm as unexpected as certain intervals of music: 'elles m'offraient indéfiniment le même charme avec une profusion inépuisable, mais sans me laisser approfondir davantage, comme ces mélodies qu'on rejoue cent fois de suite sans descendre plus avant dans leur secret' (I, 138). A macrometaphorical relationship is thus also established between the effect produced by flowers and the feeling engendered by the Vinteuil Sonata – the music which pervades almost all milieus explored in *A la recherche du temps perdu*. The flowers also inspire the narrator with that rapture that he feels on seeing a work by his favourite painter: 'Puis je revenais devant les aubépines comme devant ces chefs-d'œuvre dont on croit qu'on saura mieux les voir quand on a cessé un moment de les regarder ...' (I, 139). In the narrator's reaction to the flowers of Swann's Way, we can perceive the cornerstone supporting the mirror relationship between art and nature in *Le temps retrouvé* (III, 889). The narrator surreptitiously draws our attention to the song of a solitary, invisible bird during one of his walks along the Méséglise (Swann's) Way: 'Divisant la hauteur d'un arbre incertain, un invisible oiseau s'ingéniait à faire trouver la journée courte ...' (I, 137). A view of steeples introduces itself along Swann's Way: the two rustic spires of St André des Champs can be seen across the fields (I, 146). We also learn that it was along the Méséglise (Swann's) Way that M. Vinteuil lives (I, 147). A scene of lesbian love which he witnesses secretly at Montjouvain along the Méséglise Way is the basis, the narrator tells us, for the connection he later establishes between sadism and art (I, 163). It is also along the Méséglise Way that the narrator becomes aware of the differences between impressions and their usual translation into expression: 'c'est cet automne-là, dans une de ces promenades, près du talus broussailleux qui protège Montjouvain, que je fus frappé pour la première fois de ce désaccord entre nos impressions et leur expression habituelle' (I, 155). Swann's Way (or Méséglise Way), therefore, is characterized primarily by flowers, a bird, steeples, M. Vinteuil (and his music), Mlle Vinteuil (and her homosexuality): phenomena which give rise collectively to the narrator's awareness of the dissimilitude between his impressions of reality and their expression.

Although the narrator implies that it is an entirely different experience to go the Guermantes' Way rather than Swann's Way ('S'il était assez simple d'aller du côté de Méséglise, c'était une autre affaire d'aller du côté de Guermantes ...' (I, 165), we discover, if we compare the phenomena encountered by the narrator along the Guermantes' Way to those experienced along the Méséglise Way, that the two ways are not as radically different as their external appearance would lead us to believe. From Swann's Way, the narrator can see the steeples of St André des Champs. Similarly, from the beginning of the Guermantes' Way, the narrator can see the steeple of Saint-Hilaire (Combray) (I, 166) and can hear its bells (I, 170). He also sees from the Guermantes' Way the twin steeples of Martinville and the steeple of Vieuxvicq (I, 180). The Méséglise Way is bordered by flowers, especially lilacs and hawthorns. Correspondingly, the Guermantes' Way passes by little gardens with clusters of dark blossoms (I, 172) and the Vivonne river, whose banks are choked with water lilies (I, 168). Whereas Swann's Way caused the narrator to recognize the disparity between external appearance and internal reality through his hidden observation of a homosexual act engaged in by Mlle Vinteuil and her friend, the Guermantes' Way teaches him the lack of correspondence between the signification of a name and that of its referent, when he sees by the roadside the ruins of the old castle of Combray, which cause the name of Combray to connote a historical city vastly different from the little town of the present (I, 167). The Méséglise Way brings the narrator to an awareness of the discrepancy between his impressions and their usual expression. In a similar vein, the Guermantes' Way frequently presents the narrator with 'obscure impressions' (such as a gleam of sunlight reflected from a stone), which appear to be concealing something. These impressions give him an unreasonable pleasure and seem to urge him to strive for a perception of what lies behind them, but he cannot yet surmise what it is that they are telling him (I, 179). Along the Méséglise Way, the narrator notices the song of a solitary bird. Swann, the man whose property borders this 'way' has a name which sounds like an English word designating a bird. Along the Guermantes' Way, the narrator compares the three steeples he can see from the road to three birds (I, 181), and later compares Mme de Guermantes to a bird (II, 62).

Both the Méséglise and the Guermantes' Way are characterized, therefore, by the following phenomena and ideas: steeples, flowers, birds, impressions, and the disparity between internal and external reality manifested through homosexuality in the case of the Méséglise Way, and through the dissimilitude between a name and its presence in the case of the Guermantes' Way. Because hawthorns and lilies, the steeples of St André des Champs and the steeples of Martinville, a bird in the forest and steeples that look like birds all constitute binary groups of externally dissimilar phenomena with components possessing an internal common nature (hawthorns and lilacs are both flowers, for example); we can see that, through these innate common denominators, the Méséglise (Swann's) Way and the Guermantes' Way are internally doubles of each other.

As well as designating two geographical locations, the two ways signify two distinctly different social spheres: Swann's Way connotes the world of the 'nouveaux riches' or haute bourgeoisie whose members' social position and wealth have arisen from capitalistic endeavours. The Guermantes' Way, on the other hand, signifies the social sphere composed of France's old noble families. Because Swann's social sphere is accessible to the narrator's own family and the Guermantes' social set is apparently not, the Guermantes' Way signifies for the young narrator a world of mystery whose reality, he assumes, must be entirely different (more gracious, more refined) than anything which comprises his own social sphere (the world of the haute bourgeoisie). We saw above that the geographical differences of the two ways are largely eliminated through their common denominators: flowers, steeples, birds, and 'impressions.' Similarly, through his social encounters with both worlds, the narrator discovers that the two opposing social spheres are not as radically different as their respective members would like to pretend. Although the narrator rarely compares one social world to the other, his individual portraits of each of the two social 'ways' interact together in the text; the sights, sounds, social mannerisms, conversations, and individuals associated with each world come into play with each other, and their common denominators consequently manifest themselves in the same way that the joining together of dissimilar phenomena in a metaphorical phrase allows their internal common essence to be revealed.

In the second part of *Du côté de chez Swann*, the narrator introduces us to the Verdurins, whose nightly gatherings are attended by a select group of 'faithful' friends, and a talented artist or musician. The Verdurins are described as 'une respectable famille bourgeoise, excessivement riche et entièrement obscure' (I, 188). Because they are rich, bourgeois, and yet lacking any historical distinction, the Verdurins are the perfect parody of the 'nouveau riche' social sphere to which the narrator and Swann both belong by birth. As the Verdurins are first introduced to us through Swann, in the volume entitled *Du côté de chez Swann*, I shall assume, for the purposes of this study, that the Verdurins pertain to Swann's Way.

The Guermantes, on the other hand, are first introduced in the novel through the eyes and imagination of the narrator as a young boy who, while listening to the curé of Combray explain the origin of some of the relics of his church (he specifically makes reference to some tombs and to the pictures depicted in the stained glass windows, I, 104), hears that the Duc and the Duchesse de Guermantes are the direct descendants of the ancient counts of Brabant – the subjects portrayed in the narrator's magic lantern projections. Being linked to a distant, mystical past totally different from his own present reality, the Guermantes come to be associated in the young narrator's mind with the colours of a tapestry or of a stained glass window. He assumes that they are not like the normal human beings in his own social sphere, but possess a different nature like beings from another century (I, 171). In this way, the Guermantes also represent a living past existing in the context of the present, like the moments of past time restored to him in his past/present reminiscences.

In the course of his initiation into society, however, and through successive acquaintance with people from both 'ways' or social sets, the narrator discovers that the 'two ways' have much in common. While still a very young boy, the narrator sees from a distance in the church of Combray, Mme de Guermantes, who has been – because of the historical past he associates with her – the subject of so many of his fanciful musings. Upon seeing her in person, he experiences a profound deception: he cannot believe that a being who he previously envisioned painted in the colours of a stained glass window should look so common: 'Jamais je ne m'étais avisé qu'elle pouvait avoir une figure rouge, une cravate mauve comme Mme Sazerat, et l'ovale de ses joues me fit tellement souvenir de personnes que j'avais vues à la maison que le soupçon m'effleura, pour se dissiper d'ailleurs aussitôt, que cette dame, en son principe générateur, en toutes ses molécules, n'était peut-être pas substantiellement la duchesse de Guermantes, mais que son corps, ignorant du nom qu'on lui appliquait, appartenait à un certain type féminin qui comprenait aussi des femmes de médecins et de commerçants. "C'est cela, ce n'est que cela, Mme de Guermantes"' (I, 175).

The lack of distinction suggested by Mme de Guermantes' physical

appearance is repeated in the physical demeanour of other members of the Guermantes' set. When Odette first sees the Marquise de Villeparisis, for example, she thinks that she is a charwoman (I, 244). Similarly, at Balbec, a barrister and his wife mistakenly assume that the Princesse de Luxembourg and the Marquise de Villeparisis are two old prostitutes. The narrator admits to himself that, on the basis of the ladies' appearance and comportment, the barrister's assumption is quite understandable (I, 703).

When he has the opportunity to meet the Guermantes in person during an evening at Mme de Villeparisis', the narrator experiences yet another disillusionment: he expects Mme de Guermantes' appearance and conversation to reflect the aura of mystery with which her name was previously associated for him. Instead, he finds her face altogether too human (II, 209), and her conversation to be limited to low and slanderous gossip (II, 210). Correspondingly, the narrator discovers that the manner of speaking of the Prince von Faffenheim totally destroys the illusions that his name suggested (II, 263), just as the Prince d'Agrigente – whose name suggests visions of a rose marble city – is in reality a vulgar drone (II, 432–3). Thus, the narrator's preliminary encounters with the Guermantes' world culminate on a note of profound disillusionment: rather than finding himself on the threshold of an enchanted kingdom, he discovers himself to be as far as possible from it. He asks himself finally if there is any basis at all for the exclusivity that the noble families grant themselves: 'Etait-ce vraiment à cause de dîners tels que celui-ci que toutes ces personnes faisaient toilette et refusaient de laisser pénétrer des bourgeoises dans leurs salons si fermés? Pour des dîners tels que celui-ci? Pareils si j'avais été absent?' (II, 544).

The source of the narrator's disenchantment resides partly in his previous refusal to acknowledge the signs indicating that the two social worlds (the bourgeoisie and the nobility) were not so different as they appeared to be. In *A l'ombre des jeunes filles en fleurs*, for example, we discovered that the Prince d'Agrigente (of the Guermantes' 'way') frequently visits Swann's house (I, 599) and conversely, Swann is repeatedly a guest of the noble families.

After he has personally made the acquaintance of the Guermantes, the narrator realizes that Swann and the Guermantes follow the same social code: 'Il y apportait d'ailleurs cette spontanéité dans les manières et ces initiatives personnelles, même en matière d'habillement, qui caractérisaient le genre des Guermantes' (II, 579). In the same way that Swann's social code is indistinguishable from the Guermantes, the

reader beings to realize that the two opposing social worlds are mirror reflections of each other. Both salons are remarkable for their self-imposed exclusivity and their apparently distinctive conventions. The narrator tells us, for example, that in order to belong to the little clan at the Verdurins', it was necessary to adhere strictly to a creed dictated by Mme Verdurin: 'Pour faire partie du "petit noyau," du "petit groupe," du "petit clan" des Verdurin, une condition était suffisante mais elle était nécessaire: il faillait adhérer tacitement à un Crédo dont un des articles était que le jeune pianiste, protégé par Mme Verdurin cette année-là et dont elle disait: "Ça ne devrait pas être permis de savoir jouer Wagner comme ça!" "enfonçait" à la fois Planté et Rubenstein et que le docteur Cottard avait plus de diagnostic que Potain' (I, 188). Similarly, we are informed in *Le côté de Guermantes* that the type of distinguished person who constituted the basis of the Guermantes' drawing room was one who had renounced everything incompatible with the wit and courtesy of the Guermantes: 'Le type des hommes distingués qui formaient le fond du salon Guermantes était celui de gens ayant renoncé volontairement (ou le croyant du moins) au reste, à tout ce qui était incompatible avec l'esprit des Guermantes, la politesse des Guermantes, avec ce charme indéfinissable odieux à tout "corps" tant soit peu "constitué"' (II, 459).

Swann was a member of the Guermantes' salon in *Du côté de chez Swann*. Correspondingly, M. de Charlus of the Guermantes' set becomes a regular member of the Verdurin salon in *Sodome et Gomorrhe*. He is, however, the second member of the nobility to be admitted to the little group, the first being Princess Sherbatoff (II, 1044). It is through Princess Sherbatoff's death, in fact, that the innate similarity of the two opposing social worlds is indicated to the narrator. In *Le Côté de Guermantes*, the narrator was deeply shocked by the cold indifference the Duc de Guermantes displayed upon hearing the news of Swann's terminal illness (II, 595–6). He encounters the same unfeeling brutality in M. Verdurin, who pretends not to know of the death of Mme Sherbatoff, as acknowledgment of the fact would require cancellation of his party: 'M. Verdurin, à qui nous fîmes nos condoléances pour la princesse Sherbatoff, nous dit: "Oui, je sais qu'elle est très mal – Mais non, elle est morte à six heures, s'écria Saniette. – Vous, vous exagérez toujours," dit brutalement à Saniette M. Verdurin, qui, la soirée n'étant pas décommandée, préférait l'hypothèse de la maladie, imitant ainsi sans le savoir le Duc de Guermantes' (III, 227–8). It is no surprise to the reader, therefore, that when M. de Charlus invites his friends from the Guermantes' set to

come to the Verdurins' to hear a concert played by Morel, the noble guests are astonished to discover that the Verdurins' world so closely resembles their own: 'somme toute, [elles] regrettaient de ne pas trouver ce salon aussi dissemblable de ceux qu'elles connaissaient, qu'elles avaient espéré, éprouvant le désappointement de gens de monde qui, étant allés dans la boîte à Bruant dans l'espoir d'être engueulés par le chansonnier, se seraient vus, à leur entrée, accueillis par un salut correct, au lieu du refrain attendu: "Ah! voyez c'te gueule, c'te binette. Ah! voyez c'te gueule qu'elle a"'(III, 245–6).

The social spheres of the bourgeoisie and the nobility that the two ways represent also come together through a play of names. Mme de Villeparisis is an example of a woman whose name and family background renders her a link between both ways. Because she is a good friend of his grandmother and seemingly part of his own world, the narrator as a young boy cannot believe that she is in reality a member of the Guermantes' social sphere:

> Ma grandmère qui à force de se désintéresser des personnes finissait par confondre tous les noms, chaque fois qu'on prononçait celui de la Duchesse de Guermantes prétendait que ce devait être une parente de Mme de Villeparisis. Tout le monde éclatait de rire; elle tâchait de se défendre en alléguant une certaine lettre de faire-part: 'Il me semblait me rappeler qu'il y avait du Guermantes là-dedans.' Et pour une fois j'étais avec les autres contre elle, ne pouvant admettre qu'il y eût un lien entre son amie de pension et la descendante de Geneviève de Brabant. (I, 104)

When the narrator's family meets Mme de Villeparisis at Balbec, however, her intimate friendship with the Princesse de Luxembourg verifies his grandmother's contention that her friend has family ties with the Guermantes. Through Mme de Villeparisis, the narrator is admitted into the Guermantes' world: she introduces him to the young Marquis de Saint-Loup, who informs him that his aunt, the Duchesse de Guermantes, is the niece of Mme de Villeparisis: 'Ma tante est la nièce de votre amie Madame de Villeparisis, elle a été élevée par elle, et a épousé son cousin qui était neveu aussi de ma tante Villeparisis, le duc de Guermantes actuel' (I, 755).

During an evening at the Guermantes' residence, the narrator learns from M. de Charlus the truth about Mme de Villeparisis' family origin: despite her historical-sounding title, the Villeparisis name was ac-

quired only a generation previously when a very rich man by the name of M. Thirion decided to call himself the Marquis de Villeparisis in order to please his wife, a member of the Guermantes family, who had married him for love (II, 293–4). The narrator feels it quite unfair that a woman whose title and name are of such recent origin should be able to maintain such close, intimate association with royal personnages, and he immediately relegates her to the other 'way' of his childhood, where he half-correctly assumed her to be a person who had nothing aristocratic about her (II, 294–5).

In *Sodome et Gomorrhe*, the narrator learns the truth about another noble title whose origin is in the mind of the rich bourgeois gentleman who created it. While dining at M. de Crecy's house, the narrator discovers that Legrandin, a friend of his family from the Méséglise Way of his childhood, has started to call himself Legrand de Méséglise (II, 1085).

In spite of the narrator's indignation at people of humble origin adopting aristocratic-sounding titles, he acknowledges the link of regional mannerisms that binds the nobility to peasants. This common denominator manifests itself in the nobility's pronunciation of regional speech and in their anecdotes about themselves into which peasants are introduced. The narrator notices, for example, a semi-peasant quality which survives in the Duchesse de Guermantes, which she enjoys emphasizing at times (III, 35), and he compares the compromises between the spontaneously provincial and the artificially literary that characterize Mme de Guermante's speech, to the dialogue of George Sand's pastoral novels or of certain legends preserved by Chateaubriand in his *Mémoires d'Outre-Tombe* (III, 35). It is significant that the narrator should compare this peasant-nobility duality to works by George Sand and Chateaubriand, as these are the literary works that later reveal to him the ability of a work of art to intimate the internal reality of things (III, 884–5, 919–20).

Although both the narrator and M. de Crecy (of the Guermantes' set) express disdain for the noble titles that some rich members of the bourgeoisie have created for themselves, we discover that these apparently bogus titles may not be any more counterfeit than some of the titles which the aristocracy has endowed on members of the lower classes whom they have adopted. Charlus brings about a merger of the two 'ways,' for example, when he adopts as his daughter a little seamstress and bestows on her the title of Mlle d'Oloron. Even before she was adopted by M. de Charlus, however, Jupien's niece represented the innate similarity of the two 'ways': her 'natural' nobility – her

charming manner, her way of speaking, her almost perfect character – previously prompted her customers, people far above her own social station, to invite her to dinner, receive her as a friend, and introduce her to their friends.

The nobility's reaction to M. de Charlus' adoption of the young seamstress provides evidence that their historical genealogies may not be as firmly grounded in the distant past as they would have others believe. In order to render Mlle d'Oloron truly acceptable, for example, the brother of Charlus – le duc de Guermantes – strongly suggests that Mlle d'Oloron is a 'natural' daughter whom Charlus has decided to recognize (III, 666). Consequently, when the Princesse de Parme arranges Mlle d'Oloron's marriage to young Cambremer, she suggests to Legrandin that his relation will be marrying someone like Mlle de Nantes – a bastard of Louis XIV who was not scorned by either the Duc d'Orléans or the Prince de Conti (III, 666). As Mlle d'Oloron's death illustrates, however, the majority of the nobility do not really care whether her title and position were created through a whim of Charlus or were the 'natural' result of a 'natural' connection, as the most important thing to most of them, the narrator realizes, is simply to have important connections. Consequently, after her death, all of the princely families in Europe – including the individuals who know the facts about Mlle d'Oloron's origin – are plunged into mourning for a simple little shop-girl, her death announcement bringing the two 'ways' together by blending names such as Jupien's with those of the noblest families (III, 671). The narrator realizes that Mlle d'Oloron's connections to Charlus will be regarded as quite genuine by succeeding generations, who will not have access to the facts. Those same future generations will accept this validity of Legrandin's self-created title – le comte de Méséglise – with equal confidence. Thus, surmises the narrator, they will assume that the 'Méséglise Way' converges with the 'Guermantes Way,' because both will appear to represent old and noble families of the same region who have most probably been allied for generations: 'Vieille noblesse de la même region, peut-être alliée depuis des générations, eussent-ils pu se dire. Qui sait? C'est peut-être une branche de Guermantes qui porte le nom des comtes de Méséglise' (III, 672).

Through their exchange of one name for another, Madame Swan and her daughter Gilberte effect a merger of the 'two ways' similar to that produced by M. de Charlus' adoption of a young seamstress. After Swann's death, Madame Swann (Odette) – now a very wealthy widow – marries le comte de Forcheville. In turn, de Forcheville adopts

Gilberte and gives her his name (III, 574). Although previously Mme de Guermantes refused to acknowledge Mme Swann's daughter socially, she now seeks out Gilberte since her name has changed to correspond to the 'Guermantes' set,' proving that the difference between the 'two ways' is the dissimilitude of their nomenclature:

> Quant à Mlle de Forcheville, je ne pouvais m'empêcher de penser à elle avec désolation. Quoi? fille de Swann, qu'il eût tant aimé voir chez les Guermantes, que ceux-ci avaient refusé à leur grand ami de recevoir, ils l'avaient ensuite spontanément recherchée, le temps ayant passé qui renouvelle pour nous, insuffle une autre personnalité, d'après ce qu'on dit d'eux, aux êtres que nous n'avons pas vus depuis longtemps, depuis que nous avons fait nous-même peau neuve et pris d'autres goûts. (III, 591)

When she marries Robert de Saint-Loup, nephew of the Duchesse de Guermantes (III, 657), Gilberte de Forcheville née Swann consolidates the merger of the 'two ways' initiated by her first change of name.

In *Du côté de chez Swann*, the narrator described the two ways as distinctly different worlds (I, 134–5). In spite of his assertion that each of the two ways was a unique entity, however, we saw that, in his preliminary descriptions of each 'way,' he inadvertently described them in very similar terms. In the middle volumes of *A la recherche du temps perdu*, we also saw that the differences between the social worlds represented by the two ways are gradually reduced through a growing awareness of their innate similarities. The two worlds become mirror reflections of each other through inter-way friendships (le Prince d'Agrigente and Swann; Charlus and the Verdurins; Swann, the narrator and the Guermantes); inter-way marriages (Jupien's niece and young Cambremer, Gilberte Swann and Robert de Saint-Loup); titles created by both the bourgeoisie and the nobility that put into question the validity of the nobility's historical origins (Jupien's niece becomes Mlle d'Oloron, M. Thirion becomes le Marquis de Villeparisis, Legrandin becomes Legrand de Méséglise); and a similar code of dress and social convention adhered to by both ways (when the Guermantes' set attends the concert at the Verdurin's, they are astonished to discover that this bourgeois salon so closely resembles their own world).

In *Le temps retrouvé*, the narrator is forced to acknowledge that, even geographically, the two ways are not as irreconcilable as he had supposed. While out for a walk with Gilberte, she suggests to him that

they can get to the Guermantes' Way by taking the Méséglise Way: ' "Si vous voulez, nous pourrons tout de même sortir un après-midi et nous pourrons alors aller à Guermantes, en prenant par Méséglise, c'est la plus jolie façon," phrase qui en bouleversant toutes les idées de mon enfance m'apprit que les deux côtés n'étaient pas aussi inconciliables que j'avais cru' (III, 693).

Several years later, in the days which follow his return to Paris from the sanatorium where he had been recovering from ill health, the narrator is presented with more evidence testifying to the amalgamation of the 'two ways.' He receives in one day for the same afternoon two invitations, which represent the 'two ways' of his childhood. One comes from la Berma. Because Swann introduced the narrator to la Berma (I, 97–8), la Berma's invitation is suggestive of Swann's Way. The second invitation comes from the Prince de Guermantes, who of course represents the Guermantes' Way (III, 856). The narrator decides to go to the Guermantes' party because he feels that, by going there, he will be brought nearer to his childhood: 'J'avais eu envie d'aller chez les Guermantes comme ci cela avait dû me rapprocher de mon enfance et des profondeurs de ma mémoire où je l'apercevais' (III, 856–7). His choice suggests the reversibility of the two ways. In his childhood, the Guermantes' residence signified for the narrator the unknowable and the unattainable (I, 171). As an adult, he aspires – by going the Guermantes' Way – to return to his childhood which was, in reality, more closely associated with Swann's Way than it was with the Guermantes'. Like the geographical merger that Gilberte noted earlier, therefore, the narrator goes by the 'Guermantes' Way' in his mind, in order to reach 'Swann's Way.' Correspondingly, in order to arrive at the new residence of the Prince de Guermantes, the narrator has to pass through streets he previously used to play in with Gilberte Swann; in order to reach the 'new' Guermantes' Way, he has to traverse a past reality which is internally linked to Swann's Way (III, 858). Arriving at the Prince de Guermantes' residence, the narrator discovers that the two ways as represented by the bourgeois salon of the Verdurins and the Guermantes' social set have once again amalgamated through marriage, as the former Mme Verdurin is now the Princess de Guermantes: 'La princesse de Guermantes en effet était morte, et c'est l'ex-madame Verdurin que le prince, ruiné par la défaite allemande, avait épousée' (III, 955). As if to make the merger of personalities of the 'two ways' complete on all levels, the narrator also discovers that Odette de Forcheville – who was previously Mme Swann – is having a love affair with the Duc de Guermantes: 'le vieux fauve dompté se rappelant qu'il était, non pas libre chez la duchesse dans ce Sahara dont le paillasson du palier marquait l'entrée, mais chez Mme de Forcheville dans la cage du Jardin des Plantes ...' (III, 1019).

It is Mlle de Saint-Loup, however, the daughter of Gilberte Swann and Robert de Saint-Loup – whom the narrator correctly perceives as a star-shaped crossroads bringing not only the great two ways together but also a network of transversals connecting these two ways to each other. In the context of his reflections on Mlle de Saint-Loup, the narrator asserts that his whole life is in some sense a prolongation of the two ways; connecting places as far apart as the Champs-Elysées, and the beautiful terrace of La Raspelière, with the result that between any slightest point of his past and all the other points, a rich network of memories gives him an almost infinite variety of connecting paths from which to choose:

> L'étonnement de ces paroles et le plaisir qu'elles me firent furent bien vite remplacés, tandis que Mme de Saint-Loup s'éloignait vers un autre salon, par cette idée du Temps passé, qu'elle aussi, à sa manière, me rendait, et sans même que je l'eusse vue, Mlle de Saint-Loup. Comme la plupart des êtres, d'ailleurs, n'était-elle pas comme sont dans les forêts les 'etoiles' des carrefours où viennent converger des routes venues, pour notre vie aussi, des points les plus différents? Elles étaient nombreuses pour moi, celles qui aboutissaient à Mlle de Saint-Loup et qui rayonnaient autour d'elle. Et avant tout venaient aboutir à elle les deux grands 'côtés' où j'avais fait tant de promenades et de rêves ... Certes, s'il s'agit uniquement de nos coeurs, le poète a eu raison de parler des 'fils mystérieux' que la vie brise. Mais il est encore plus vrai qu'elle en tisse sans cesse entre les êtres, entre les événements, qu'elle entre-croise ces fils, qu'elle les redouble pour épaissir la trame, si bien qu'entre le moindre point de notre passé et tous les autres un riche réseau de souvenirs ne laisse que le choix des communications. (III, 1029–30)

As well as describing the network of personal connections which caused the two ways to amalgamate (Swann told him about Balbec, and it is at Balbec that he met Saint-Loup of the Guermantes' Way; he first meets Odette – the lady in pink – at his uncle's house, and she later is connected by marriage to the houses of Swann and Guermantes; the butler at that same uncle's house was the father of Morel, who was the lover of both Charlus and Saint-Loup, etc.), the narrator also compares Mlle de Saint-Loup to his idea of 'time past'; and thus establishes a macrometaphorical link between the two ways, his previous experiences of involuntary memory (past/present reminiscences), and all of the truths that the latter revealed to him about the nature of internal reality, metaphor, and art.

Although the narrator does not explain the exact nature of the correspondence between Mlle de Saint-Loup, the two ways and his idea of past time, his comparison invites us to superimpose the 'two ways' onto his past/present reminiscences; and by doing so, we can perceive the common denominators that cause these two dissimilar phenomena to reflect each other. The narrator's experiences of involuntary memory are the result of the repetition in the present of an action, sound, scent, or object originally experienced in the past, which, through the common denominator it establishes between past and present, allows the past to re-emerge and be experienced in the context of the present moment. If Mlle de Saint-Loup is the crossroads between the two ways, then she is like the common essence of a past and a present experience. In Chapter 2, I exposed the parallels established by the narrator between past/present reminiscences and metaphorical structure. Mlle Swann, therefore, is not only like the essence that binds two times to each other but is also the macro-incarnation of the innate common reality shared by two dissimilar phenomena, which reveals itself through the combination of those phenomena in a metaphorical phrase.

The mirror relationship established between Mlle de Saint-Loup and the essence revealed through both poetic metaphor and natural analogies such as past/present reminiscences indicates that the 'two ways' are one of the fundamental binary structures of *A la recherche du temps perdu*, which cause the text in its entirety to assume the form and movement of signification of a metaphorical phrase. Earlier in *Le temps retrouvé*, the merger of the two ways brought about by the marriage of Gilberte Swann to Robert de Saint-Loup was described as 'tout un roman' (III, 962). In the passage just examined, the narrator asserts that his whole social life (which is to be the subject of his proposed novel) is a prolongation of the 'two ways' (III, 1029–30). In *Du côté de chez Swann*, the narrator told us that Combray is at the intersection of the two ways (I, 134), and then subsequently compared his memories of the village to works of art:

> Elle a d'ailleurs pour ces reconstitutions des données plus

> précises que n'en ont généralement les restaurateurs: quelques
> images conservées par ma mémoire, les dernières peut-être
> qui existent encore actuellement, et destinées à être bientôt
> anéanties, de ce qu'était le Combray du temps de mon enfance;
> et parce que c'est lui-même qui les a tracées en moi avant de
> disparaître, émouvantes – si on peut comparer un obscur por-
> trait à ces effigies glorieuses dont ma grand'mère aimait à me
> donner des reproductions – comme ces gravures anciennes de
> la Cène ou ce tableau de Gentile Bellini, dans lesquels l'on voit
> en un état qui n'existe plus aujourd'hui le chef-d'oeuvre de
> Vinci et le portail de Saint-Marc. (I, 166)

If the narrator's whole life is a prolongation of the two ways, and if his social life is the subject of the novel, then the novel is like Combray. Just as Combray, at the intersection of two ways, is like a work of art, so the 'two ways' are the fundamental girders of a work of art – *A la recherche du temps perdu* – which are joined through analogy to the other primary metaphor-like opposition of the novel – time lost and time regained.

PAST/PRESENT/METAPHOR/ART/LIFE

In the final volume of a novel whose subject is the search for lost time, the narrator of *A la recherche du temps perdu* ultimately discovers that past time may be restored to him through the creation of a work of art:

> Car les êtres qui, par leur méchanceté, leur nullité, étaient
> arrivés malgré nous à détruire nos illusions, s'étaient réduits
> eux-mêmes à rien et séparés de la chimère amoureuse que
> nous nous étions forgée, si alors nous nous mettons à travailler,
> notre ame les élève de nouveau, les identifie, pour les besoins
> de notre analyse de nous-même, à des êtres qui nous auraient
> aimé, et dans ce cas la littérature, recommençant le travail
> défait de l'illusion amoureuse, donne une sorte de survie à des
> sentiments qui n'existaient plus. (III, 904–5)

In Chapter 2, we saw that he reaches this conclusion after conducting an investigation into the nature of three 'intimation' experiences, which produced in him an inexplicable happiness that had also been given to him by various other experiences in the past. In the course of his analysis, he realizes that these three experiences were all catalysed by his chance re-encounter in the present of a sensation originally experienced in the past and thus, through the intermediary of the sensation common to the past and the present, a moment of past time was momentarily restored to him in a pure, atemporal state (see p 20). The narrator subsequently comprehends that his true self or internal being is able to recognize itself as such in this extratemporal essence and emerge into reality. Only through the miracle of an analogy (in this case, the superimposition of a past moment onto a present moment) is his true being able to reveal itself; and it is only this being which has the ability to recover past time (lost time), which his memory and his active intelligence are both incapable of recovering:

> Je glissais rapidement sur tout cela, plus impérieusement sollicité que j'étais de chercher la cause de cette félicité, du caractère de certitude avec lequel elle s'imposait, recherche ajournée autrefois. Or cette cause, je la devinais en comparant ces diverses impressions bienheureuses et qui avaient entre elles ceci de commun que je les éprouvais à la fois dans le moment actuel et dans un moment éloigné, jusqu'à faire empiéter le passé sur le présent, à me faire hésiter à savoir dans lequel des deux je me trouvais ... Cela expliquait que mes inquiétudes au sujet de ma mort eussent cessé au moment où j'avais reconnu inconsciemment le goût de la petite madeleine, puisqu'à ce moment-là l'être que j'avais été était un être extra-temporel ... Cet être-là n'était jamais venu à moi, ne s'était jamais manifesté, qu'en dehors de l'action, de la jouissance immédiate, chaque fois que le miracle d'une analogie m'avait fait échapper au présent. Seul, il avait le pouvoir de me retrouver les jours anciens, le temps perdu, devant quoi les efforts de ma mémoire et de mon intelligence échouaient toujours. (III, 871)

As a direct result of his analysis of the nature of the past/present 'intimation' experiences and their effect on him, the narrator understands that art may intimate the internal reality of things to us by duplicating through metaphorical structure the superimposition of dissimilar phenomena which occurs naturally in life experiences (III, 889, see p 17).

Since I am attempting to demonstrate that, structurally, the whole of *A la recherche du temps perdu* is a macrometaphor, it is significant (in view of the relationship between past/present reminiscences and metaphor) that a macro past/present dichotomy spans the totality of the novel. The first volume of Proust's work – *Du côté de chez Swann* – ends with the assertion that time is irrevocably lost: 'La réalité que j'avais connue n'existait plus ... le souvenir d'une certaine image n'est que le regret d'un certain instant; et les maisons, le routes, les avenues, sont fugitives, hélas! comme les années' (I, 427), and the title of the final volume of the novel – *Le temps retrouvé* – suggests that the time which had previously been lost has now been regained (III, 871–2). The body of the novel, *A la recherche du temps perdu*, is the recounting of that lost time which allows the narrator's past sensations and experiences to have a sort of second life (see p 33).

Although the structure and effect of all the recurring phenomena in *A la recherche du temps perdu* resemble the structure and effect of metaphor, the past/present reminiscences are the only 'natural' phenomena examined that the narrator classifies specifically as analogies (III, 889). Thus, the analogical bonds and subliminal macrometaphorical links established between the past/present reminiscences and other recurring phenomena in the novel clarify the common metaphorical nature that all of these experiences share. A comparison of the entities, sensations, and conditions that engender past/present analogies (words, objects, sounds, actions, dreams, etc.) will also enable us to perceive the metaphorical quality of many facets of life experience and of our perception of them.

Through a common effect (the ability to recover lost time) or by means of an analogy, the past/present reminiscences are intricately connected in the text to the nature of sleep, dreams, art, writing, literature, and the life of a human being. Phenomena that give rise to past/present 'intimation' experiences include the steeple of Combray, objects from the past re-encountered in the present (the tea and the madeleine, a window frame, the book *François le Champi*), words common to two situations or times, a sound or tactile sensation common to two situations, a physical resemblance between family members of different ages, a personality common to two times, a manner of pronunciation common to two times, a body part associated with two different activities, a street visited at different times, the events of war, and names.

In general, past/present reminiscences are metaphorical in nature because they bring together, through the intermediary of a common sensation, dissimilar times and situations whose common essence is subsequently illuminated through their juxtaposition. In the course of *A la recherche du temps perdu*, two distinct kinds of past/present superimpositions occur, which suggest to the narrator two different kinds of truths. The totally involuntary sort of past/present superimposition, such as that catalysed by the madeleine dipped in tea, intimates to the narrator an internal reality that transcends the two times and places whose juxtaposition produced it. Other past/present superimpositions voluntarily performed by the narrator such as his comparison of Rachel's past and present reality (II, 161) also reveal truths shared by different times and circumstances, but the narrator classifies these truths revealed through the work of the active intelligence as more superficial than those revealed through natural or poetic analogies. Nevertheless, he asserts that truths disengaged by the intelligence also have a place in literature because they reflect truths disengaged by involuntary comparisons, and thus place the latter in relief:

> Je sentais pourtant que ces vérités que l'intelligence dégage
> directement de la réalité ne sont pas à dédaigner entièrement,
> car elles pourraient enchâsser d'une matière moins pure,
> mais encore pénétrée d'esprit, ces impressions que nous apporte
> hors du temps l'essence commune aux sensations du passé et
> du présent, mais qui, plus précieuses, sont aussi trop rares pour
> que l'oeuvre d'art puisse être composée seulement avec elles.
> Capables d'être utilisées pour cela, je sentais se presser en moi
> une foule de vérités relatives aux passions,* aux caractères,
> aux moeurs.
>
> ---
>
> *Chaque personne qui nous fait souffrir peut être rattachée par
> nous à une divinité dont elle n'est qu'un reflet fragmentaire et
> le dernier degré, divinité (Idée) dont la contemplation nous
> donne aussitôt de la joie au lieu de la peine que nous avions.
> (III, 898–9)

In view of the connection that the narrator establishes between the nature of his past/present reminiscences and the mysterious effect produced by literature in *Le temps retrouvé*, it is significant that these two phenomena are introduced consecutively to the reader in *Du côté de chez Swann*: immediately after reflecting on the cause of the mysterious intonation that seemed to emanate from *François le Champi* when his mother read it to him (I, 41) the narrator considers the possibility of the past being restored to him as it really existed, as compared to the residue of a past revived by memory (I, 44). The narrator's musings on the possible means through which time may be restored are immediately followed by his description of an experience that has much in common with the recovery of lost souls described in a Celtic myth (see pp 37-8): he takes some tea with a madeleine one cold day in winter, and immediately experiences an exquisite pleasure which contains no suggestion of its origin. Although conscious that the sensation is connected with the tea and cake, he feels that it is infinitely transcendental: 'Je sentais qu'elle était liée au goût du thé et du gâteau, mais qu'elle le dépassait infiniment, ne devait pas être de même nature' (I, 45). The narrator tries to apprehend the image he feels stirring in his depths but at first to no avail. Suddenly, however, the memory returns: the taste he has just experienced is the same as that of the little crumb of madeleine which on Sunday mornings at Combray he used to take, when he was much younger, from Aunt Léonie. Like the phenomena joined together in a metaphorical phrase, the tea and the madeleine are externally dissimilar objects that give rise to a transcendental, third term (in this case, a feeling of inexplicable happiness). It is not the objects themselves which give rise to this effect, however, but the two times and circumstances that are able to merge through the intermediary of their common denominator – the taste of the tea and the madeleine.

The experience engendered by the tea and the madeleine serves as a miniature which mirrors the macro-structure of the *Recherche*: just as the middle volumes of the novel apparently emerged from the interaction of the first two books which Proust wrote (*Du côté de chez Swann*, *Le temps retrouvé*, see p 33), so the subjects which will constitute the main avenues of the narrator's 'recherche' emerge from his past/present reminiscence: 'C'est ainsi que je restais souvent jusqu'au matin à songer au temps de Combray, à mes tristes soirées sans sommeil, à tant de jours aussi dont l'image m'avait été plus récemment rendue par la saveur – ce qu'on aurait appelé à Combray le "parfum" – d'une tasse de thé' (I, 186). While 'remembering' Combray, the narrator describes the steeples of Combray and Martinville, the reversibility of art and life (as demonstrated by the Giotto frescoes and the pregnant servant girl), the 'two ways' ('le Côté de chez Swann' and 'le Côté de Guermantes'), the bipolarity of exterior and interior reality (as demonstrated by the hawthorns, Legrandin, Vinteuil's daughter, Gilberte, and the condition of homosexuality), and the disparity between names and the presences to which they refer (as manifested by the name of Combray and the past reality it connotes). Among the memories induced by the tea and the madeleine are recollections of two phenomena which give rise to other past/present reminiscences: the steeple of Combray (I, 67), and the ruins of the castle of Combray, located along the Guermantes' Way (I, 167).

As the novel unfolds, we find that the metaphor-like superimposition of two times and realities effected by the tea and the madeleine, the steeples, and the ruins of the castle of Combray is repeated by a myriad of other phenomena and life experiences – some of which we have already discussed – including the Vinteuil Sonata, sleep, words, gestures, people, objects, body parts, personality traits, pronunciation, works of literature, and writing.

Part I ('Combray') of *Du côté de chez Swann* presents us with involuntary past/present reminiscences engendered through the intermediary of an object common to the past and to the present (the object referred to in the Celtic myth, the steeple, the ruins of Combray, the tea, and the madeleine); whereas Part II ('Un Amour de Swann') introduces a form of past/present superimposition that is more the work of the active intelligence than the chance re-encounter of an entity from the past in the present. Although the entity common to two times and two realities is still present, it paradoxically emphasizes their differences rather than their common denominator. In the case of Odette, for example, we saw that her present life as Swann's mistress is apparently incompatible with her past reality as a courtesan who began her career when sold as a young teenager by her mother, even though these two realities are irrevocably linked in their common denominator – the human being who represents both of them (I, 313-14). Similarly, the Verdurins' salon – which was originally viewed by Swann as an example of genuine life–comes to represent for him a debased form of life, even though the same people continue to frequent it (I, 287). Although the past/present superimpositions of dissimilars engendered by Odette's being and the Verdurin salon do not disengage any transcendental reality, they reveal a truth about the human condition in time, which puts into relief those transcendent, extratemporal truths that are suggested by the narrator's involuntary past/present reminiscences.

In *A l'ombre des jeunes filles en fleurs*, the narrator proposes that past time may be regained through a deep sleep: 'je tombais dans ce sommeil lourd où se dévoilent pour nous le retour à la jeunesse, la reprise des années passées, des sentiments perdus' (I, 819, see p 67). He does not explain at this point why sleep can effect a return to past time, but he previously suggested in *Du côté de chez Swann* that the sleeper has in a circle about him different times and years which he can perceive simultaneously. Because this ordered procession may become jumbled, the sleeper will perceive in the context of his present reality different times and places: 'Un homme qui dort tient en cercle autour de lui le fil des heures, l'ordre des années et des mondes. Il les consulte d'instinct en s'éveillant et y lit en une seconde le point de la terre qu'il occupe, le temps qui s'est écoulé jusqu'à son réveil; mais leurs rangs peuvent se mêler, se rompre' (I, 5).

Some words that Albertine utters to the narrator in the course of her suggestion that he come and spend the evening by her bedside exercise on the narrator an effect similar to that produced by the tea and the madeleine: '"Alors, à tout à l'heure. Venez tôt, pour que nous ayons de bonnes heurs à nous," ajouta-t-elle en souriant. A ces mots, je remontai plus loin qu'aux temps où j'aimais Gilberte, à ceux où l'amour me semblait une entité non pas seulement extérieure, mais réalisable' (I, 931). Similarly, in *Le côté de Guermantes II*, the re-entry of Albertine into the narrator's life precipitates the juxtaposition of two different milieus and time periods – the narrator's past in Balbec and his present reality in Paris:

> Tout d'un coup, sans que j'eusse entendu sonner, Françoise vint ouvrir la porte, introduisant Albertine qui entra souriante, silencieuse, replète, contenant dans la plenitude de son corps, préparés pour que je continuasse à les vivre, venus vers moi, les jours passés dans ce Balbec où je n'étais jamais retourné. Sans doute, chaque fois que nous revoyons une personne avec qui nos rapports – si insignifiants soient-ils – se trouvent changés, c'est comme une confrontation de deux époques ... Elle semblait une magicienne me présentant un miroir du Temps. En cela elle était pareille à tous ceux que nous revoyons rarement, mais qui jadis vécurent plus intimement avec nous. (II, 350–1)

We saw in *Du côté de chez Swann* that Odette is characterized by a discrepancy between her past and present realities. We also perceived that her dual personality resembles the structure of past/present reminiscences and metaphor, in that she brings together in her person two dissimilar times and circumstances. In *Le côté de Guermantes I*, a second character is introduced – Rachel – who duplicates the apparently irreconcilable past/present duality of Odette's personality. In the case of Rachel, however, the parallel between metaphor, her dual character and the past/present reminiscences is more explicit than in the case of Odette, as the narrator and Saint-Loup can see both of her realities simultaneously – one nature appearing beside the other, like a sort of contradictory double – in the same manner that two dissimilar phenomena are joined together in a metaphorical phrase: 'Je crois pourtant que, précisément ce matin-là, et probablement pour la seule fois, Robert s'évada un instant hors de la femme que, tendresse après tendresse, il avait lentement composée, et aperçut tout d'un coup à quelque distance de lui une autre Rachel, un double d'elle, mais absolument différent et qui figurait une simple petite grue' (II, 161). I suggested previously that the past/present duality of Odette's and Rachel's personalities resembles structurally the duality of body and spirit in any human being (II, 298), and the duality of internal reality and external appearance inherent in the nature of homosexuality (see p 57).

The narrator discovers that an experience of involuntary memory may be precipitated through the repetition of a psychological condition. On the first night of his second visit to Balbec, his state of mind and body duplicates the physical and mental state he experienced the night of his first visit to Balbec. Consequently, when he bends over to undo his boots, a vision of his grandmother is restored to him, exactly as she had been on that first night of his arrival. Just as he later realizes in *Le temps retrouvé* that a past/present reminiscence restores to him a moment of 'pure' time, so he realizes now that he has not just experienced a memory of his grandmother, but the essence of her living reality:

> Mais à peine eus-je touché le premier bouton de ma bottine, ma poitrine s'enfla, remplie d'une présence inconnue, divine, des sanglots me secouèrent, des larmes ruisselèrent de mes yeux. L'être qui venait à mon secours, qui me sauvait de la sécheresse de l'âme, c'était celui qui, plusieurs années auparavant, dans un moment de détresse et de solitude identiques, dans un moment où je n'avais plus rien de moi, était entré, et qui m'avait rendu à moi-même, car il était moi et plus que moi (le contenant qui est plus que le contenu et me l'apportait). Je venais d'apercevoir, dans ma mémoire, penché sur ma fatigue, le visage tendre, préoccupé et déçu de ma grand'mère, telle qu'elle avait été ce premier soir d'arrivée, le visage de ma grand'mère, non pas de celle que je m'étais étonné et reproché de si peu regretter et qui n'avait d'elle que le nom, mais de ma grand'mère véritable dont, pour la première fois depuis les Champs-Elysées où elle avait eu son attaque, je retrouvais dans

un souvenir involontaire et complet la réalité vivante.
(II, 755–6)

It is at Balbec also that, in the course of a conversation with Albertine, some words she utters resuscitate a past scene for him which, when compared to Albertine's present reality, allows him to perceive an inexpressed 'truth' that he would never have been able to ascertain otherwise. Albertine's casual admission that Mlle Vinteuil's 'friend' was one of her closest friends, and that she is almost as intimate with Mlle Vinteuil herself serves as a 'Sesame' (II, 1127 – 8) for the narrator: 'Nous pouvons avoir roulé toutes les idées possibles, la vérité n'y est jamais entrée, et c'est du dehors, quand on s'y attend le moins, qu'elle nous fait son affreuse piqûre et nous blesse pour toujours' (II, 1114). Albertine's words – 'C'est Mlle Vinteuil' – provoke in the present a past drama in the narrator's life – his hidden observation of Mlle Vinteuil and her girlfriend making love. Through the intermediary of this person (Mlle Vinteuil) common to the past and the present, the past scene associated with this woman is restored to the narrator and, when superimposed upon Albertine's present reality, reveals the unexpressed 'truth' about her bisexual nature.

By describing Albertine's words as an 'open sesame,' the narrator allows macrometaphorical connections to establish themselves between this experience of involuntary reminiscence, his former description of a dream narrated in *A l'ombre des jeunes filles en fleurs*, wherein he saw himself as a character in a tale from the *Thousand and One Nights* (I, 820), and other events compared to the *Thousand and One Nights* (M. de Charlus being beaten in a homosexual brothel (III, 832), the third intimation experience described in *Le temps retrouvé* (III, 868), the Vinteuil Sonata (III, 249).

The past/present reminiscence born from Albertine's words is immediately followed by two similar experiences linked to the former experience by common elements. When his mother appears suddenly in the room beside him, the narrator thinks that he is seeing a vision of his grandmother, as her grey hair, aging cheeks, troubled eyes, and even the dressing gown which she wears seem to belong more to his grandmother than to the youthful 'maman' that he knew in his childhood (II, 1128–9). The common resemblance heightened by aging causes the two characters (the mother and the grandmother) and two realities (the past and the present) to become superimposed one upon the other. Then, his mother indicates to him a sunrise visible through the window, and the window frame causes the narrator to recall another scene which he saw through a window: Mlle Vinteuil making love to her girlfriend. In the vision the narrator sees in the present, however, Albertine has taken the place of Mlle Vinteuil's friend. Thus, the 'truth' disengaged by the past/present reminiscence (Albertine's bisexuality) superimposes itself upon the internal reality brought into the context of the present through another past/present reminiscence (the window in Montjouvain/the window in Balbec), and reveals in pictorial form the internal reality which was intimated through the first past/present intimation resuscitated by Albertine's admission that she was Mlle Vinteuil's friend. The narrator suggests that the superimposition of the two scenes results in a vision that is like a 'painted view':

> elle me montra la fenêtre. Mais derrière la plage de Balbec, la mer, le lever du soleil, que maman me montrait, je voyais, avec des mouvements de désespoir qui ne lui échappaient pas, la chambre de Montjouvain où Albertine, rose, pelotonnée comme une grosse chatte, le nez mutin, avait pris la place de l'amie de Mlle Vinteuil et disait avec des éclats de son rire voluptueux: 'Hé bien! si on nous voit, ce n'en sera que meilleur. Moi! je n'oserais pas cracher sur ce vieux singe?' C'est cette scène que je voyais derrière celle qui s'étendait dans la fenêtre et qui n'était sur l'autre qu'un voile morne, superposé comme un reflet. Elle semblait elle-même, en effet, presque irréelle, comme une vue peinte. (II, 1129–30)

When viewed from the perspective of the totality of the novel, the art-like quality induced by the transposition of the scenes highlights the connections the narrator perceives in *Le temps retrouvé* between the nature of the past/present reminiscences, the perception of an internal reality, and the creation of a work of art as a means of intimating the true nature of reality.

In *La prisonnière*, we discover that the characteristic speech patterns of the nobility inspire past/present superimpositions also: the archaic, peasant-like pronunciation of some words functions like a museum allowing a past reality to actualize or become present: 'S'il n'y avait aucune affectation, aucune volonté de fabriquer un langage à soi, alors cette façon de prononcer était un vrai musée d'historie de France par la conversation' (III, 35). Because of their deep, historical roots, the nobility also represents for the narrator a living past (I, 171, 174–5). Even after he meets Mme de Guermantes in person and discovers that in her appearance and conversation she resembles a common bourgeois woman more than the mythical ancestors he previously associated with her, her name still continues to conjure up for him a past reality like that depicted in the stained glass windows of the church of Combray (II, 209, 229–30). By giving rise to a past recall effect, the noble names cause the narrator's extensive investigation of the dual relationship of a name to its referent to become linked subterraneously to the network of past/present reminiscences.

In *Le côté de Guermantes II*, the re-entry of Albertine into the narrator's life caused the juxtaposition of two times and places: the past shared with her in Balbec, and his present life in Paris (II, 350–1). In *Sodome et Gomorrhe*, some words uttered by Albertine serve as the 'open sesame' which restores a past scene to him (II, 1127–8). In *La prisonnière*, we discover that Albertine's external circumstances have changed radically now that she is the narrator's 'caged' mistress. Because he feels for Albertine the same desire as in the past, however, his feeling causes him to see behind her in Paris, her past reality in Balbec (III, 67–8). The narrator draws a parallel between the past/present superimposition evoked by Albertine's presence and the similar past/present comparison that Rachel's presence catalysed for Saint-Loup. His comparison of the two women to each other not only clarifies the effect they both produce and the process that engenders it, but also reveals another characteristic they share: they are both actresses. Whereas Rachel was previously an actress on the stage of a theatre, the narrator describes Albertine as an actress of the beach who played her roles in the theatre of nature (III, 68). La Berma is also an actress. While watching her performance of Phèdre, the young narrator realized that la Berma's repetition of the text functions as a supplementary envelope which clarifies the truth that the author intended to express:

> tout cela, voix, attitudes, gestes, voiles, n'était, autour de ce corps d'une idée qu'est un vers (corps qui, au contraire des corps humains, n'est pas un obstacle opaque, mais un vêtement purifié, spiritualisé), que des enveloppes supplémentaires qui, au lieu de la cacher, rendaient plus splendidement l'âme qui se les était assimilées et s'y était répandue, que des coulées de substances diverses, devenues translucides, dont la rayon central et prisonnier qui les traverse et rendre plus étendue, plus précieuse, et plus belle la matière imbibée de flamme où il est engainé. (II, 48–9)

In this way, the interaction of a theatrical text with its representation

resembles in structure and effect a past/present reminiscence: the text is a past experience which repeats itself in the present at the moment of its performance – the intermediary that allows the truth enshrined in itself to be recognized in its present repetition. Because Rachel and Albertine are both actresses and both responsible for engendering past/present superimpositions, a subtle parallel is established between their natures and a dramatic text. Albertine also functions as the common denominator that links the network of past/present reminiscences (which embraces art and writing) to the narrator's explorations of the nature of homosexuality, as she is one of the novel's most predominant homosexual personalities, and also an agent frequently connecting two times and places.

M. de Charlus reinforces the subliminal bond between the condition of homosexuality and the nature of the past/present reminiscences that Albertine initiates. When the narrator unexpectedly encounters M. de Charlus on the street, the dissimilitude between M. de Charlus' present appearance (a huge hulk) and his former reality (a haughty stranger) is like two times and two realities coming together in one being. Moreover, we saw in 'Exterior/Interior' that M. de Charlus' present appearance is like an external manifestation of a sickness that was formerly internal, causing the unexpressed past/present comparison engendered by M. de Charlus' change of appearance to represent also the revelation of an internal reality. Because this change of appearance is the result of his homosexual nature, the condition of homosexuality, the past/present reminiscences and the metaphorical process become linked to each other (see pp 55–6).

While reminiscing about the times that Albertine played Vinteuil's sonata and other works of music on the pianola in his apartment in Paris, the narrator describes the instrument as a scientific magic lantern which, by offering music from different times, conjured up visions of different places and diverse works of art which then projected themselves onto the walls of his room in Paris. He also comments that his room contained another work of art more precious than all of the others – Albertine herself who, through his friendship and protection, became his creation. Regarding her as he might observe a work of art causes him to reflect on the two times and realities which her bodily presence brings together: by watching her legs work the pedals of the pianola, for example, he is reminded of a former scene at Balbec when she pedalled a bicycle. Albertine's transformation into a work of art is the result of the difference between her past and present reality – a difference which enhances those elements (her legs, her neck, her bodily presence) common to both times:

> Je la regardais. C'était étrange pour moi de penser que c'était elle, elle que j'avais crue si longtemps impossible même à connaître, qui aujourd'hui, bête sauvage domestiquée, rosier à qui j'avais fourni le tuteur, le cadre, l'espalier de sa vie, était ainsi assise, chaque jour, chez elle, près de moi, devant le pianola, adossée à ma bibliothèque. Ses épaules, que j'avais vues baissées et sournoises quand elle rapportait les clubs de golf, s'appuyaient à mes lèvres. Ses belles jambes, que le premier jour j'avais imaginées avec raison avoir manoeuvré pendant toute son adolescence les pédales d'une bicyclette, montaient et descendaient tour à tour sur celles du pianola, où Albertine, devenue d'une élégance qui me la faisait sentir plus à moi, parce que c'était de moi qu'elle lui venait, posait ses souliers en toile d'or. (III, 382)

Just as Albertine's words 'c'est Mlle Vinteuil' previously acted as the key which revealed to him the 'truth' about her sexual nature, so the narrator discovers, after Albertine's death in *Albertine disparue*, that words and situations which duplicate those previously associated with her serve as a 'magique Sésamé' opening the door of the past and giving to Albertine a second life: 'Et même une syllabe commune à deux noms différents suffisait à ma mémoire – comme à un électricien qui se contente du moindre corps bon conducteur – pour rétablir le contact entre Albertine et mon coeur' (III, 358).

Several years separate the events narrated in *Albertine disparue* and *Le temps retrouvé*, as the narrator spends several years in a sanatorium recovering from ill health. When he emerges from the hospital, he finds himself relocated in a world quite different from the Paris that he remembers, because France is at war with Germany. The changes that Paris and its inhabitants have undergone in his absence give rise to some past/present comparisons which are capital in linking together the network of recurring themes in the novel. The march of allied troops through the streets of Paris, for example, reminds him of the Paris of 1815, when a similar march of troops occurred. Their variegated uniforms also remind him of an imaginary exotic city:

> Là, l'impression d'Orient que je venais d'avoir se renouvela, et d'autre part à l'évocation du Paris du Directoire succéda celle du Paris de 1815. Comme en 1815 c'était le défilé le plus disparate des uniformes des troupes alliées; et parmi elles, des Africains en jupe-culotte rouge, des Hindous enturbannés de blanc suffisaient pour que de ce Paris où je me promenais je fisse

toute une imaginaire cité exotique, dans un Orient à la fois
minutieusement exact en ce qui concernait les costumes et la
couleur des visages, arbitrairement chimérique en ce qui concernait le décor, comme de la ville où il vivait Carpaccio fit une
Jérusalem ou une Constantinople en y assemblant une foule
dont la merveilleuse bigarrure n'était pas plus colorée que celle-
ci. (III, 763)

The narrator does not compare the troops to a scene from the *Thousand and One Nights*, but the exotic, oriental scene they suggest to him evokes that literary work. In the midst of this 'oriental' crowd, the narrator perceives a tall, stout man whose appearance suggests to him an actor or a painter, and the sodomist scandals often associated with artists. The man is M. de Charlus (III, 763). Since the 'oriental' scene (which recalls another past war) includes a character (M. de Charlus) whom we know to be a homosexual and whose appearance is now described as that of an actor or a painter, it functions as a crossroads bringing together four of the elements that have been subjects of the narrator's 'recherche': the past/present reminiscences, homosexuality, the creation of a work of art, and the *Thousand and One Nights* analogies.

In 'The Two Ways/Metaphor/Art' we saw that the network of past/present reminiscences is linked integrally to the 'two ways' – the social and geographical binary structure that functions as one of the two main girders structuring the novel (the other being time lost/time regained). In *Le temps retrouvé*, the narrator receives an invitation to attend an afternoon tea party at the Guermantes. In order to reach the Prince de Guermantes' new residence, he has to traverse territory associated in the past with Swann's Way and doing so, feels himself soar towards the silent heights of memory:

les rues par lesquelles je passais en ce moment etaient celles,
oubliées depuis si longtemps, que je prenais jadis avec Françoise
pour aller aux Champs Elysées. Le sol de lui-même savait où
il devait aller; sa résistance était vaincue. Et, comme un aviateur
qui a jusque-là péniblement roulé à terre, "décollant" brusquement, je m'élevais lentement vers les hauteurs silencieuses
du souvenir ... Je ne traversais pas les mêmes rues que les
promeneurs qui étaient dehors ce jour-là, mais un passé glis-
sant, triste et doux. (III, 858)

Shortly after arriving at the Guermantes' new residence, the narrator

experiences the first of the three 'intimation' experiences that lead to his discovery of the process by which past time may be restored. Repeated sips of the tea with the madeleine brought back memories of Combray to the narrator in *Du côté de chez Swann*. Similarly, rocking back and forth upon the uneven paving stone restores to him in *Le temps retrouvé* the original vision of Venice, where he had once experienced the same sensation as he stood upon two uneven stones in the Baptistry of St Mark's (III, 867). In Chapter 2, we saw that the narrator's analysis of his past/present reminiscences leads him to realize the true nature of reality and the means whereby that reality may translate itself into a work of art (see pp 17–27). Just as the past/present 'intimations' restored a moment of time to him, he now comprehends that, through its ability to intimate the internal reality of things to us, a work of art or literature may also recover past time for us (III, 896). In the process of creating a work of literature, the mind of the artist/writer reconsiders the people and situations he has encountered in his life and translates them into literature; thus a sort of second life is given to sentiments that apparently no longer existed (III, 905, see pp 24–5, 121). The narrator refers specifically to the 'amorous illusions' of his own life which will be resurrected by the translation of the women who provoked them into his literary work. The many love affairs recounted in the novel (Swann/Odette, Saint-Loup/Rachel, the narrator/Gilberte, the narrator/Albertine) are consequently linked to the narrator's discussions about the recovery of lost time and the past/present reminiscences, and a structural parallel and effect common to both kinds of experiences is revealed: just as the superimposition of a past moment onto the reality of the present disengages an atemporal moment which is neither of the past nor of the present, so an amorous relationship between two people engenders a third reality – love – which is different from both partners in the relationship.

The past/present reminiscences provide the narrator with the natural model for the device (metaphor) that enables an artist to express the internal reality of things through art (III, 889). He realizes, however, that sensations of the same genre as those engendered by the madeleine dipped in tea have already been recorded in literature. He makes specific reference to passages from Chateaubriand's *Mémoires d'Outre-Tombe*, Gérard de Nerval's *Sylvie*, and to some verses of Baudelaire, from *Les Fleurs du mal*. It is noteworthy that these three passages recording sensations similar to the narrator's past/present reminiscences depict phenomena which are also integral subjects of the narrator's life experience. Chateaubriand, for example, described

how the twittering of a thrush during a solitary walk caused his father's estate to appear before his eyes:

> N'est-ce pas à une sensation du genre de celle de la madeleine qu'est suspendue la plus belle partie des *Mémoires d'Outre-Tombe*: 'Hier au soir je me promenais seul ... je fus tiré de mes réflexions par le gazouillement d'une grive perchée sur la plus haute branche d'un bouleau. A l'instant, ce son magique fit reparaître à mes yeux le domaine paternel; j'oubliai les catastrophes dont je venais d'être le témoin, et, transporté subitement dans le passé, je revis ces campagnes où j'entendis si souvent siffler la grive.' (III, 919)

Similarly, we saw in 'The Two Ways/Art/Metaphor' that birds are associated with both 'ways' in the *Recherche* (see pp 109–10), and with the steeples of Combray and Martinville (see pp 95–6, 100).

The narrator specifically mentions another passage from Chateaubriand's *Mémoires* which describes how the scent of heliotrope issuing from a flowering bean patch brings with it the changed sky and environment associated with this exiled plant:

> Et une des deux ou trois plus belles phrases de ces *Mémoires* n'est-elle pas celle-ci: 'Une odeur fine et suave d'héliotrope s'exhalait d'un petit carré de fèves en fleurs; elle ne nous était point apportée par une brise de la patrie, mais par un vent sauvage de Terre-Neuve, sans relation avec la plante exilée, sans sympathie de réminiscence et de volupté. Dans ce parfum non respiré de la beauté, non épuré dans son sein, non répandu sur ses traces, dans ce parfum changé d'aurore, de culture et de monde, il y avait toutes les mélancolies des regrets, de l'absence et de la jeunesse.' (III, 919)

We have seen that flowers played a key role in the narrator's life, and were frequently associated with both of the 'two ways,' with the nature of homosexuality, with the Vinteuil Sonata, and with the relationship of a writer's past life to the works he creates (see pp 62–3, 107–8, 160–1). The hawthorns of Swann's Way also represented the disparity between external appearance and internal reality, as their almond fragrance suggested they were something they were not (I, 113).

In the case of Baudelaire's work, past/present reminiscences of the type engendered by the madeleine and the twittering of the thrush are numerous, except that this time the poet seeks in a woman the analogies that will inspire him:

> Un de ces chefs-d'oeuvre de la littérature française, *Sylvie*, de Gérard de Nerval, a, tout comme le livre des *Mémoires d'Outre-Tombe* relatif à Combourg, une sensation du même genre que le goût de la madeleine et 'le gazouillement de la grive.' Chez Baudelaire enfin, ces réminiscences, plus nombreuses encore, sont évidemment moins fortuites et par conséquent, à mon avis, décisives. C'est le poète lui-même qui, avec plus de choix et de paresse, recherche volontairement, dans l'odeur d'une femme par exemple, de sa chevelure et de son sein, les analogies inspiratrices qui lui évoqueront 'l'azur du ciel immense et rond'[11] et 'un port rempli de flammes et de mâts.'[12]
> (III, 919–20)

Similarly, we saw that the narrator perceives his own past love affairs as material for the work of literature he intends to write.

The narrator is about to search his memory for passages in Baudelaire describing transposed sensations, when he suddenly finds himself in the main drawing room of the Guermantes' residence, in the middle of a party which is to assume a special significance in his eyes. The narrator's observations about the people at the party lead us to understand that the gathering is unique because the altered appearances of the guests cause different times to converge and to reveal the effects of time as an artist. The narrator has not seen the majority of the guests at the party for many years. Consequently, he is impressed by the radical disparity between the past and the present appearances of these people – an incongruity that forces him to search beneath the surface for the common denominators which link an apparent stranger to a person he knew in the past:

> La transformation que les cheveux blancs et d'autres éléments encore avaient opérée, surtout chez les femmes, m'eût retenu avec moins de force si elle n'avait été qu'un changement de couleur, ce qui peut charmer les yeux, mais, ce qui est troublant pour l'esprit, un changement de personnes. En effet, 'reconnaître' quelqu'un, et plus encore, après n'avoir pas pu le reconnaître, l'identifier, c'est penser sous une seule dénomination deux choses contradictoires, c'est admettre que ce qui était ici,

> l'être qu'on se rappelle n'est plus, et que ce qui y est, c'est un être qu'on ne connaissait pas; c'est avoir à penser un mystère presque aussi troublant que celui de la mort dont il est, du reste, comme la préface et l'annonciateur. (III, 939)

In attempting to perceive the common factors linking two apparently contradictory realities, the narrator mentally duplicates – although he does not say this – the preliminary task performed by a poet or an artist when creating a metaphor. He frequently discovers that a certain rosiness of complexion or a name is the only factor linking dissimilar past and present realities associated with one being: 'On me disait un nom et je restais stupéfait de penser qu'il s'appliquait à la fois à la blonde valseuse que j'avais connue autre fois et à la lourde dame à cheveux blancs qui passait pesamment près de moi. Avec une certaine roseur de teint, ce nom était peut-être la seule chose qu'il y avait de commun entre ces deux femmes ...' (III, 939). Thus, the name of a person functions like those other objects, words, gestures, or sensations common to the past and the present (such as the tea and the madeleine) which previously brought together in the narrator's mind two dissimilar times and circumstances, and clarified an extratemporal essence common to them both. The radical disparity between the past and present appearance of the guests at the party also recalls the altered appearance of the lime blossoms used by the narrator's Aunt Léonie to make the tea he used to drink with her at Combray: 'c'était bien des tiges de vrai tilleuls comme ceux que je voyais avenue de la Gare, modifiées, justement parce que c'étaient non des doubles, mais elles-mêmes et qu'elles avaient vieilli. Et chaque caractère nouveau n'y étant que la métamorphose d'un caractère ancien, dans de petites boules grises, je reconnaissais les boutons verts qui ne sont pas venus à terme ...' (I, 51). Yet another bridge thus establishes itself between the first and last books of the *Recherche* which represent structurally the two poles of the primary macrometaphor (time lost/time regained) from which the body of the novel arises.

Although time may cause one entity to assume two apparently irreconcilable natures, it can also reveal common features that link family members to each other. Through time, for example, Gilberte's face has come to resemble her mother's, with the result that, when the narrator looks at Gilberte, two times and two faces superimpose themselves, and the comparison clarifies their common nature. For this reason, the narrator describes time as an artist, who creates metaphors by bringing together and revealing the common nature of distinctly different entities:

> 'Au lieu de votre beau nez droit on vous a fait le nez crochu
> de votre père que je ne vous ai jamais connu.' Et en effet c'était
> un nez nouveau et familial. Bref l'artiste, le Temps, avait 'rendu' tous ces modèles de telle façon qu'ils étaient reconnaissables; mais ils n'étaient pas ressemblants, non parce qu'il les
> avait flattés, mais parce qu'il les avait vieillis. Cet artiste-là,
> du reste, travaille fort lentement. Ainsi cette réplique du visage
> d'Odette, dont, le jour où j'avais pour la première fois vu
> Bergotte, j'avais aperçu l'esquisse à peine ébauchée dans le
> visage de Gilberte, le Temps l'avait enfin poussée jusqu'à
> la plus parfaite ressemblance, pareil à ces peintres qui gardent
> longtemps une œuvre et la complètent année par année.
> (III, 935–6)

The narrator described in *Sodome et Gomorrhe* a family resemblance between his mother and his grandmother, that caused two times and two realities to superimpose themselves upon each other (II, 1128–9). Similarly, the resemblance noted at the party causes two books (*Sodome et Gomorrhe* and *Le temps retrouvé*), two times (the past and the present) and two milieus (Balbec and Paris) to converge macrometaphorically, even though the narrator does not compare these two scenes explicitly.

Marcel realizes that social changes, like the changes in people he knew, can also reveal important truths: 'De changements produits dans la société je pouvais d'autant plus extraire des vérités importantes et dignes de cimenter une partie de mon œuvre qu'ils n'étaient nullement, comme j'aurais pu être au premier moment tenté de le croire, particuliers à notre époque' (III, 967). He does not specify what these truths are or how they reveal themselves through change, but we can surmise – by applying to society the same mechanism that changes in people engendered – that alterations in social structure cause us to compare a society's past and present reality, and thus allow us to perceive internal truths common to society and to the human condition which transcend external differences wrought by time.

Through his written account of his own past life, the narrator understands that he will not only recover his past, but will also enable his readers to perceive their own true past (their true inner 'being'):

> Seul il exprime pour les autres et nous fait voir à nous-même
> notre propre vie, cette vie qui ne peut pas 's'observer,' dont
> les apparences qu'on observe ont besoin d'être traduites et souvent lues à rebours et péniblement déchiffrées. (III, 896)

> Mais pour en revenir à moi-même, je pensais plus modestement

> à mon livre, et ce serait même inexact que de dire en pensant
> à ceux qui le liraient, à mes lecteurs. Car ils ne seraient pas,
> selon moi, mes lecteurs, mais les propres lecteurs d'eux-mêmes,
> mon livre n'étant qu'une sorte de ces verres grossissants com-
> me ceux que tendait à un acheteur l'opticien de Combray; mon
> livre, grâce auquel je leur fournirais le moyen de lire en
> eux-mêmes. (III, 1033)

In the course of reading the narrator's 'past,' the reader will unconsciously compare it with his own life experience and will consequently recognize the atemporal 'truths' common to both past experiences. Thus, the interaction of reader and book catalyses a process that is not only like a metaphor but also like a past/present reminiscence.

The narrator is quite aware that the subject-matter of his work might inadvertently repeat truths expressed by other writers from other epochs:

> Non pas que je prétendisse refaire, en quoi que ce fût, les
> *Mille et une Nuits*, pas plus que les *Mémoires* de Saint-Simon,
> écrits eux aussi la nuit, pas plus qu'aucun des livres que
> j'avais aimés, dans ma naïveté d'enfant, superstitieusement
> attaché à eux comme à mes amours, ne pouvant sans horreur
> imaginer une œuvre qui serait différent d'eux. Mais, comme Elstir
> Chardin, on ne peut refaire ce qu'on aime qu'en le renonçant.
> Ce serait un livre aussi long que les *Mille et une Nuits* peut-être,
> mais tout autre. Sans doute, quand on est amoureux d'une
> œuvre, on voudrait faire quelque chose de tout pareil, mais il
> faut sacrifier son amour du moment, ne pas penser à son
> goût, mais à une vérité qui ne vous demande pas vos préfé
> rences et vous défend d'y songer. Et c'est seulement si on la
> suit qu'on se trouve parfois rencontrer ce qu'on a abandonné,
> et avoir écrit, en les oubliant, les 'Contes arabes' ou les
> '*Mémoires* de Saint-Simon' d'une autre époque. (III, 1043-4)

Images and sensations that the narrator's work shares with previous works will cause past works to emerge into the context of the present, and the past/present comparisons that they give rise to will illuminate a truth common to two epochs.

In the concluding paragraph of *A la recherche du temps perdu*, the pattern traced by human life is likened to 'living stilts' which grow higher than church steeples:

> Je venais de comprendre pourquoi le duc de Guermantes, dont j'avais admiré, en le regardant assis sur une chaise, combien il avait peu vieilli bien qu'il eût tellement plus d'années que moi au dessous de lui, dès qu'il s'était levé et avait voulu se tenir debout, avait vacillé sur des jambes flageolantes comme celles de ces vieux archevêques sur lesquels il n'y a de solide que leur croix métallique et vers lesquels s'empressent des jeunes séminaristes gaillards, et ne s'était avancé qu'en tremblant comme une feuille, sur le sommet peu praticable de quatre-vingt-trois années, comme si les hommes étaient juchés sur de vivantes échasses, grandissants sans cesse, parfois plus hautes que des clochers, finissant par leur rendre la marche difficile et perilleuse, et d'où d'un coup ils tombaient. (III, 1047–8)

Because the stilts on which a human being is perched begin to grow in youth and reach their full height just before death, the narrator's analogy implies that life constantly brings together two realities – the distant past (the bottom of the stilts) and the present (the top of the stilts). Like the parallel lines which outline the steeple tower and converge at its topmost pinnacle, the past/present stilts representing a person's life converge in one body.[13] In 'Exterior/Interior' I observed that the dual nature (body/spirit, male/female) of the human personality renders it a metaphor-like structure. The narrator's binary image of the growing stilts reflects the metaphorical nature of the human personality and of humanity in general: the human person, like the stilts, is the common nature which links together epochs vastly separated in time and space:

> Du moins, si elle m'était laissé assez longtemps pour accomplir mon oeuvre, ne manquerais-je pas d'abord d'y décrire les hommes (cela dût-il les faire ressembler à des êtres monstrueux) comme occupant une place si considérable, à côté de celle si restreinte qui leur est réservée dans l'espace, une place au contraire plongée sans mesure – puisqu'ils touchent simultanément, comme des géants plongés dans les années, à des époques si distantes, entre lesquelles tant de jours sont venus se placer – dans le Temps. (III, 1048)

The past/present reminiscences, therefore, not only furnish the natural model for the metaphorical process which allows an artist to intimate the true nature of reality through a work of art, but serve also as reflections of the inherent nature of the human condition.

ART/LIFE/METAPHOR

As if to illustrate in reverse the reflective bond which the narrator perceives in *Le temps retrouvé* between past life experiences and the creation of a work of art, Proust includes in his novel a multitude of 'art/life' analogies, wherein characters and situations in the 'present' time of the novel are compared to 'past' works of art. These 'real-life' reflections of art include the pregnant servant girl in the narrator's household, Bloch, la Berma, Odette, Mme Verdurin, several people at a party whom the narrator characterizes as 'racial archetypes,' Mme de Guermantes, one of Swann's associates, the people at Saint-Euverte's concert, Albertine, M. de Charlus, a glass vendor in Venice, Combray, a landscape the narrator sees while out riding around La Raspelière, Mme Swann's drawing room, the steeple of Combray, the magic lantern, a dream, flowers, names, the past/present reminiscences, homosexuality, the two ways, war, and love. These comparisons not only foreshadow the narrator's hypothesis that art and life co-exist in a metaphor-like, reflective relationship, but also establish through the common term (a work of art) present in each of them, macrometaphorical correspondences among the people, places, objects, and circumstances that are all compared to works of art.

In 'Steeples/Art/Metaphor,' I illustrated that the structure of the steeple of Combray – and the impression given by it – reflects the metaphorical process. In Chapter 2, I mentioned that, for Proust's narrator, the basic building block of art is metaphor. Even if an analogy were not drawn between the steeples and art, therefore, a macrometaphorical correspondence would engender itself between them through their common metaphor-like nature. Proust consolidates their connection, however, in a comparison: the narrator's grandmother saw in the steeple the same simplicity which made her love nature and great works of art (I, 64 see p 96). I also mentioned in Chapter 4 that, shortly after alluding to the artistic quality of the steeple of Saint-Hilaire, the narrator explores another parallel between life experience and art – the resemblance of the pregnant kitchen girl in his Aunt Léonie's kitchen to the allegorical figure of Charity in Giotto's frescoes. 'Il fallait que ces Vertus et ces Vices de Padoue eussent en eux bien de la réalité puisqu'ils m'apparaissaient comme aussi vivants que la servante enceinte, et qu'elle-même ne me semblait pas beaucoup moins allégorique' (I, 82). In later years, the narrator realizes that the special beauty of these frescoes arose from symbols: 'Mais plus tard j'ai compris que l'étrangeté saisissante, la beauté spéciale de ces fresques tenait à la grande place que le symbole y occupait, et que le fait qu'il fût représenté, non comme un symbole puisque la pensée symbolisée n'était pas exprimée, mais comme réel, comme effectivement subi ou matériellement manié, donnait à la signification de l'œuvre quelque chose de plus littéral et de plus précis, à son enseignement quelque chose de plus concret et de plus frappant' (I, 82). Depicted as real things, the symbols of the frescoes demonstrate the interchangeability of the real and the symbolic, of art and life; a reversibility put in relief by the pregnant servant girl, who paradoxically appears as allegorical in her nature as the frescoes appear to be real. From the perspective of the totality of the text, these symbols – depicted as 'real things' – not only reflect the servant girl, but life experience in general, in which characters, milieus and events are symbols to which the narrator must restore true meaning by rendering them into a work of art: 'Il me fallait rendre aux moindres signes qui m'entouraient (Guermantes, Albertine, Gilberte, Saint-Loup, Balbec, etc.) leur sens que l'habitude leur avait fait perdre pour moi' (III, 897).

Before the narrator recognized the resemblance between the pregnant servant girl and one of Giotto's frescoes, Swann had indicated the resemblance to him: when inquiring after the condition of the girl, he would always ask, 'Comment va la Charité de Giotto?' (I, 80). Swann also compares one of his business associates to Giotto's 'Injustice' (I, 327), and notices a similar sort of resemblance between Bloch – the narrator's friend – and Bellini's portrait of Mahomet II: the same arched eyebrows, hooked nose, and prominent cheekbones (I, 97). In a similar vein, Swann tells the narrator that la Berma's acting will give him 'une vision aussi noble que n'importe quel chef-d'œuvre' (I, 98).

Swann finds a peculiar fascination in tracing in the paintings of the old Masters the individual features of men and women he knows (I, 222–3). Possibly, the narrator suggests, Swann has enough artistic temperament to be able to find a genuine satisfaction in watching the individual features of his associates take on a more general significance when he sees them uprooted and disembodied through the similarity shared by a historic portrait and a modern 'original' (I, 223). Like a metaphor, Swann's comparison of live people to works of art clarifies their common feature, endowing it with a more general significance and releasing it from the external circumstances in which it is embodied. In the totality of the text, therefore, Swann's comparisons of real-life characters to works of art illustrate the mirror relationship perceived by the narrator in *Le temps retrouvé* between an author's past life experience and the works of art drawn from it (III, 899, 902–5). In the case of Odette, Swann identifies her with Botticelli's painting of Zipporah to such an extent that Odette and the painting become totally interchangeable: when he draws towards him the photograph of Zipporah, he imagines that he is holding Odette to him (I, 225). After he has fallen in love with Odette, his attempts to discover the truth about her life and her daily activities seem to Swann to be on a level with the deciphering of manuscripts, or the interpretation of old monuments. Odette is a literary work whose meaning he must discover:

> Et tout ce dont il aurait eu honte jusqu'ici, espionner devant une fenêtre, qui sait? demain peut-être, faire parler habilement les indifférents, soudoyer les domestiques, écouter aux portes, ne lui semblait plus, aussi bien que le déchiffrement des textes, la comparaison des témoignages et l'interprétation des monuments, que des méthodes d'investigation scientifique d'une véritable valeur intellectuelle et appropriées à la recherche de la vérité ... Il éprouvait une volupté à connaître la vérité qui le passionnait dans cet exemplaire unique, éphémère et précieux d'une matière translucide, si chaude et si belle. (I, 274)

In addition to the large number of comparisons that he draws between life and art (Bloch/Mahomet II, Odette/Zipporah, the servant girl/Giotto's 'Charity,' la Berma/great art, Odette/manuscript, business associate/Giotto's 'Injustice'), Swann forges an integral link between art and life experience for yet another reason: he sees the advantage of a life of leisure in the time that it gives him to perceive life situations more interesting and more romantic than those in novels (I, 193); thus, life experience and a work of art are totally interchangeable for him.

In *Le temps retrouvé*, the narrator proclaims that all of his life experience, which is to be the matter with which he will create his literary work, can be traced back to the 'two ways.' Because Swann introduced him to both social milieus, he describes Swann as the 'tender stalk' which supported his whole life: 'En somme, si j'y réfléchissais, la matière de mon expérience, laquelle serait la matière de mon livre, me venait de Swann ... Pédoncule un peu mince peut-être pour supporter ainsi l'étendue de toute ma vie (le "côté de Guermantes" s'étant trouvé en ce sens ainsi procéder du "côté de chez Swann")' (III, 915). Swann is the stalk supporting the narrator's life for yet another reason that is not expressed explicitly. Because a writer's life is the source of his literary work, the narrator realizes that his life experience and his book will reflect each other (III, 899, 904). Being the stalk that supports his life experience, Swann is also the stalk around which the narrator's novel will build itself. As Swann epitomizes the human being who perceives the reversibility of art and life experience, the duality of art and life is the stalk supporting the narrator's life and his literary work. The 'two ways' and the interchangeability of art and life being incarnated in Swann, he initiates and sums up in himself a macrometaphorical link between the 'two ways' and the mirror relationship of art and life.

Like Swann, the narrator perceives resemblances between works of art and his own life experiences. We saw that he compares his childhood memories of Combray to the old engravings of the 'Cenacolo' or a certain painting by Gentile Bellini, in which one sees, in a state in which they no longer exist, the masterpiece of Leonardo and the portico of St Mark's (I, 166, see p 212). He also frequently compares events in his life to scenes from the *Thousand and One Nights* (see pp 67–8, 129).

Bergotte – the writer whose works are held in great esteem by the young narrator – compares la Berma's physical appearance during a performance of *Phèdre* to certain classical statues which she had possibly never seen: a Hesperid carved in the same attitude upon a metope at Olympia, or the beautiful, primitive virgins at Erechteum. Bergotte suggests that, by duplicating the appearance of these works, la Berma intimates the presence of a more primitive art in *Phèdre* (I, 560). The innate similarity between Racine's *Phèdre* and archaic Greek art manifests itself in Bergotte's own writing: in one of his volumes, he addresses a famous invocation to these statues (I, 560). As Bergotte's writings and Racine's *Phèdre* both recall a more ancient, primitive art form, their hermeneutical interaction with these former works possibly would clarify a nature common to works of art from different epochs. The narrator realizes, however, that Bergotte's writing resembles the smartness of Mme Swann's drawing room more than the ancient Greek statues he addresses. Consequently, life experience (Mme Swann's drawing room) and art (Bergotte's writing) begin to function as commentaries one upon the other: 'Mais enfin il y a entre ce que fut l'élégance du salon de Mme Swann et tout un côté de l'oeuvre de Bergotte des rapports tels que chacun des deux peut être alternativement, pour les vieillards d'aujourd'hui, un commentaire de l'autre' (I, 561).

In *Le côté de Guermantes II*, the narrator suggests that Elstir's paintings are remarkable because they illustrate the representation of one thing through another: 'Dès lors n'est-il pas logique, non par artifice de symbolisme mais par retour sincère à la racine même de l'impression, de représenter une chose par cette autre que dans l'éclair d'une illusion première nous avons prise pour elle?' (II, 419). Duplicating the optical illusion inherent in a first impression, Elstir's paintings are 'doubles' of life experience, which clarify the essential metaphorical nature of human perception – its tendency to represent one thing by another.

Comparisons are also frequently drawn between people and existing works of art in *Le côté de Guermantes*. The graceful appearance of Mme de Guermantes, for example, is likened to an elegant poem: 'attendant le départ de cette grande dame qui, dans sa toilette simple, savait, par la grâce de sa marche (toute différente de l'allure qu'elle avait quand elle entrait dans un salon ou dans une loge), faire de sa promenade matinale – il n'y avait pour moi qu'elle au monde qui se promenât – tout un poème d'élégance et la plus fine parure, la plus curieuse fleur du beau temps' (II, 59).

Some people whom the narrator encounters in Mme de Villeparisis' drawing room remind him of museum pieces, because the features of the live models duplicate the archetypal features portrayed in ancient sculpture (II, 191). Like a metaphor, his comparison of those living models to works of art which portray their racial features liberates the 'soul' common to the life and the work of art which embodied it: 'C'est l'âme (ou plutôt le peu de chose auquel se réduit, jusqu'ici du moins, l'âme, dans ces sortes de matérialisations), c'est l'âme, entrevue auparavant par nous dans les seuls musées, l'âme des Grecs anciens, des anciens Juifs, arrachée à une vie tout à la fois insignifiante et transcendentale, qui semble exécuter devant nous cette mimique déconcertante' (II, 191).

In *Le côté de Guermantes II*, the characteristic features of noble families are compared to the signature of a painter in whom Marcel has lost interest: 'Je lisais le crochet que faisait le nez du duc de Châtellerault comme la signature d'un peintre que j'aurais longtemps étudié, mais qui ne m'intéressait plus du tout' (II, 431). We saw that he also likens the pattern traced by the intertwined genealogies of the noble families to a finished work of art in which each part derives its sense from its relationship to the other parts (II, 537, see p 81).

Le Baron de Charlus is described as an artist who can restore to members of the nobility the charm and mystery associated with their names that their physical presences frequently destroyed. His stories about the genealogical origins of the nobility fire the narrator's imagination and cause him to forget how much the noble guests had disappointed him: 'Parlant en artiste, il pouvait tout au plus dégager le charme fallacieux des gens du monde' (II, 567). Although the narrator does not explain why M. de Charlus is an artist, a comparison of the effect produced by his stories with the consequences attributed to art in *Le temps retrouvé* will clarify the analogy for us. Just as the function of an artist (and the work of art) is to undo the masking imposed upon reality by passions, intellect, and habit, and to make us travel back to the depths where reality lies (III, 896), so M. de Charlus' stories restore to the noble guests an internal reality which their own vulgar presences concealed. The narrator's comparisons of Mme de Guermantes to a poem, of the intertwined genealogies of the nobility to a finished work of art, of M. de Charlus to an artist link the network of life/art analogies in the *Recherche* with the investigation of the ambiguous relationship of a name to its presence. M. de Charlus also being a homosexual, the artistic qualities attributed to him tend to reinforce the analogical connections drawn in the novel between the condition of homosexuality and art.

In *Sodome et Gomorrhe*, Mme Verdurin regards her regular social evenings as fragile works of art that could be shattered by one false note: 'des fameux mercredis, chefs-d'oeuvre incomparables et fragiles, pareils à ces verreries de Venise qu'une fausse note suffit à briser' (II, 885). By reflecting an earlier metaphor in *Du côté de chez Swann* (I, 227) likening Mme Verdurin to a statue, this comparison establishes a bridge between the different times (past/present), milieus (Paris/La Raspelière) and characters (Swann/the narrator) associated with Mme Verdurin at the time that each of these analogies is drawn.

While out riding on horseback one day, the narrator encounters a landscape that duplicates exactly a mountainous, marine scene which Elstir had painted in two watercolours. After mentally superimposing the natural scene upon the painted scene, he experiences a feeling of transcendence, as if transported to a place far beyond the world of today:

> Un instant, les rochers dénudés dont j'étais entouré, la mer qu'on apercevait par leurs déchirures, flottèrent devant mes yeux comme des fragments d'un autre univers: j'avais reconnu le paysage montagneux et marin qu'Elstir a donné pour cadre à ces deux admirables aquarelles, 'Poète rencontrant une Muse,' 'Jeune homme rencontrant un Centaure,' que j'avais vues chez la duchesse de Guermantes. Leur souvenir

> replaçait les lieux où je me trouvais tellement en dehors du
> monde actuel que je n'aurais pas été étonné si, comme le jeune
> homme de l'âge anti-historique que peint Elstir, j'avais, au
> cours de ma promenade, croisé un personnage mythologique.
> (II, 1028–9)

The mirror relationship of Elstir's painting to nature (the view seen by the narrator) and the transcendental effect to which their rapport gives rise illustrate the metaphor-like correspondence that the narrator perceives between life experience and works of art in *Le temps retrouvé* (III, 889, 899, 904–5).

In *La prisonnière*, the narrator attempts to incorporate life experience with art. As a result of this amalgamation, he discovers that real-life experience begins to assume for him the quality of imagination of a work of art. While looking at one of Elstir's works, reading one of Bergotte's books or listening to the Vinteuil Sonata, he unconsciously conjures up the dreams that Albertine had inspired in him long ago – visions that had been stifled by the routine of everyday life. As a result of this amalgamation, life experience and art are both enhanced: the book that he is reading or the work of art that he is observing is enriched by its association with his dreams of Albertine (a life experience), and correspondingly, Albertine is transported out of the tangible world and is free to play in the fluid space of the mind. Through her association with a work of art, Albertine assumes, for the narrator, the appearance of a work of art: 'Elle avait à ce moment-là l'apparence d'une oeuvre d'Elstir ou de Bergotte, j'éprouvais une exaltation momentanée pour elle, la voyant dans le recul de l'imagination et de l'art' (III, 56). Transported into a transcendent space, Albertine recalls Odette of *Du côté de chez Swann*, as she too was able to enter into a world of dreams as a result of her resemblance to Botticelli's painting (I, 225).

While reflecting on the works of art which enter his rooms through Albertine's playing of the pianola, the narrator realizes that his room contains another work of art more precious than all the others – Albertine herself:

> Mais ma chambre ne contenait-elle pas une œuvre d'art plus
> précieuse que toutes celles-là? C'était Albertine elle-même. Je la
> regardais. C'était étrange pour moi de penser que c'était elle,
> elle que j'avais crue si longtemps impossible même à connaître,
> qui aujourd'hui, bête sauvage domestiquée, rosier à qui

j'avais fourni le tuteur, le cadre, l'espalier de sa vie, était ainsi assise, chaque jour, chez elle, près de moi, devant la pianola, adossée à ma bibliothèque. (III, 382)

I observed that Albertine's transformation into 'a work of art' is the result of the difference between her past and present reality, and that the past/present duality inherent in her is the direct result of the narrator's 'shaping' of her life (see pp 132–3). Similarly, in order to create a work of art, a writer must 'prune' his own past life into generalities, and then translate those generalities into writing, with the result that a past life becomes the internal double of a work of art existing in the context of the present. Through Albertine, therefore, the art/life correspondences discussed in the novel become macrometaphorically connected to the network of past/present reminiscences that form an essential part of the narrator's life experience. As the condition of homosexuality is frequently linked analogically in the *Recherche* to the nature of flowers, the narrator's comparison of Albertine to a rosebush trimmed to a pleasing shape (III, 382) reinforces the macrometaphorical correspondences which have previously been established between homosexuality and art (see pp 59–64).

In *La fugitive*, the narrator attempts to make a life situation reflect art: fearing that his love affair with Albertine is on the verge of crumbling, he attempts to force her hand by creating a situation which will demand that she profess her feeling for him. In doing so, he tries to duplicate in his own life a situation whose elements (a man, a woman, one who loves more than the other, a forced confrontation) have already come together and played themselves out as visible drama in Racine's *Phèdre* (III, 458–60).

Shortly after his attempt to make life duplicate art, the narrator discovers evidence that an episode in Albertine's life may have been rendered into a work of art. After her death, the narrator learns of Albertine's lesbian encounters on the banks of the Loire with a young laundress and her friends (III, 524–5). While reflecting on the changing perceptions of Albertine's personality that these revelations bring with them, the narrator is reminded of two paintings by Elstir depicting nude women against a leafy background. In one of them, one of the girls is raising her foot as Albertine must have raised hers when she offered it to the laundress. The narrator also realizes that the raising of the thigh in the painting made the same swan's neck curve with the angle of the knee that was made by the droop of Albertine's thigh when she was lying by his side on his bed (III, 155). The text does not state that Albertine was the real-life model for these paintings, but her previous acquaintance with Elstir at Balbec (I, 844) indicates that she might well have been.

The mirror relationship that the narrator perceives between Albertine and art repeats itself after her death with another of his female acquaintances: he wishes to bring to Paris with him a rosy-cheeked young glass vendor because 'c'était un vrai Titien à acquérir avant de s'en aller' (III, 640).

In *Le temps retrouvé*, several more analogies are drawn that establish direct links between the art/life duality frequently alluded to by the narrator, and some of the other major recurring themes of the novel: homosexuality, the past/present reminiscences, the 'two ways,' and writing. After witnessing the beating of M. de Charlus by two 'ruffians' in Jupien's homosexual brothel, the narrator tells Jupien that his establishment is worse than a madhouse, since the mad fantasies of the lunatics who inhabit it are played out as actual drama: while watching M. de Charlus being beaten, he thought he had arrived, like the Caliph in the *Thousand and One Nights*, in the nick of time to rescue a man from affliction. In fact, he realizes, it was a different tale he had enacted before him – the one in which a woman, who has been turned into a dog, willingly submits to being beaten in order to regain her true form (III, 832, pp 67–8). The art/life comparison that the fictional incident inspires establishes a connection between a literary work and the condition of homosexuality, which reinforces the theoretical connection between sadism and melodrama that the narrator perceived years earlier at Montjouvain, after Mlle Vinteuil and her girlfriend spit upon the portrait of her father before they made love together (I, 163). The subterranean links established among life, art, and homosexuality through the intermediary of these comparisons (M. de Charlus/the *Thousand and One Nights*, and Mlle Vinteuil/melodrama) help to clarify another connection between the condition of homosexuality and the relationship of a writer's past life to his future literary work. In *Sodome et Gomorrhe*, the narrator compared a homosexual act to the chance fertilization of a flower by a honey bee (II, 604–7). In *Le temps retrouvé*, homosexuality is linked to the mirror relationship of life experience and art by another 'plant' comparison: the narrator likens his past life experience to the albumen of a germ cell which existed only for the nourishment of the plant – his literary work (III, 899). The network of connections established among the *Thousand and One Nights*, the life/art analogies, homosexuality, and writing expands itself to embrace the network of past/present reminiscences also: when he wipes his mouth with a napkin in the Guermantes' library, the sensation makes him feel as if he is a character in one of the tales of the *Thousand and One Nights* who unwittingly accomplishes the very rite that causes a genie to appear. In the narrator's case, however, the rubbing does not conjure up a genie, but a vision of the past, because the napkin he uses to wipe his mouth has exactly the same degree of stiffness as the towel with which he used to dry his face at Balbec (III, 868). A texture common to the past and the present allowed a past moment to emerge into the context of the present. Similarly, the *Thousand and One Nights* (a common term to which the following entities are all compared) allows a macrometaphorical link to establish itself between homosexuality, the past/present reminiscences, and the mirror relationship of art and life experience.

Life and literature may also reflect each other through the circumstances of war: in the course of a discussion with Albertine about the war in which France is engaged with Germany, the narrator realizes that he was impressed in the beginning by the fighting in France because the trenches reminded him of similar trenches first encountered in the writings of Mme de Sévigné (III, 982). Gilberte tells the narrator that Saint-Loup, before his death, was most impressed by the war because it repeated manoeuvres that occurred in previous wars and by doing so, recalled past history to him. Saint-Loup had noted, for example, that the English made use of a tactic that was utilized by the Chaldeans at the dawn of history (III, 982). By resurrecting past events and also recalling similar circumstances recorded in literary works, the events of war catalyze yet another subterranean link between the past/present reminiscences, the art/life comparisons, and the writing of a literary work.

Gilberte's former love for Saint-Loup is compared to a novel: 'Ainsi peut-être la vue d'Andrée rappelait à Gilberte ce roman de jeunesse qu'avait été son amour pour Robert' (III, 984). We saw earlier that the apparently impossible merger of the 'two ways' realized through the marriage of Gilberte de Forcheville née Swann (of Swann's Way) to Robert de Saint-Loup (of Guermantes' Way) is also described as 'tout un roman' (III, 962).

After intermittently describing – through the course of the novel – the mirror relationship linking real-life entities and situations to pre-existent works of art, the narrator ultimately concludes, in *Le temps retrouvé*, that art and life experience are doubles of each other because life experiences are the source materials for a work of art (III, 904–5). The relationship of an artist's life to the work of art he creates duplicates the structure of a past/present reminiscence: they both entail elements common to the past and to the present that allow a past reality to re-emerge into the context of the present. Similarly, the art/life comparisons linking people, places and situations in the narrator's life to pre-existent works of art illuminate the essential reality common to the past and the present, life and art. Thus, the individual art/life analogies are microreflections of the primary macrometaphor of the work – time lost/time gained – which, in its largest sense, is the life experience of the narrator translating itself into *A la recherche du temps perdu*.

WORKS OF ART IN THE NOVEL/THE NOVEL/METAPHOR/ART

While telling his life story, the narrator frequently alludes to works of art – literary works, musical compositions, theatrical performances, sculptures, and painting – and repeatedly compares one art form to another: the effect produced by a remarkable prose passage, for example, is likened to an interlude of music (I, 93). Through the intermediary of these cross-references, his critical commentaries on paintings, literary works, and musical compositions imply that all works of art give rise to a similar effect and possibly manifest a common structural nature. The narrator presents his general theories about the nature of art in the final volume of the novel – *Le temps retrouvé*. At the moment that he formulates them, however, he has not only been reflecting on works of art in general but on life experiences that produce in him a certain inexplicable happiness similar to the sensation provoked by a work of art such as the Vinteuil Septet:

> Mais au moment où, me remettant d'aplomb, je posai mon pied sur un pavé qui était un peu moins élevé que le précédent, tout mon découragement s'évanouit devant la même félicité qu'à diverses époques de ma vie m'avaient donnée la vue d'arbres que j'avais cru reconnaître dans une promenade en voiture autour de Balbec, la vue des clochers de Martinville, la saveur d'une madeleine trempée dans une infusion, tant d'autres sensations dont j'ai parlé et que les dernières œuvres de Vinteuil m'avaient paru synthétiser. (III, 866)

The narrator perceives a common denominator in each experience (two times and realities are superimposed upon each other with the result that their common essential nature – their essence – is momentarily allowed to appear), which allows him to discern the true nature of reality and the process that an artist/writer must use to express that reality to us in his work: he must duplicate the rapport between dissimilar phenomena that occurs naturally, and the only device that can accomplish this task is metaphorical structure (III, 889). It appears to be natural phenomena encountered in the course of his life experience, therefore, that suggest to the narrator the essential character of art.

Long before he experiences his moment of epiphany about the nature of art in the Guermantes' library, however, the narrator has analysed and described the structure and/or effect of various works of art (musical compositions, literary works, paintings) which struck him, at various times in his life, as remarkable experiences. Some of these works are 'real' works that exist outside of Proust's text: *François le Champi* by George Sand, novels by Thomas Hardy, Dostoievsky, Honoré de Balzac, Gérard de Nerval, Madame de la Fayette, reminiscences by Chateaubriand, poetry by Baudelaire, letters by Mme de Sévigné, the opera *Tristan und Isolde* by Wagner. In addition, there are other works of art analysed that exist only in the context of *A la recherche du temps perdu*: Bergotte's novels, Elstir's paintings, and Vinteuil's musical compositions. Michel Butor, in *Les Oeuvres d'art imaginaires chez Proust*, suggests that these 'imaginary' works fabricated by Proust reflect some 'real' works of the nineteenth century. The sonata with its remarkable little phrase, for example, had previously appeared in *Jean Santeuil*, where it was directly attributed to Saint-Saens.[14] Although Proust never mentions Saint-Saens' name in *A la recherche du temps perdu*, the sonata for piano and violin which is attributed to Vinteuil is suggestive of the sonata for piano and violin by Saint-Saens. Butor comments: 'on connaît une sonate pour piano et violon de Saint-Saens, mais dans le passage de Jean Santeuil que j'ai cité, il n'est question que de piano. De même la sonate de Vinteuil est écrite pour piano et violon, mais elle apparaît tout d'abord, et le plus souvent, sous la forme de sa réduction pour piano seul.'[15] Butor suggests that, although Proust compares a section of the sonata to a passage from *Tristan*, the work also brings to mind a few other unnamed composers of the nineteenth century, especially Schumann and Debussy. Thus, Vinteuil's work may be a composite of late nineteenth-century music.[16] Butor also suggests that 'Elstir' – the name of the painter whose work frequently appears in the novel – is a Gallicized anagram for Whistler,[17] and proposes that Elstir's work is inspired by a certain number of turn-of-the-century works (a Manet, certain Monets, Whistlers, obviously some Degas) and by several Japanese artists, particularly Housaki.[18] Albeit the composition of Elstir's 'Le Port de Carquethuit' originated apparently in Proust's imagination, Butor suggests that the narrator's analysis of the painting constitutes an extraordinary analysis of the painting of the period.[19] Proust does not just imitate the painting of that era, however, but surpasses it: where paintings by Monet depict compositional metaphors in thicknesses of matter (rocks depicted like wool, for example), Proust describes two reverse metaphorical ensembles in 'Le Port de Carquethuit' (marine terms to describe the earth, terrestrial terms to describe the sea) that are a remarkable equivalent to twentieth-century surrealist painting. Butor proposes that Elstir's paintings are suggestive of themes that were worked out almost literally by the surrealist painter Magritte.[20]

Whether he is discussing imaginary works that are composite depictions of nineteenth-century art forms, or 'real' works of art such as George Sand's *François le Champi*, the narrator's commentaries upon works of art perform two structural functions in the vast macrometaphor which constitutes *A la recherche du temps perdu*: they serve as concrete illustrations of his theoretical assertions about the nature of art which are presented in *Le temps retrouvé*, and they also act as models which mirror (and illuminate) the structure of the *Recherche*. Also, the two macrometaphorical relationships (works of art in novel/theories about art in novel; structure of works of art in novel/structure of novel itself) arising from the narrator's commentaries on works of art reveal the common denominator that Proust's novel shares with some other works of art and possibly, with all works of art. In the following pages, I hope to show that the basic structure of all of the works examined critically by the narrator is metaphorical structure.

In the introductory paragraph of the *Recherche*, the narrator mentions that, after falling asleep while reading, he seemed to become the subject of his book but he does not tell us its name. He does, however, tell us the name of the first novel that he read as a young boy: *François le Champi* by George Sand. Novels being a new experience for him, even the title of the book appeared to represent something undefinable and mysterious (I, 41, see p 37). The narrator first attributed this sense of mystery to the obscure name of François le Champi itself. Later in life, however, he is obliged to admit that part of the obscurity associated with the book resulted from his tendency to daydream while reading, and from his mother's habit of leaving out all the love scenes when she read the story to him (I, 42). The true cause of the mysterious emanation arising from the novel is not recognized by the narrator, however, but by his grandmother, who chose the four pastoral novels of George Sand as a birthday present to her grandson because they were to her examples of novels that were well-written (1, 39). The narrator mentions that his grandmother preferred old things because they bring with them a vision of the past ('une fleurette, un sourire, quelquefois une belle imagination du passe,' 1, 41). Similarly, she regarded the pastoral novels of George Sand as examples of good writing because, like 'antique furniture,' they are full of references and expressions that have fallen out of use in everyday language but which have returned as imagery:

> Or, justement, les romans champêtres de George Sand qu'elle me donnait pour ma fête, étaient pleins, ainsi qu'un mobilier ancien, d'expressions tombées en desuétude et redevenues imagées, comme on n'en trouve plus qu'à la campagne. Et ma grand'mère les avait achetés de préférence à d'autres comme elle eût loué plus volontiers une propriété où il y aurait eu un pigeonnier gothique ou quelqu'une de ces vieilles choses qui exercent sur l'esprit une heureuse influence en lui donnant la nostalgie d'impossibles voyages dans le temps. (1, 41)

The effect produced by these obsolete expressions in George Sand's novels suggests the sensation initially engendered by the narrator's past/present 'intimations.' When the narrator partakes of the tea and the madeleine with his mother, for example, he instantly experiences an exquisite pleasure that does not carry with it any suggestion of its origin (1, 45) but compels him to reflect upon itself in an effort to recognize its source. Similarly, the antiquated expressions in George Sand's novels fill his grandmother with a nostalgic longing to make impossible journeys through the realms of time. In *Le temps retrouvé*, the narrator subjects all of his past/present intimations to analysis and discovers why they conjure up in him the same inexplicable happiness: as they all begin with an encounter in the present of an object or sensation originally experienced in the past, they cause two times to become superimposed one upon the other, thus allowing an extratemporal 'essence' to reveal itself. Correspondingly, the archaic expressions in George Sand's novels cause a former time and reality to be conjured up in the context of the reader's present, plunging him into an extratemporal world that is neither in the past where the expressions originated nor in the present where the book is being read.

The narrator tells us that his grandmother preferred photographs of an artist's interpretation of a scene to an actual photograph of the place itself, because the latter appeared to her to be vulgar and utilitarian. She attempted to overcome the banality inherent in a photograph by allowing it to serve the function of a supplementary layer or filter through which she could perceive another work of art. Instead of photographs of Chartres cathedral, for example, she would request photographs of 'Chartres Cathedral by Corot' (I, 40). Sometimes, she would attempt to postpone the moment of contact with vulgar reality even further still by procuring, instead of photographs, old engravings (I, 40). In the grandmother's attempts to overcome the commercial banality of the mechanical photograph by substituting for it several thicknesses of art, we can see the origin of the narrator's own theories about the function of art as an optical instrument whose projection upon our lived experience reveals the true nature of reality to us (III, 911).

As well as describing his reaction to a 'real' novel (*François le Champi*) which exists outside of *A la recherche du temps perdu*, the narrator also introduces, in *Du côté de chez Swann*, an imaginary work which exists only in the context of his reminiscences – Bergotte's novel. Proust does not provide us with sufficient information about Bergotte's work (a few quotations, a few general comments, details on a single volume, his monograph on Racine) to enable us to see Bergotte as a reflection of a specific writer of the period, but the details that he does give us enable us to see the writer's imaginary works as a reflection of what literature should accomplish, according to the criteria that the narrator establishes in *Le temps retrouvé*. Bergotte and his novel may be fictitious creations originating in Proust's imagination; nevertheless they are introduced to Bloch and subsequently to the narrator by 'le père Leconte' (I, 90), whose name strongly suggests Leconte de Lisle, a nineteenth-century French poet and a foremost leader of the 'l'art pour l'art' movement.[21] The narrator compares his first impression of Bergotte's novel to an elusive air of music running through his head: 'Mais au sujet de Bergotte, il avait dit vrai. Les premiers jours, comme un air de musique dont on raffolera, mais qu'on ne distingue pas encore, ce que je devais tant aimer dans son style ne m'apparut pas' (I, 93). A macrometaphorical correspondence establishes itself between Bergotte's novel and the Vinteuil Sonata through the intermediary of this comparison, as the latter work is the air of music most frequently alluded to in the *Recherche*.

His continued reflection on the novel reveals to the narrator the rare, almost archaic phrases that Bergotte utilizes at certain points. Through these archaic phrases, Bergotte's novel also macrometaphorically aligns itself with *François le Champi*, which is likewise full of 'antique' expressions utilized as imagery. The narrator's grandmother felt that these obsolete expressions produced a nostalgic longing for impossible journeys through the realms of time. When the narrator encounters archaic phrases in Bergotte's work, he realizes that they coincide with a hidden flow of harmony: 'Puis je remarquai les expressions rares, presque archaïques qu'il aimait employer à certains moments où un flot caché d'harmonie, un prélude intérieur, soulevait son style' (I, 94). This parallel (archaic phrases/prelude in the work) establishes an opposition of equivalence between its terms, abrogating the distinction between a musical composition and a literary work by rendering them interchangeable. At the moments that the archaic phrases coincide with a harmony in the work, Bergotte also expresses to the narrator a whole system of philosophy and ideas through the use of marvelous imagery. Continuing the analogy he previously established between a musical prelude and the literary work, the narrator compares the inspiration derived from this imagery to the 'sound of harps': 'C'était aussi à ces moments-là ... qu'il exprimait toute une philosophie nouvelle pour moi par de marveilleuses images dont on aurait dit que c'était elles qui avaient éveillé ce chant de harpes qui s'élevait alors et à l'accompagnement duquel elles donnaient quelque chose de sublime' (I, 94). According to the narrator, the strength of Bergotte's imagery resides in its power to reveal beauty that had hitherto been imperceptible to him, and to drench him with its essence: 'Chaque fois qu'il parlait de quelque chose dont la beauté m'était restée jusque-là cachée, des forêts de pins, de la grêle, de Notre-Dame de Paris, d'*Athalie* ou de *Phèdre*, il faisait dans une image exploser cette beauté jusqu'à moi' (I, 95). Thus, Bergotte's writing illustrates the power which the narrator attributes to metaphor and art many years later (in *Le temps retrouvé*), when he asserts that a work of art can only suggest the internal reality of things by duplicating – through the metaphorical process – the 'natural' conditions which reveal the rapport between objects (III, 889). While proclaiming his desire to obtain from Bergotte an all-comprehensive metaphor upon everything in the world, which would clarify the meaning of things for him (I, 95, he does not realize that by showing him the power of poetic imagery – its ability to reveal the essence of things – Bergotte has already provided him with the key which will render everything meaningful for him – metaphor itself.

Marcel's youthful reaction to Bergotte's writing also illustrates the theories about the mirror relationship of art and life experience which he formulates years later (III, 911, 1033). While reading Bergotte's novels, he frequently discovers that a page of the book expresses ideas which he attempted to write himself. He discovers incidents described in the novels (a joke about an old family servant, for example) which reflect perfectly his own life experience, and he consequently realizes that his own existence and the realms of truth which Bergotte's writings represent for him are less widely separated than he supposed:

> Un jour, ayant rencontré dans un livre de Bergotte, à propos d'une vieille servante, une plaisanterie que le magnifique et solennel langage de l'écrivain rendait encore plus ironique, mais qui était la même que j'avais souvent faite à ma grand'mère en parlant de Françoise, une autre fois où je vis qu'il ne jugeait pas indigne de figurer dans un de ces miroirs de la vérité qu'étaient ses ouvrages une remarque analogue à celle que j'avais eu l'occasion de faire sur notre ami M. Legrandin (remarques sur Françoise et M. Legrandin qui étaient certes de celles que j'eusse le plus délibérément sacrifiées à Bergotte, persuadé qu'il les trouverait sans intérêt), il me sembla soudain que mon humble vie et les royaumes du vrai n'étaient pas aussi séparés que j'avais crus, qu'ils coïncidaient même sur certains points, et de confiance et de joie je pleurai sur les pages de l'écrivain comme dans les bras d'un père retrouvé. (I, 96)

The narrator compares the dissemination of Bergotte's writings to the scattering of seeds, which at first rarely took root, but later flowered profusely throughout Europe and America:

> Je n'étais pas tout à fait le seul admirateur de Bergotte; il était aussi l'écrivain préféré d'une amie de ma mère qui était très lettrée; enfin pour lire son dernier livre paru, le docteur du Boulbon faisait attendre ses malades; et ce fut de son cabinet de consultation, et d'un parc voisin de Combray, que s'envolèrent quelques-unes des premières graines de cette prédilection pour Bergotte, espèce si rare alors, aujourd'hui universellement répandue, et dont on trouve partout en Europe, en Amérique, jusque dans le moindre village, la fleur idéale et commune. (I, 94–5)

I observed that flowers are frequently linked metaphorically in the

Recherche to most of the other recurring phenomena of the novel which we have been examining: 'the two ways' (I, 135, 138, 168, 169, 172), homosexuality (II, 604–5, 631) a passage of music (the Vinteuil Sonata, I, 138), a work by his favourite painter (Elstir, I, 139), La princesse de Guermantes (and consequently, to the duality of names/presences, II, 41), Albertine (III, 69), Swann (III, 915), a chapel (reminiscent of the church of Combray, I, 138), the obscure impressions (such as those feelings produced by the drinking of the tea and the madeleine, III, 375), etc. I also mentioned that, in *Sodome et Gomorrhe*, the narrator concludes his discussion of homosexuality and the fertilization of flowers with the statement that these exceptional entities are a vast crowd, the reason for which will be disclosed at the end of the book (II, 631). Although I find no succinct explanation in *Le temps retrouvé* as to why the 'orchids' and 'bees' are so numerous, there is another 'plant' analogy: the narrator compares his past life experience to the albumen of a germ cell which existed only to produce and nourish the plant – his future literary work (III, 899). Before seeds, plants, and flowers were compared to anything else in the novel, however, they were linked analogically in *Du côté de chez Swann* to the dissemination of Bergotte's novel. Thus, the ultimate clue that the narrator promised to reveal in the last volume of the work is already presented in the first volume in the guise of an analogical link between the dissemination of writing and the scattering of seeds (plants). A comparison of all terms woven together through this metaphorical labyrinth of 'plants' allows us to perceive that the recognition of an innate similarity upon which a homosexual coupling depends or as a result of which a flower is fertilized by a honeybee is like the intuitive perception of the innate similitude of dissimilars upon which our knowledge of the internal reality of things is based, and which is expressed to us through the device of metaphor in a literary work. A book also intimates the internal reality of things to us through the process of recognition of internal doubles: the reader sees a reflection of his own 'true' self in the work of art. When viewed from the perspective of the totality of the text, the 'literary work/plant' analogies common to the first and last volumes of the novel not only reinforce each other, but also bring together the terms of the primary macrometaphor of the novel (time lost/time regained) which are associated with the first and last volume of the novel. This latter correspondence recalls to itself the narrator's assertion in *Le temps retrouvé* that the creation of a work of art is the only means by which lost time may be regained (III, 899).

The narrator does not provide us with sufficient information about the structure of Bergotte's novel to enable us to perceive it as a work-of-art-as-metaphor, but he does emphasize the transcendent effect produced by the poetic metaphors in Bergotte's work. However, the second 'imaginary' work of art introduced in *A la recherche du temps perdu* – the Vinteuil Sonata – is structurally presented to us in such a way that we can see the work of art itself as a macromodel of metaphor. The sonata is introduced into the context of the novel through Swann, a character who is integrally linked to art and metaphor on many levels (see pp 144–5). Upon hearing the opening bars of an unnamed sonata played one evening at the Verdurin's salon, Swann realizes that he is hearing the same mysterious composition first encountered a year before:

> Swann trouvait en lui, dans le souvenir de la phrase qu'il avait entendue, dans certaines sonates qu'il s'était fait jouer, pour voir s'il ne l'y découvrirait pas, la présence d'une de ces réalités invisibles auxquelles il avait cessé de croire et auxquelles, comme si la musique avait eu sur la sécheresse morale dont il souffrait une sorte d'influence élective, il se sentait de nouveau le désir et presque la force de consacrer sa vie.
> (I, 211)

The invisible reality suggested by the sonata reflects macrometaphorically the internal reality of things alluded to by the narrator in *Le temps retrouvé*, which can only be apprehended through metaphor in a work of art (III, 889). During the narrator's description of Swann's second encounter with the sonata, the musical composition is compared to the sea, to roses and to a mysterious, unknown woman. In view of my attempt to establish that Proust perceived a common denominator characterizing all works of art (whether literary works, musical compositions, paintings, or sculptures), the comparison linking the movement of the sonata to the waves of the sea is especially remarkable, as it establishes a subtle relationship between the Vinteuil Sonata and another 'imaginary' work of art introduced into the second book of the novel – Elstir's painting 'Le Port de Carquethuit' (I, 208).

Just as Marcel later compares the effect of the sonata to a dawn of lilied meadows (III, 250) and to a geranium scent (III, 375), so Swann now likens its harmony to the odour of roses circulating in the evening air: 'il avait cherché à recueillir la phrase ou l'harmonie – il ne savait lui-même – qui passait et qui lui avait ouvert plus largement l'âme, comme certaines odeurs de roses circulant dans l'air humide du soir ont la propriété de dilater nos narines' (I, 208–9). We saw earlier that plants are also linked analogically to Bergotte's novel and to most of the other recurring themes of the novel: homosexuality, the two ways, Albertine, Swann, Mme de Guermantes, the name/presence duality, and the nature of writing. The analogy linking the effect produced by the sonata to an unknown woman causes an unvoiced parallel to arise between the sonata and Albertine – the narrator's greatest love, whom he frequently describes as impossible to know, to decipher or to understand, and who is later depicted as a living work of art created by himself (III, 382).

Prior to the introduction of the Vinteuil Sonata into the narration of the *Recherche*, the narrator compared the sight of three steeples (the twin steeples of Martinville joined by the steeple of Vieuxvicq) to three flowers painted on the sky and to three maidens described in a legend (I, 182). Through the common terms (flowers, women) that are compared to Vinteuil's sonata and to the steeples, a macrometaphorical link is forged between them:

> Vinteuil's sonata/scent of a rose/a mysterious woman
> the three steeples/three flowers/three women
> Vinteuil's sonata = the steeples.

In 'Steeples/Art/Metaphor,' I concluded that the steeples serve as the key hieroglyphic figure of *A la recherche du temps perdu* because their shape structurally duplicates the metaphorical process which, according to the narrator's assertions in *Le temps retrouvé*, is the basic building block of art. Thus, the analogical similarities that link the sonata to the steeples suggest the art-like character of the steeples and the metaphorical nature of the sonata.

The impression produced by the sonata is not only like a 'mysterious woman,' but is also 'sine materia': 'Une impression de ce genre, pendant un instant, est pour ainsi dire "sine materia." Sans doute les notes que nous entendons alors, tendent déjà, selon leur hauteur et leur quantité, à couvrir devant nos yeux des surfaces de dimensions variées, à tracer des arabesques, à nous donner des sensations de largeur, de ténuité, de stabilité, de caprice' (I, 209). The 'sine materia' impression engendered by the sonata resembles the exquisite, undefinable happiness produced by the past/present 'intimation' experiences and the obscure impressions, and also evokes the impression beyond the realm of articulation that the narrator defines, in *Le temps retrouvé*, as the only criterion for truth, which must be apprehended through metaphor in order to be incorporated into a work of art: 'Seule l'impression, si chétive qu'en semble la matière, si insaisissable la trace, est un criterium de vérité ...' (III, 880).

We observed above that a subterranean link is established between the Vinteuil Sonata and Elstir's painting 'Le Port de Carquethuit,' when the narrator compares the harmony of the music to the waves of the sea. He consolidates this correspondence between the two art forms by proposing that, both being 'avant-garde' art, the paintings of Biche (the young artist patronized by the Verdurins, who later changes his name to Elstir (III, 720) resemble Vinteuil's music: the Cottards (a bourgeois couple whose artistic inclinations typify the public's taste in art) are incapable of finding, either in Vinteuil's sonata or in Biche's (Elstir's) paintings, that which constitutes for them beauty or harmony in art. Both artists have forsaken the generally accepted forms of reality in their efforts to produce a work of art (I, 213). The narrator does not clarify the structural similarities shared by Elstir's paintings and Vinteuil's sonata which cause them to be innovations, but he does offer us at different times in the text structural analyses of both art forms which allow us to perceive the common structural principles that they manifest.

After his evening at the Verdurins', when he heard the Vinteuil Sonata for the second time, Swann has it replayed for him in order that he may disentangle from his confused impressions about it an understanding of how it is constructed. He encounters it yet another time during a concert at the Saint-Euverte's, and reflects on the discoveries that he made about the sonata when he submitted it previously to analysis. He attributes the sonata's impression of a contracted sweetness to the closeness of the intervals between the five main notes which compose it and to the constant repetition of two of those notes:

> Quand après la soirée Verdurin, se faisant rejouer la petite phrase, il avait cherché à démêler comment à la façon d'un parfum, d'une caresse, elle le circonvenait, elle l'enveloppait, il s'était rendu compte que c'était au faible écart entre les cinq notes qui la composaient et au rappel constant de deux d'entre elles qu'était due cette impression de douceur retractée et frileuse; mais en réalité il savait qu'il raisonnait ainsi non sur la phrase elle-même, mais sur de simples valeurs, substituées pour la commodité de son intelligence à la mystérieuse entité qu'il avait perçue, avant de connaître les Verdurin, à cette soirée où il avait entendu pour la première fois la sonate. (I, 349)

Like Mme de la Fayette's *La Princesse de Clèves* and Chateaubriand's *René* (I, 350), the sonata represents for him an original conception of love and happiness. Even when he is not thinking of the little phrase, Swann realizes that it exists latent in his mind: 'Même quand il ne pensait pas à la petite phrase, elle existait latente dans son esprit au même titre que certaines autres notions sans équivalent, comme la notion de lumière, de son, de relief, de volupté physique, qui sont les riches possessions dont se diversifie et se pare notre domaine intérieur' (I, 350). The music's ability to suggest immateriality reminds Swann of some themes in *Tristan*: both musical compositions present themselves as special, distinctive ornaments of the human soul (I, 350). It reminds him of other concepts without material equivalent (such as light, sound, desire, perspective) which are a part of everyday, lived experience, and thus illustrates the mirror relationship between art and life experience that the narrator recognizes much later in *Le temps retrouvé* (III, 899, 904). By specifically categorizing 'desire' and 'perspective' as doubles of the impression left in his mind by the sonata, the narrator causes macrometaphorical parallels to establish themselves between the sonata and persons and objects associated with desire and perspective in the text of *A la recherche du temps perdu*. Physical desire, for example, is a prime factor not only in Swann's life during his long relationship with Odette, but also in the narrator's life when he falls in love first with Gilberte, and then with Albertine. 'Perspective' brings to mind Elstir's paintings; we are told in *A l'ombre des jeunes filles en fleurs* that Elstir's primary technique in painting consists of attempts to represent an object from the perspective of our initial impression of it rather than from a traditional perspective (I, 835).

After his brief reflections on the impressions engendered by the sonata, Swann listens again to the musical composition and realizes that the introductory phrase, of which he is so fond, disappears but then reappears at the end of the last movement, after a long passage which Mme Verdurin's pianist had omitted. Swann realizes that this missing passage contains some memorable ideas that he had not noticed on first hearing the sonata but which he now recognizes. One after the other, all the scattered themes that make up the composition reduce themselves into its culminating impression, 'comme si elles se fussent, dans le vestiaire de sa mémoire, débarrassées du déguisement uniforme de la nouveauté' (I, 351).

In view of my attempt to establish a common structural nature linking these diverse works of art to each other and to the novel *A la recherche du temps perdu*, it is significant that the basic components of

Swann's structural analysis of the Vinteuil Sonata (five main notes, two major recurring themes, a long middle passage in which apparently new themes merge into the composition of the original phrase) reflect the structure of the totality of the *Recherche*. Like the five main notes which make up the sonata, there are five principal themes that serve as structural girders supporting the plot of the novel: (1) the two ways, (2) the past/present reminiscences (time lost/time regained), (3) the duality of names and their designated presences, (4) homosexuality, and (5) love. In addition, there are five principal characters or families whose lives and actions illustrate the five main themes: (1) the narrator, (2) Swann, (3) the Guermantes, (4) Albertine, and (5) Charlus. Swann suggested that two of the five key themes of the sonata constantly repeated themselves. Similarly, the 'two ways' and 'time lost/time regained' are the interlocking cornerstones of the novel from which and around which all of the other themes are built. Swann remarked that the Vinteuil Sonata contained a long middle passage that was frequently omitted by performers, who may have found it redundant, but which contained apparently new themes which ultimately merged into the impression of the primary phrase of the work. Likewise, *A la recherche du temps perdu* contains an extensive, middle passage (*A l'ombre des jeunes filles en fleurs*, *Le côté de Guermantes*, *Sodome et Gomorrhe*, *La prisonnière*, *La fugitive*) whose 'new developments' are reflections or variations of material introduced in the first volume of the novel – *Du côté de chez Swann* – and reiterated in the final volume – *Le temps retrouvé*. Just as all of the variations introduced in the long, middle passage of the sonata merge into a culminating impression, of which the introductory phrase is the clearest manifestation, so we have seen in the course of our investigation of the labyrinth of intertwining themes which composes *A la recherche du temps perdu*, that all symbols, entities, and ideas explored in the middle volumes of the novel have their roots in the first volume; and through the metaphorical parallels (macrometaphorical connections) established between dissimilar phenomena by innate similarities, all of these themes ultimately divest themselves of their external variations and accumulatively give rise to a unified impression that is their internal similarity – a metaphor-like binary structure.

Swann compares Vinteuil's variations on a theme to an experiment whose purpose is to discover the secret laws that govern an unknown force: 'O audace aussi géniale peut-être, se disait-il, que celle d'un Lavoisier, d'un Ampère, l'audace d'un Vinteuil expérimentant, découvrant les lois secrètes d'une force inconnue, menant à travers l'inexploré, vers le seul but possible, l'attelage invisible auquel il se fie et qu'il n'apercevra jamais' (I, 351). Although neither Swann nor the narrator describes the exact nature of the secret law that Vinteuil uncovers, they do remind us at this time that the sonata, in its most essential form, is a dialogue between violin and piano which resembles the mating song of two birds – the primal couple when there were only two beings on earth (I, 351–2, see p 44). Their analogy emphasizes the mirror resemblance between the structure of the sonata and the 'original' conditions which engendered life, and also establishes a macrometaphorical connection between the sonata and other entities in the novel that have been associated with birds: the two ways (I, 137, 181), Mme de Guermantes (II, 62), Swann of 'Swann's Way,' the steeple of Combray which frequently had flocks of birds issuing forth from its windows (I, 63), and the narrator's commentary on a selection from Chateaubriand's *Mémoires d'Outre-Tombe* in which the sound of a lone thrush catalyses an experience of involuntary memory, resurrecting in the author's mind memories of his childhood (III, 919).

The dialogue of the sonata is also described as the perfect language that transcends speech – the signified concept which speech aspires to: 'La suppression des mots humains, loin d'y laisser régner la fantaisie, comme on aurait pu croire, l'en avait éliminée; jamais le langage parlé ne fut si inflexiblement nécessité, ne connut à ce point la pertinence des questions, l'évidence des réponses' (I, 351). Swann's analysis of the Vinteuil Sonata plays a major role in clarifying the qualities of a work of art that allow it to transcend differentiated thought processes. He emphasizes the dual nature of the musical composition – an intertwining of dissimilars (piano and violin) which, after dividing and splitting itself into multiple hues of the primary harmony, gives rise to an ethereal impression that both transcends material reality and suggests the primeval origin of all life. Upon hearing the multiple themes of the sonata dissolve into one basic form, Swann feels that he is assisting at the mystery of its birth ('Swann écoutait tous les thèmes épars qui entreraient dans la composition de la phrase, comme les prémisses dans la conclusion nécessaire, il assistait à sa genèse,' I, 351). Correspondingly, during the performance of the sonata, he feels in the room a 'magic presence' which had not been there previously: 'Swann n'osait pas bouger et aurait voulu faire tenir tranquilles aussi les autres personnes, comme si le moindre mouvement avait pu compromettre le prestige surnaturel, délicieux, et fragile qui était si près de s'évanouir' (I, 352). This 'magic presence' born from the dialogue of the sonata is like the 'essence' or internal reality disengaged by the union of dissimilars in a metaphor.

Swann compares the stage on which the performers play to an altar: 'La parole ineffable d'un seul absent, peut-être d'un mort (Swann ne savait pas si Vinteuil vivait encore), s'exhalant au-dessus des rites de ces officiants, suffisant à tenir en échec l'attention de trois cents personnes, et faisait de cette estrade où une âme était ainsi evoquée un des plus nobles, autels où pût s'accomplir une cérémonie surnaturelle (I, 352–3). His analogy (stage/altar) engenders another intratextual parallel between the steeple of Combray and the sonata, as the word 'altar' immediately conjures up a vision of the church that the steeple indicates.

In the second volume of the novel, *A l'ombre des jeunes filles en fleurs*, the narrator tours Elstir's studio at Balbec and is able to study close to their source the artist's celebrated paintings. His analysis of Elstir's paintings is paramount in establishing the common metaphorical nature which a painting and a literary work share, and the phenomena that he encounters upon entering and leaving the studio are equally significant, as their close proximity to Elstir's work reinforces the metaphorical bonds which the narrator establishes between these entities and works of art in other parts of the novel.

In order to reach Elstir's studio, the narrator must traverse a small garden of begonias (I, 834). These flowers summon up in the reader's mind the hawthorns and other flowers that the narrator encountered during his walks along the 'two ways,' which suggested to him then a rhythm as unexpected as certain intervals of music (I, 138) and inspired him with the same rapture that he felt upon seeing a work by his favourite painter (I, 139). The flowers also bring to mind the nature of homosexuality which is frequently linked metaphorically to flowers (II, 604–7). Upon leaving the studio, the narrator sees Albertine Simonet upon her bicycle. Several years later, after Albertine has become his mistress in Paris, the narrator describes her as a work of art he has created, like a rosebush he might have pruned into a pleasing shape (III, 382). In *Le temps retrouvé*, the mirror relationship between a literary work and the life of its author is compared to the symbiotic relationship of the albumen of a germ cell to the future plant that it nourishes (III, 899). In *Du côté de chez Swann*, the dispersal of Bergotte's novels is compared to the dissemination of seeds (I, 94–5). Thus, phenomena associated with art that are metaphorically linked to flowers in other sections of the novel converge in the garden of begonias at the entrance to Elstir's studio.

After submitting the Vinteuil Sonata to analysis, Swann compared Vinteuil's variation on a theme to an experiment to discover the secret laws that govern an unknown force (1, 351). Similarly, Elstir's studio appears to the narrator as the laboratory for a new sort of creation of the world: 'Et l'atelier d'Elstir m'apparut comme le laboratoire d'une sorte de nouvelle création du monde, où, du chaos que sont toutes les choses que nous voyons, il avait tiré, en les peignant sur divers rectangles de toile qui étaient posés dans tous les sens, ici une vague de la mer écrasant avec colère sur le sable son écume lilas, là un jeune homme en coutil blanc accoudé sur le pont d'un bateau' (1, 834).

Swann never mentioned metaphor in connection with Vinteuil's sonata, but we hypothesized that, through their common elements (a binary structure, a union of dissimilars which gives rise to a third 'presence' or reality), a relationship establishes itself between the sonata and the process of metaphor, as defined by the narrator in *Le temps retrouvé*. In the case of Elstir's paintings, the narrator forges a direct link between the structural principles underlying them and metaphor. He perceives that the charm of each of the paintings resides in a sort of metamorphosis of the thing represented in it, and compares the effect produced by Elstir's 'metaphors' to a renaming procedure – taking away the accepted names of things and endowing them with new names – thus consolidating the correspondence between the nature of a work of art and the narrator's investigation of the divergent relationship of a name and the presence to which it refers: 'Naturellement, ce qu'il avait dans son atelier, ce n'était guère que des marines prises ici, à Balbec. Mais j'y pouvais discerner que le charme de chacune consistait en une sorte de métamorphose des choses représentées, analogue à celle qu'en poésie on nomme métaphore, et que, si Dieu le Père avait créé les choses en les nommant, c'est en leur ôtant leur nom, ou en leur en donnant un autre, qu'Elstir les recréait' (1, 835).

The narrator suggests that Elstir's paintings depict those rare moments when we see nature with poetic vision, as she actually is. One of the metaphors that occurs most commonly in his paintings is a comparison of land to sea, which suppresses every line of demarcation between them (1, 835–6). In 'Le Port de Carquethuit,' for example, Elstir planes down the difference between (or reveals the innate similarity of) land and sea by using only marine terms to depict the little town portrayed in the painting, and only urban terms to depict the sea in front of the town. The roofs of the houses, for example, are overtopped by masts, making the vessels to which they belong appear to be built on land. The churches of Criquebec, on the other hand, are

seen in the far distance surrounded by water on all sides. On the beach in the foreground, the painter has executed his work in such a way that there is no fixed boundary, no absolute line of demarcation, between land and sea. The result of this sustained superimposition and/or reversal of marine and urban terms is that the whole painting gives the impression of a landscape in which the sea entered into the land, in which the land was already subaqueous, and in which the population was amphibian (I, 836). In their superimposition of one reality upon another (marine terms applied to urban reality, for example), Elstir's paintings not only reflect metaphorical structure but also manifest an innate similarity to many of the other major recurring symbols and phenomena that pervade the *Recherche*. The magic lantern, for example, was regarded by the young narrator as a device for producing mysteriously transcendent effects, because its superimposition of a coloured picture upon the existing reality of the room gave rise to an intermingling of two realities (I, 10). Similarly, when reflecting upon the 'two ways' in *Du côté de chez Swann*, the narrator perceived them as two distinct entities which together possessed a cohesion or unity that pertains only to creations of the mind because, despite their dissimilarity, he could think of one only in terms of the other (I, 134). We saw that the frequent superimposition of one 'way' upon the other in the context of the narrator's reminiscence of his life experience allows the reader (and ultimately the narrator) to perceive their innate resemblance. Just as Elstir, when painting, had to strip himself of every intellectual concept in order to achieve his effects (I, 840), so the narrator later suggests in *Le temps retrouvé* that the task of an artist is to undo for us the work of the intellect, the passions, and daily habit, in order that we may experience our true impressions of reality – as it actually is – before our conceptions of it are altered by the nomenclatures attached by our intellect (III, 896). In their metaphor-like composition which results from their creator's perception of reality, therefore, Elstir's paintings illustrate the theories about art, metaphor, and reality that the narrator expounds in *Le temps retrouvé*.

In *Du côté de chez Swann*, Swann felt the presence of a nature common to the Vinteuil Sonata and a theme from *Tristan*, because both compositions represented to him an aspect of the human condition which was moving and profound (I, 350). In *La prisonnière*, many years later, the narrator also notices a resemblance between the sonata and *Tristan*: he compares his perception of their similitude to the smile of an old friend of the family who perceives a trace of the grandfather in the gesture of the grandson who had never set eyes on him: 'En jouant

cette mesure, et bien que Vinteuil fût là en train d'exprimer un rêve qui fût resté tour à fait étranger à Wagner, je ne pus m'empêcher de murmurer: "Tristan," avec le sourire qu'a l'ami d'une famille retrouvant quelque chose de l'aïeul dans une intonation, un geste du petit-fils qui ne l'a pas connu' (III, 158–9). The innate resemblance that links the two musical compositions is like a sensation common to two times and circumstances which, when encountered in the present, causes a moment from the past (in which that sensation was previously experienced) to emerge into the context of the present. Earlier, while admiring the Guermantes' collection of Elstir's paintings in *Le côté de Guermantes II*, the narrator perceived resemblances between the 'avant-garde' works of Elstir and the 'traditional' paintings of Chardin and Perroneau (II, 419–20), and also between two canvases as apparently different as Manet's 'Olympia' and a masterpiece by Ingres (II, 420, see p 77). All such intertextual connections reflect the narrator's many past/present reminiscences, such as that precipitated by the taste of the madeleine dipped in tea.

Although he does not immediately clarify the nature of the similarity between the Vinteuil Sonata and Wagner's *Tristan*, the narrator's subsequent discussion about the latter work discloses structural affinities shared by Wagner's music, Vinteuil's sonata, Balzac's *La Comédie Humaine* and Victor Hugo's *La Légende des Siècles*. The narrator associates reality in the work of Wagner with the composition's insistent, fleeting themes, which withdraw only to return, being alternatively vague, distant, detached, and then pressingly near, internal, and organic (III, 159). Swann, in *Du côté de chez Swann*, was similarly impressed with the recurring motifs of the sonata, which emerged only to disappear, and then re-emerged later in the composition (I, 210).

The narrator remarks in *La prisonnière* that Wagner's music allows him to go deep into himself and there make a new discovery that his life experience had not revealed to him. Similarly, in *Du côté de chez Swann*, Swann perceived in the sonata the presence of an invisible reality in which he had ceased to believe but to which he now aspired to consecrate his life (I, 211). Thus, both Wagner's *Tristan* and the Vinteuil Sonata accomplish the function that the narrator later attributes to art in *Le temps retrouvé* – it allows us to return to the depths of ourselves: c'est ce travail que l'art défera, c'est la marche en sens contraire, le retour aux profondeurs où ce qui a existé réellement gît inconnu de nous, qu'il nous fera suivre' (III, 896).

During his brief analysis of Wagner's *Tristan*, the narrator establishes a parallel between the harmony of Wagner's composition and the colours of Elstir's paintings – both forms of art reveal a 'two-fold difference' to him. The first half of the 'two-fold difference' consists of the essential quality of another person's sensations that the work of art makes visible, and which life experiences such as love for another person do not reveal: 'Diversité double. Comme le spectre extériorise pour nous la composition de la lumière, l'harmonie d'un Wagner, la couleur d'un Elstir nous permettent de connaître cette essence qualitative des sensations d'un autre où l'amour pour un autre être ne nous fait pas pénétrer' (III, 159). In their power to present different, internal perceptions of reality to him, Tristan and Elstir's paintings illustrate another characteristic attributed by the narrator in *Le temps retrouvé* to a work of art:

> car le style pour l'écrivain, aussi bien que la couleur pour le peintre, est une question non de technique mais de vision. Il est la révélation, qui serait impossible par des moyens directs et conscients, de la différence qualitative qu'il y a dans la façon dont nous apparaît le monde, différence qui, s'il n'y avait pas l'art, resterait le secret éternel de chacun. Par l'art seulement nous pouvons sortir de nous, savoir ce que voit un autre de cet univers qui n'est pas le même que le nôtre, et dont les paysages nous seraient restés aussi inconnus que ceux qu'il peut y avoir dans la lune. Grâce à l'art, au lieu de voir un seul monde, le nôtre, nous le voyons se multiplier et, autant qu'il y a d'artistes originaux, autant nous avons de mondes à notre disposition, plus différents les uns des autres que ceux qui roulent dans l'infini ... (III, 895–6)

Although the uniquely different perceptions of reality presented by different works of art would appear to indicate that there is no common denominator shared by all works of art, the second half of the 'two-fold difference' revealed by *Tristan* establishes the nature of the correspondence which causes one work of art to reflect another one. The narrator remarks that, as well as revealing to him a difference between his personal perception of the world and an artist's, a painting by Elstir or music by Wagner divulges a diversity within the work itself, which arises from its presentation of many different realities as individual figures; the completeness of the music (in the case of Wagner) consists of the joyous clash of sounds (or colours, in the case of Elstir), which weave themselves into an orchestral whole, without losing their original nature:

> Puis, diversité au sein de l'œuvre même, par le seul moyen
> qu'il y a d'être effectivement divers: réunir diverses individua-
> lités. Là où un petit musicien prétendrait qu'il peint un
> écuyer, un chevalier, alors qu'il leur ferait chanter la même
> musique, au contraire, sous chaque dénomination, Wagner met
> une réalité différente, et chaque fois que paraît son écuyer, c'est
> une figure particulière, à la fois compliquée et simpliste, qui,
> avec un entrechoc de lignes joyeux et féodal, s'inscrit dans l'im-
> mensité sonore. (III, 159)

In view of my attempt to demonstrate that metaphorical structure is the essential pattern reflected in all of the recurring phenomena in *A la recherche du temps perdu*, Wagner's and Elstir's preservation of the individuality of diverse elements within their works would appear to render their works radically different from Proust's work. It is precisely the diverse elements combined in these works, however, that make them parallel the metaphorical process and the architectonic structure of *A la recherche du temps perdu*. After submitting his past/present reminiscences to analysis in *Le temps retrouvé*, the narrator realizes that, through a sensation common to the past and to the present, a moment of past time is able to emerge into the context of the present where the past scene momentarily grapples with the actual scene 'like a wrestler.' Neither the past nor the present scene loses its individuality, as the narrator perceives both scenes separately. Nevertheless, their super-imposition clarifies their common nature – the atemporal sensation which caused the two scenes to come into conflict with each other ('Toujours, dans ces résurrections-là, le lieu lointain engendré autour de la sensation commune s'était accouplé un instant, comme un lutteur, au lieu actuel. Toujours le lieu actuel avait été vainqueur; toujours c'était le vaincu qui m'avait paru le plus beau ...,' (III, 874–5). After the past/present reminiscences have led the narrator to comprehend the nature of internal reality and how it may intimate itself through art, he hypothesizes that the internal reality of things can be revealed only by the combination of dissimilar phenomena in a metaphor. To the extent that metaphor entails the combination of dissimilar phenomena, the joyous feudal clash of individual elements in Wagner's opera constitutes a metaphor-like structure.

Let us turn to the individuality of the diverse elements of *A la recherche du temps perdu*. Although my attempt to establish metaphor as the common structural model for all recurring phenomena in the *Recherche* apparently would entail an abrogation of difference between these entities, we must not forget that the common nature of these individual elements only reveals itself through their textual superimposition, or through metaphorical cross-references which describe one entity in terms of another. When the 'two ways' are first presented to us, for example, they are depicted as entities which are so vastly different that the narrator had to go out different sides of the house in order to reach each respective 'way' (I, 134). Nevertheless, we have seen that the superimposition of the individual descriptions of each 'way' in the text reveals the existence of innate similarities which the narrator does not immediately acknowledge, but which become apparent to him as his experience with both 'ways' increases.

Similarly, despite the clash of individual elements which Wagner's *Tristan* represents for the narrator, he perceives in the work that same unity which characterizes all the greatest works of the nineteenth century. He envisions this unity arising in part from the attitudes expressed in prefaces written after the books themselves. He perceives the preface as a 'musician's cadence' rather than a 'scholarly precaution,' however, as the unity which the preface imposes upon the work is an ulterior, rather than an artificial unity, because it is the expression of the unity that the author himself – after completing his work – discovered existing among its diverse elements, which had only to be brought together for that unity to reveal itself. In Wagner's case, the narrator hypothesizes that the composer realized he had written a tetralogy only when he recognized that all three completed works revolved around a similar theme. Wagner must have felt, at that moment, the same exhilaration as Balzac when he recognized an innate similarity in his existing works, and decided to bring them all together in a cycle in which the same characters would reappear. The unity that both Wagner and Balzac perceived in their works is an unconscious unity which emerges like a fragment – composed separately – from the composition of the work itself:

> Unité ultérieure, non factice, sinon elle fût tombée en poussière comme tant de systématisations d'écrivains médiocres qui, à grand renfort de titres et de sous-titres, se donnent l'apparence d'avoir poursuivi un seul et transcendant dessein. Non factice, peut-être même plus réelle d'être ultérieure, d'être née d'un moment d'enthousiasme où elle est découverte entre des morceaux qui n'ont plus qu'à se rejoindre; unité qui s'ignorait, donc vitale et non logique, qui n'a pas proscrit la variété, refroidi l'exécution. (III, 161)

When he examined Elstir's paintings in his studio at Balbec, the narrator perceived 'unity' in those compositions also, arising from the sustained comparisons inscribed in them: 'Une de ces métaphores les plus fréquentes dans les marines qu'il avait près de lui en ce moment était justement celle qui, comparant la terre à la mer, supprimait entre elles toute démarcation. C'était cette comparaison, tacitement et inlassablement répétée dans une même toile, qui y introduisait cette multiforme et puissant unité' (I, 835–6). Through this common 'unity' that they all manifest, a macrometaphorical connection establishes itself in the reader's mind among Elstir's paintings, Wagner's operas, and Balzac's novels. The unity of Elstir's paintings having been attributed to the metaphorical comparisons in them, their internal link with these other works suggests that their unity may result from 'metaphors' also.

During an evening at the Verdurins', the narrator hears a new work performed whose origin is unknown to him. While listening to its introductory bars, the narrator feels like a lost character in the *Thousand and One Nights*, who waits for the appearance of a genie to show him his way. At that moment, a 'genie' in the form of the little phrase from the Vinteuil Sonata appears and immediately indicates to him the origin of the composition (III, 249).

After listening to Vinteuil's larger masterpiece,[22] the narrator realizes that, although the sonata indicated the 'way' of the septet to him, it is not the septet's way itself, as the two compositions – though equally beautiful – are radically different in tone: 'Tandis que la Sonate s'ouvrait sur une aube liliale et champêtre, divisant sa candeur légère mais pour se suspendre à l'emmêlement léger et pourtant consistant d'un berceau rustique de chèvrefeuilles sur des géraniums blancs, c'était sur des surfaces unies et planes comme celles de la mer que, par un matin d'orage, commençait au milieu d'un aigre silence, dans un vide infini, l'œuvre nouvelle …' (III, 250).

The 'two ways' of the sonata and the septet suggest the 'two ways' of the narrator's childhood (le côté de Guermantes and le côté de chez Swann), as they were first described as distinctly different entities also (I, 134). We saw that, despite their external, diametrically opposed natures, the 'two ways' manifest many innate similarities. Similarly, after listening to the septet, the narrator realizes that, although the sonata is as calm, timid, and detached in tone as the septet is anxious, pressing, and imploring, the two compositions are nevertheless the 'same prayer':

> ces deux interrogations si dissemblables qui commandaient le mouvement si différent de la sonate et du septuor, l'une brisant

> en courts appels une ligne continue et pure, l'autre ressoudant en une armature indivisible des fragments épars, l'une si calme et timide, l'autre si pressante, anxieuse, implorante, c'était pourtant une même prière, jaillie devant différents levers de soleil intérieurs, et seulement réfractée à travers les milieux différents de pensées autres, de recherches d'art en progrès au cours d'années où il avait voulu créer quelque chose de nouveau. Prière, espérance qui était au fond la même, reconnaissable sous ses déguisements dans les diverses œuvres de Vinteuil, et d'autre part qu'on ne trouvait que dans les œuvres de Vinteuil. (III, 255)

The macrocomparison of the two musical compositions gives rise to an effect which is like that produced by the comparison of two objects in a metaphorical phrase: it reveals their innate similarity.

In *La prisonnière*, the narrator frequently asks Albertine to play Vinteuil's music for him on the pianola. His prolonged reflections on the music lead him to some conclusions about the nature of a work of art in general and its relationship to other works of art. He suggests that it is the unoriginal parts of a musical composition that remind us of other works. When he first heard the Vinteuil Septet at the Verdurins', for example, the phrases in the music which seemed most remarkable to him were those whose origin he could not immediately discern, but later identified with other musical compositions (III, 373). On the other hand, phrases that first seemed ugly and discordant later appear to him as the most beautiful parts of the composition. He attributes the initial disappointment which these phrases produce to the artist's effort to unravel the initial impression and lay bare the truth (III, 373), and contends that this question (how the ugly may become beautiful) is at the centre of all questions about the truth of art and the immortality of the soul. His suggestion that a preliminary impression of ugliness may arise from the artist's attempts to shatter our common perceptions recalls his previous observations about Elstir's works whose strength resided in their ability to recapture our initial impression of an object (I, 838). Just as Swann previously described the sonata as the perfect language that transcends speech (I, 351), so the narrator proposes that Vinteuil's music has something in it which is truer, more real than the ideas expressed by any book of his acquaintance: musical sounds can reproduce the interior point of a sensation, whereas literary translations of that sensation can only explain it or analyse it:

> Par instants je pensais que cela tenait à ce que ce qui est senti
> par nous de la vie, ne l'étant pas sous forme d'idées, sa traduc-
> tion littéraire, c'est-à-dire intellectuelle, en rend compte, l'ex-
> plique, l'analyse, mais ne le recompose pas comme la musique
> où les sons semblent prendre l'inflexion de l'être, reproduire
> cette pointe intérieure et extrême des sensations qui est la partie
> qui nous donne cette ivresse spécifique que nous retrouvons
> de temps en temps et que, quand nous disons: 'Quel beau
> temps! quel beau soleil!' nous ne faisons nullement connaître
> au prochain, en qui le même soleil et le même temps éveillent
> des vibrations toutes différentes. (III, 374)

His observations about the power of music indicate a difference in the degree to which different art forms may express reality, but they do not negate the possibility of a common means of achieving that end. He is reminded at this time of the resemblance between the impression produced by certain phrases of Vinteuil and the peculiar pleasure he felt at other moments of his life, such as the times when he gazed at the steeples of Martinville, saw the three trees along a road near Balbec, or tasted the cup of tea accompanied by the madeleine (III, 374). We have seen that his analysis of these obscure impressions and experiences of involuntary memory leads him to discover the nature of internal reality and the means by which a literary work may express that true nature of things through metaphorical structure. Despite his contention, therefore, that music can intimate more truly the nature of things because it can avoid the intellectualization which the use of words entails, his subsequent discoveries in *Le temps retrouvé* about internal reality and how it may intimate itself through the use of metaphor reaffirms the equivalence previously established between a literary work (Bergotte's novel) and a musical work in *Du côté de chez Swann* (I, 93).

His reflections on Vinteuil's music also lead the narrator to discuss with Albertine what constitutes a work of genius. He suggests to her that a work of genius gives us access to an unknown world which no other composer/writer has ever made us see (III, 375), and which reveals itself in all of a great artist's works, with the result that he creates only a single work or refracts through various mediums an identical beauty (III, 375). When we read the narrator's assertion, we are not only reminded of the 'common prayer' evoked by Vinteuil's works ('prière, espérance qui etait au fond le même,' III, 255), but also of the 'morceau idéal' that the young narrator recognized in one of Bergotte's novels years earlier, which appeared to sum up the essential quality evoked by all his novels (I, 94). The narrator's conclusions about the repetitive nature of an artist/writer/composer's works are not based entirely on 'imaginary' works of art which exist solely in the context of *A la recherche du temps perdu*, but are founded also on his observations of other literary and artistic masterpieces which have an existence 'in reality' outside of the context of Proust's novel. He specifically refers to the works of Thomas Hardy, Stendhal, Dostoievsky, and Vermeer.

In the case of Thomas Hardy's novels, the narrator remarks that, as a result of the common themes and imagery which characterize all of his works, they can be laid one upon another like the vertically piled houses depicted in one of the stories:

> je revins aux tailleurs de pierre de Thomas Hardy. 'Vous vous rappelez assez dans *Jude l'Obscur*, avez-vous vu dans *la Bien-Aimée*, les blocs de pierre que le père extrait de l'île venant par bateaux s'entasser dans l'atelier du fils où elles deviennent statues; dans *les Yeux bleus*, le parallélisme des tombes, et aussi la ligne parallèle du bateau, et les wagons contigus où sont les deux amoureux, et la morte; le parallélisme entre *la Bien-Aimée* où l'homme aime trois femmes, *les Yeux bleus* où la femme aime trois hommes, etc., et enfin tous ces romans superposables les uns aux autres, comme les maisons verticalement entassées en hauteur sur le sol pierreux de l'île?' (III, 376–7)

He observes that, in the case of Stendhal, all his novels are characterized by a certain sense of altitude presented in combination with the life of the spirit: the lofty place in which Julien Sorel is imprisoned, for example, bears an innate resemblace to the tower on the summit in which Fabrice is confined and the abbey in which the Abbé Blanès pores over his astrology (III, 377). Vermeer's paintings are similarly described as fragments of an identical world, in which are re-created the same table, the same carpet, the same woman, the same rare beauty; together constituting a unique enigma (III, 377). He perceives an identical beauty manifesting itself in all of Dostoievsky's novels through the 'Dostoievsky woman' who, with her mysterious face and engaging nature that changes abruptly from good to intolerably insolent, is always the same (III, 377). As in Vermeer's paintings, the narrator sees in Dostoievsky's novels the creation of a certain soul, a certain colour of fabrics and places. He later suggests to Albertine that Dostoievsky's novels could collectively be described as the story of a crime ('l'Histoire d'un Crime,' III, 379). As a result of his comparison of the structural nature of Vermeer's paintings to a structural similarity manifested by the novels of Dostoievsky and Hardy, the line of demarcation between these apparently different media of expression is once more put into question.

The repetition of themes and imagery not only manifests itself in a series of novels by one author, however, but in a single novel also, especially if the work is long. To illustrate his theory, the narrator refers to a certain scene in a carriage which reappears frequently in Tolstoi's *War and Peace* (III, 378). In the introduction to this section, I suggested that the narrator's critical analyses of 'real' works of art reveal important truths about the structure of literature in general, which serve as a mirror that renders intelligible the apparent structural complexity of *A la recherche du temps perdu*. Just as similar themes and imagery reappear constantly in the complete works of a single author such as Dostoievsky, or in a single long work like those written by Tolstoi, so the same images and themes (the magic lantern, the two ways, internal and external reality, etc.) recur in the seven books of the *Recherche*, with the result that these books superimpose themselves one upon the other, and through their common images and themes, merge into a common 'prayer' or impression. In this book, I have attempted to illustrate that the impression engendered by all Proust's books and images is a reflection of the innate, metaphorical nature of all works of art.

We have seen that the narrator frequently describes one work of art in terms of another art form. He previously compared, for example, the unity he perceived in the musical compositions of Wagner and Vinteuil to the unity inherent in the literary works of Balzac (III, 160–1). Correspondingly, during his conversation with Albertine, he stresses that, despite the 'originality' of a work of genius, similar techniques may manifest themselves in diverse works of the same art form (two literary works by different authors, for example) or in different art forms (a novel and a painting). He perceives a technique common to the letters of Mme de Sévigné and the novels of Dostoievsky, that is also inherent in the paintings of Elstir: instead of presenting things in their logical sequence (the effect beginning with the cause), they first show us the effect, or the illusion that strikes us. Thus, the actions of Dostoievsky's characters seem at first as misleading as those effects in Elstir's paintings in which the sea appears to be in the sky:

Il est arrivé que Mme de Sévigné, comme Elstir, comme Dos-

toievsky, au lieu de présenter les choses dans l'ordre logique,
c'est-à-dire en commençant par la cause, nous montre d'abord
l'effet, l'illusion qui nous frappe. C'est ainsi que Dostoievsky
présente ses personnages. Leurs actions nous apparaissent aussi trompeuses que ces effets d'Elstir où la mer a l'air d'être dans
la ciel. Nous sommes tout étonnés après d'apprendre que cet
homme sournois est au fond excellent, ou le contraire. (III, 378–9)

If we submit the narrator's two examples (Dostoievsky's method of presenting his characters, Elstir's device of superimposing apparently incompatible entities upon each other) to analysis, we perceive that the common technical device utilized by the two is not a simple presentation of the effect before the cause but more essentially, a depiction on the same plane of apparently incompatible terms (sea/sky; good/evil) in such a way that their internal correspondence is suggested. If we compare this technique to the narrator's definition of metaphor in *Le temps retrouvé*, we can see that Elstir's and Dostoievsky's common method of composition is metaphorical structure (III, 889). However, whereas a metaphorical phrase links two dissimilar phenomena together in a poetic image, the metaphors present in Elstir's and Dostoievsky's work consist of the linking of contradictory elements in the work as a whole, with the result that the work is itself a metaphor.

The narrator includes in his reminiscences a lengthy passage from one of the 'Goncourt's unpublished journals,' although the selection is really a pastiche of those works. This literary excerpt is different from any of the other works referred to in *A la recherche du temps perdu*, as it is an example for him of what true literature is not! After reading the pages, the narrator feels profoundly disappointed:

C'était un volume du journal inédit des Goncourt.
  Et quand, avant d'éteindre ma bougie, je lus le passage que je
transcris plus bas, mon absence de dispositions pour les lettres,
pressentie jadis du côté de Guermantes, confirmée durant
ce séjour dont c'était le dernier soir – ce soir des veilles de
départ où, l'engourdissement des habitudes qui vont finir
cessant, on essaie de se juger – me parut quelque chose de
moins regrettable, comme si la littérature ne révélait pas de
vérité profonde; et en même temps il me semblait triste que
la littérature ne fût pas ce que j'avais cru. (III, 708–9)

Despite the lack of any profound truth inscribed in the pages of

Goncourt, he still feels compelled to read them because they depict a reality which he had experienced in his own life: an evening with the Verdurins: 'D'autre part, moins regrettable me paraissait l'état maladif qui allait me confiner dans une maison de santé, si les belles choses dont parlent les livres n'étaient pas plus belles que ce que j'avais vu. Mais par une contradiction bizarre, maintenant que ce livre en parlait, j'avais envie de les voir' (III, 709).

Whereas the narrator later proclaims (in *Le temps retrouvé*) that the reflective relationship between a literary work and its reader disengages their common truth and allows the reader to recognize his true self (III, 911), the pages from the Goncourt journal[23] only impress him with their banality and inaccurate depiction of the Verdurins as he knew them (III, 722-3), and make him wonder if characters in literature owe their prestige only to the illusory magic of literature itself (III, 723). Although he rejects Goncourt's pages as bad literature, the characters and milieus described in them (the Verdurins, their guests, their salon) inspire him to reflect on the qualities that characterize a writer. He reaffirms his former hypothesis that it is not the best-informed man who becomes a writer but the one who knows how to become a mirror which can reflect his life experience and the characters who are a part of it, commonplace though they may be (III, 722).

It is not until years later, after he has emerged from the sanatorium where he has been recovering from ill health, that the narrator realizes why the Goncourt pages (and the realistic school of writing which they represent) fail to be a work of literature in the true sense of the word. I observed that his three simultaneous experiences of involuntary memory lead him to analyse his past/present 'intimations' and all other experiences which produced in him a similar feeling of inexplicable happiness, in order to identify the common conditions that gave rise to them. The sensation engendered by Vinteuil's last work is described at this time as the synthesis of all the experiences that produced a similar, inexplicable happiness (III, 866). Soon after his analysis of these sensations, the narrator encounters another object from the past which not only precipitates another experience of involuntary memory, but also reveals to him the true nature of reality and the process that a work of art must embody if it is to express this reality to us. Ironically, the revelatory object is a copy of the novel *François le Champi*, the little book first encountered in early childhood which intimated to him then that literature could reveal a reality truer than life experience (I, 41-2). This time, however, it is not the text of the novel that suggests the true nature of reality in him, but the effect produced by the physical re-encounter of the book-as-object-from-the-past. The title of the novel not only resuscitates its essence for him, but the book-as-object-from-the-past evokes his former self at the time that he first encountered it and a thousand, trifling details associated with the book then and with his former self (III, 884–5).

Because of the ability of this single object to conjure up a whole world of sights, sounds, and objects associated with it, the narrator realizes that reality does not lie in a cinematographic depiction of objects, but in a certain rapport between objects, and the sensations and memories which they evoke (III, 889). He consequently understands that the kind of literature which contents itself with describing things by making of them a miserable abstract of lines and surfaces is – though it calls itself 'realistic' literature – the furthest removed from reality (III, 889), and in order to intimate the true nature of reality to us, an artist/writer must rediscover the rapport that exists naturally between dissimilar phenomena, and express it by duplicating, through the use of metaphor, the comparison of dissimilar objects which occurs naturally (III, 889).

The narrator does not state that the past/present reminiscence engendered by *François le Champi* is a natural metaphor, but we can perceive that the experience is metaphorical in the truest sense of the word, as it entails the superimposition of two realities (the past and the present), and the consequent clarification of a reality common to them both – the true 'being' of the narrator and the essence of the novel *François le Champi*.

The narrator does not establish any connection between the style of writing of the little novel and the effect engendered by the book when he re-encounters it. Nevertheless, the past/present reminiscence catalysed by *François le Champi* in the present reflects the "past/present" effect engendered by its 'antique' expressions which inspired in the narrator's grandmother 'la nostalgie d'impossibles voyages dans le temps' (I, 41). This double common denominator (*François le Champi*, a past/present reminiscence) linking two times in the narrator's life not only suggests a correspondence between the conditions that engender a past/present reminiscence naturally and the imagery in a literary work that produces a similar effect, but also reinforces the primary macrometaphor of the *Recherche* (time lost/time regained), by bringing together the first and last volumes of the work (*Du côté de chez Swann, Le temps retrouvé*) which represent 'time lost' and 'time regained' respectively.

The narrator classifies Vinteuil's last musical compositions as the quintessential expression of the many sensations and experiences that produced in him a similar inexplicable happiness. Although he never describes the structure of Vinteuil's music in terms of metaphorical structure, he does link it to the past/present reminiscences through the common effect to which they give rise. We saw previously that, from the perspective of the totality of the text, a macrometaphorical correspondence establishes itself between Swann's structural analyses of the sonata (in which he describes the sonata as a dialogue of piano and violin suggesting another reality to him, I, 351–2) and the narrator's definition of metaphor in *Le temps retrouvé* (which he defines as the combination of two dissimilar realities linked by a composite style, in such a way that their common internal reality is revealed). Through the network of metaphorical cross-references that link the Vinteuil Sonata to other works of art or to other media of artistic expression (an interlude of music/imagery in Bergotte's novels [I, 93], the Vinteuil Sonata/Elstir's paintings [I, 213], the Vinteuil Sonata/Tristan [I, 350], the Vinteuil Sonata/a line of poetry [I, 352], the Vinteuil Sonata/Tristan/Balzac's *La Comédie Humaine*, Hugo's *La Légende des Siècles* [III, 160–2], the Vinteuil Sonata/colours [III, 250, 255, 256, 374, 375], the Vinteuil Sonata/novels of Thomas Hardy, Dostoievsky, Stendhal/paintings by Vermeer, III, 376–7), a rapport establishes itself between those other works and metaphorical structure. Thus, the Vinteuil Sonata – like the steeple of Combray – functions as an element of architectonic design: its outlines superimposed upon other works of art illuminate their metaphor-like nature.

In addition to those works of art that the narrator submits to structural analysis in the course of his reminiscences (Vinteuil's compositions, Bergotte's novel, Elstir's paintings, Wagner's Tristan, the collected works of Hardy, Dostoievsky, Stendhal, Balzac, Vermeer), there are other works of art metaphorically connected to events in *A la recherche du temps perdu* by means of the common images they depict. In 'Art/Life/Metaphor,' we saw that the narrator frequently compares incidents in his own life experience to events described in the Arabian masterpiece, the *Thousand and One Nights* (see p 129). We also saw, in 'Past/Present/Metaphor/Art/Life,' that the narrator acknowledges the repetitive nature of his future literary work: sensations such as those engendered by the madeleine dipped in tea have already been recorded in other literary works, such as Chateaubriand's *Mémoires d'Outre-Tombe* and Gérard de Nerval's *Sylvie* (III, 919). The narrator realizes too that his work may repeat truths expressed by other writers from other epochs (III, 1044). Although he does not specify the consequences of the play of doubles which his work will engender when it inadvertently duplicates other writer's images and truths, we can perceive – on the basis of the intertextual investigations that he has conducted in *A la recherche du temps perdu* – that it will give rise to bonds of a macrometaphorical kind that will not only bring past works of art into the context of the present but will also cast light on the common truths that they express. Comparative structural analyses of those works will reveal common structural devices used by their creators to suggest these common truths.

6 Conclusion: Literature as Macrometaphor

PROUST'S 'RECHERCHE': THE WORK OF ART AS METAPHOR

In 'Works of Art in the Novel/The Novel/Metaphor/Art,' we saw that Proust's generalized usage of the word 'metaphor' is illustrated most clearly in his application of the term to Elstir's paintings: 'Mais j'y pouvais discerner que le charme de chacune consistait en une sorte de métamorphose des choses représentées, analogue à celle qu'en poésie on nomme métaphore ...' (I, 835). I mentioned that the narrator categorizes Elstir's painting 'le Port de Carquethuit' as an example of this kind of metaphor, because it illustrates the utilization of marine terms to depict the town and urban terms to depict the sea, with the result that the sea seems to enter into the land, and vice versa, abrogating any fixed line of demarcation between the two apparently dissimilar phenomena (I, 836). The narrator's application of the term 'metaphor' to the painting illustrates that Proust is not utilizing the word to signify a poetic trope, but to designate the structural mechanism (the superimposition of dissimilar phenomena upon each other) which metaphor-understood-as-a-poetic-trope has traditionally effected on a linguistic level, by combining two words together in the links of a single poetic image. In the case of Elstir's paintings, however, the metaphor does not consist of the combination of two words, but of two distinct physical realities – water and land – and all of the diverse phenomena (houses, churches, people, boats, masts) associated with both media, which are superimposed visually upon each other: colour upon colour, land terms (roofs, churches) upon marine terms (masts, water). Dissimilar entities overlaid upon each other in the painting (masts/houses, church/water, sun/waves, alabaster/seafoam) function as subsidiary metaphorical structures that all converge in the primary macrometaphor – water/land – which expresses itself through the totality of the painting:

> les toits étaient dépassés (comme ils l'eussent été par des cheminées ou par des clochers) par des mâts, lesquels avaient l'air de faire des vaisseaux auxquels ils appartenaient, quelque chose de citadin, de construit sur terre, impression qu'augmentaient d'autres bateaux, demeurés le long de la jetée, mais en rangs si pressés que les hommes y causaient d'un bâtiment à l'autre sans qu'on pût distinguer leur séparation et l'interstice de l'eau, et ainsi cette flotille de pêche avait moins l'air d'appartenir à la mer que, par exemple, les églises de Criquebec qui, au loin, entourées d'eau de tous côtés parce qu'on les voyait sans la ville, dans un poudroiement de soleil et de vagues, semblaient sortir des eaux, soufflées en albâtre ou en écume et, enfermées dans la ceinture d'un arc-en-ciel versicolore, former un tableau irréel et mystique. Dans le premier plan de la plage, le peintre avait su habituer les yeux à ne pas reconnaître de frontière fixe, de démarcation absolue, entre la terre et l'océan. (I, 836)

In the course of our investigation of *A la recherche du temps perdu*, we saw that the structure of the totality of the novel resembles the structure of the metaphors depicted in it (one example of those 'metaphors' being Elstir's paintings). Just as Elstir's 'le port de Carquethuit' consists of many minor metaphors (church/sea, for example) which accumulatively culminate in the realization of the totality of the painting as a macrometaphor (land/sea), Proust's *A la recherche du temps perdu* presents many different entities, phenomena, and ideas (the magic lantern, the steeples, the two ways, dreams, art/life comparisons, works of art such as Vinteuil's musical compositions, Elstir's paintings, Bergotte's novels, homosexual characters – Albertine, Charlus, Saint-Loup, Morel, Andrée – the past/present reminiscences, the duality of names/presences) that individually function as metaphorical structures, and accumulatively culminate in the realization of the primary macrometaphor which expresses itself through the totality of the novel – time lost/time regained. In turn, the macrometaphor 'time lost/time regained' reflects the inherent metaphorical nature of a work of art: its ability to regain 'past time' through the reflective bonds that arise first of all between the subject matter of the work and the past life experience of its author (III, 899), and secondly, between the literary text and its reader (III, 1033). By reducing human experience to general laws and thereby acting as a mirror in which we can perceive our internal reality, a work of art allows us to perceive the 'truth' about our own life experience (III, 900, 905, 911, 1033). The primary macrometaphor of *A la recherche du temps perdu* is not only 'time lost/time regained,' therefore, but also the opposition through which the analogy realizes itself: 'life experience/a work of art.' Life and art being internal doubles of each other, their similitude suggests that they may share the same innate structural principles.

By submitting some natural phenomena that he has experienced in the course of his life to analysis (the past/present reminiscences, the obscure impressions), the narrator perceives the true nature of reality: that it is not a simple, cinematographic depiction of objects, lines and surfaces, but the rapport between these objects (III, 889). In order for art to depict the true reality of things, the narrator realizes that an artist/writer must express the relationship between objects by duplicating the mechanism which occurs naturally in life experience or nature (the superimposition of dissimilar phenomena, as a result of which their innate similarity reveals itself), and the device that allows him to duplicate this process is metaphor (III, 889). Metaphor is thus a reflection of the 'law of life' which the narrator defines in *La prisonnière* as 'the coupling of contrary elements': 'D'autre part, l'accouplement des éléments contraires est la loi de la vie, le principe de la fécondation et, comme on verra, la cause de bien des malheurs' (III, 108). In *Du côté de chez Swann*, we are told that the Vinteuil Sonata reflects the 'law of life': Swann compares the coupling of the piano and violin in the sonata to the mating song of two birds, which took place at the beginning of the world when there were only those two upon the earth (I, 351–2). Like the two primary terms (sea/land) which interact together to produce the metaphor representing itself in Elstir's 'le Port de Carquethuit,' Vinteuil's musical metaphor constructs itself from the interaction of the two primary instruments with which the work is performed – the piano and the violin. The consequent variations on the primary melody performed by the two instruments converge upon that dialogue itself and clarify the inherent principle of the work: the law of life and art.

In 'Works of Art in the Novel/The Novel/Metaphor/Art,' I examined the narrator's structural analyses of works of art in order to determine whether or not these works of art were metaphorical in nature, and whether or not they reflected the structure of *A la recherche du temps perdu*. We saw that the three works which are most frequently submitted to analysis and which most clearly demonstrate the principle of art-as-metaphor are 'imaginary' works existing only in the context of *A la recherche du temps perdu*: Bergotte's novels, Vinteuil's musical compositions, and Elstir's paintings. We also saw, however, that the characteristics of these works reminded us of several famous paintings, musical compositions and literary schools of expression, existing in a historical reality outside of Proust's novel. We consequently interpreted Proust's three 'imaginary' works of art as composite depictions of literary, musical, and artistic schools of expression prevalent in the late nineteenth and early twentieth centuries. In addition, we saw that Proust compares the structures of and the effects engendered by these imaginary artistic masterpieces to 'real' works of art which originate outside of his novel – George Sand's *François le Champi*, Wagner's *Tristan*, novels by Mme de la Fayette, Thomas Hardy, Dostoievsky, Balzac, Hugo, de Nerval; paintings by Vermeer, poetry by Baudelaire, reminiscences by Chateaubriand, letters by Mme de Sévigné. Through these comparisons which link 'real' works of art to 'imaginary' works of art, Proust implies the existence of general laws common to his literary work and to other works of art. In Chapters 2–5 we saw that the structure of Proust's novel illustrates his theoretical assertions about the work-of-art-as-metaphor, and reflects on a macroscale the structure of those 'imaginary' works of art described in its context.

Let us review the structural characteristics which render *A la recherche du temps perdu* a macrometaphor, and which allow it to stand as an illustration of the work-of-art-as-metaphor:

(1) a binary opposition which embraces the totality of the novel, as illustrated by 'time lost/time regained';

(2) the introduction of oppositions at the level of milieus, characterizations, symbols, and ideas, whose dichotomous relationships give rise to investigations which ultimately illustrate the common essential nature of the two poles of the opposition; as illustrated by the narrator's investigation of the lack of correspondence between the external appearance and internal reality of the homosexual characters depicted in *A la recherche du temps perdu*, the incongruity of the movements of signification engendered by the names of people and places and the reality of the presences to which those names refer; the apparent dissimilitude of the 'two ways' (two geographical locations which also represent two social spheres – the haute bourgeoisie and the old nobility); the conflict between two times and places engendered by a past/present reminiscence; and the comparison of life experience to works of art;

(3) the superimposition of apparently dissimilar phenomena one

upon the other through their contiguity in the text. This device allows similarities shared by dissimilars to reveal themselves to the reader, even though the existence of these common factors is not directly acknowledged in the text. We saw that the first part of *Du côté de chez Swann* illustrates the above technique: it consists primarily of an enumeration of many diverse characters, experiences, and ideas which are not directly related to each other in any way except that they are all experienced by the narrator: the reflective relationship of a reader and his book, a dream, a magic lantern show, the two ways, the hawthorns, the steeple and church of Combray, a past/present reminiscence, the reflective relationship of art and life, the lack of correspondence between external reality and internal appearance as manifested by Mlle Vinteuil and M. Legrandin, etc. The close proximity of these phenomena in the text allows the reader to perceive the factors common to all of them which are 'unvoiced' at this time.

(4) the conversion of these distinctly different entities, binary oppositions, symbols upon each other, through the establishment of cross-referential comparisons (the magic lantern is linked analogically to the nature of the Guermantes family, for example, III, 884).

(5) the presence of a 'key' passage in the work that acts as a mirror which reveals the common essential nature of all of the ideas, structures, symbols, and characterizations depicted in the composition. In the case of Proust's novel, the narrator's description of metaphor and its relationship to art, life experience, and the internal reality of things is the cipher which clarifies – through reflection – the metaphor-like nature of the characterizations, themes, and other phenomena depicted in the work.

(6) the presence of a hero or narrator who resides at the point of intersection of the binary oppositions which compose the primary structure of the novel. He is the one who is allowed to see both sides of the coin from the point of view of an external observer, and consequently perceives simultaneously with his reader the 'truth' which intimates itself through the confrontation of opposites. The engendering of consciousness in the narrator, therefore, corresponds with the disengagement of the internal 'truth' of the novelistic experience through the macrometaphor of the text itself.

We saw in 'Works of Art in the Novel/The Novel/Metaphor/Art' (Chapter 5) that Proust frequently demonstrates the common essential nature shared by different art forms through cross-referential comparisons and comparative structural analyses. The Vinteuil Sonata, for example, is likened to Mme de la Fayette's *La princesse de Clèves* and

Chateaubriand's *René*, because all works represent to Swann an original conception of love and happiness (I, 350). Through the intermediary of their common ability to reveal a 'two-fold difference' to him, the narrator draws another parallel between the harmony of Wagner's *Tristan* and the colours of Elstir's paintings (III, 159). He perceives a technique common to the letters of Mme de Sévigné and the novels of Dostoievsky, which is also inherent in the paintings of Elstir: instead of presenting things in their logical sequence (the effect beginning with the cause), the works first show us the effect, or the illusion that strikes us: the actions of Dostoievsky's characters first seem as misleading as those effects in Elstir's paintings where the sea appears to be in the sky (III, 378). Proust thus implies that the metaphorical structure which he attributes to Elstir's paintings in *A l'ombre des jeunes filles en fleurs* (I, 836) is the same metaphorical mechanism which he recognizes as the fundamental building block of art in general and literary works in particular, in *Le temps retrouvé*: 'la vérité ne commencera qu'au moment où l'écrivain prendra deux objets différents, posera leur rapport, analogue dans le monde de l'art à celui qu'est le rapport unique de la loi causale dans le monde de la science, et les enfermera dans les anneaux nécessaires d'un beau style' (III, 889). The form which Proust chose to express his theory of the nature of art and its relationship to reality, however, was the novelistic genre. Although he conducts cursory, comparative analyses of other art forms (musical compositions, paintings, poetry) in that work, Proust's most eloquent illustration of his theory of art is the novel in which he expresses it – *A la recherche du temps perdu*.

Like Proust, we must acknowledge the strong possibility that this pattern of development – the text as macrometaphor – manifests itself not only in other art forms, but in other literary genres such as the short story, theatre, and poetry. In Sophocles' Theban plays, for example (*Oedipus Rex*, *Oedipus at Colonus*, *Antigone*), we can see at work a play of oppositions (will of the gods, will of man, light/darkness, ignorance/enlightenment, innocence/responsibility, life/death) whose common essential natures reveal themselves through the escapades of diametrically opposed character types (Oedipus/Creon, Antigone/Creon), whose conflicts reveal their innate similarities. Although Creon in *Antigone* denounces Antigone and her father Oedipus for their 'stubborn spirit,' he is ultimately forced to acknowledge that he is also cursed by his 'stubborn will.' Antigone, by choosing to defy her uncle (her 'internal' double) at the cost of her own life, earns 'a living death, but a name undying.' Conversely, Creon (the 'survivor' of the struggle) proclaims that, although 'living,' he is already dead: 'I am nothing. I have no life.' Oedipus, the source of the conflict depicted in Sophocles' three Theban plays, is the incarnation of metaphor, as he represents in one being two apparently distinct entities – son/husband. Like his offspring whose natures are as dual as his own (daughters/sisters, sons/brothers), the unnamed gift which Oedipus offers to Athens in *Oedipus at Colonus* is possibly the law of life or 'truth' as the coupling of contradictory opposites, which has represented itself through his tortured body:

> OEDIPUS
> I come to offer you
> A gift – my tortured body – a sorry sight;
> But there is value in it more than beauty.
> ...
> THESEUS
> When will this gift be known for what it is?
> OEDIPUS
> When I am dead, and you have buried me.[1]

Metaphor can only reveal the internal truth between dissimilar phenomena through closure – the combination of dissimilar phenomena in the links of a single image or work. Similarly, the 'truth' about Oedipus' life can only reveal itself after his death, which renders his life a totality.

INTERTEXTUAL MACROMETAPHORS: CONDUCTING RESEARCH WITH A TELESCOPE

In *Le temps retrouvé*, after he has discovered the rule of metaphor and the reflective relationship it establishes between nature and a work of art, the narrator begins writing his own literary work. He compares his investigatory method to conducting research with a telescope – bringing together separate worlds which are situated in reality a great distance from each other, but which reflect each other because they manifest the same general laws:

> Bientôt je pus montrer quelques esquisses. Personne n'y comprit rien. Même ceux qui furent favorables à ma perception des vérités que je voulais ensuite graver dans le temple, me félicitèrent de les avoir découvertes au 'microscope' quand je m'étais

> au contraire servi d'un télescope pour apercevoir des choses, très petites en effet, mais parce qu'elles étaient situées à une grande distance, et qui étaient chacune un monde. Là où je cherchais les grandes lois, on m'appelait fouilleur de détails. (III, 1041)

Just before commencing his literary work, Proust's narrator comments that, because his novel will reflect 'general laws' which will express themselves through generalized characters and situations which are reduced from multiple real-life personalities and events (III, 900), his literary creation will inevitably duplicate truths expressed in previous works of art. He perceives that some of the experiences which gave him his happiest moments have already been recorded in literature. Gérard de Nerval in *Sylvie* and Chateaubriand in *Mémoires d'Outre-Tombe* previously documented sensations the same as that engendered by his experience of the tea and the madeleine, for example (III, 919–20). The narrator consequently realizes that, in order to write his own 'original' literary work, he must renounce all previous literary works – even those which are dearest to him – and be guided instead by an inner truth which bids itself be written. By following the dictates of this truth which originates in himself, however, he understands that he will stumble upon what he has renounced, because the truth written into his book will reflect the truth expressed in previous literary works:

> on ne peut refaire ce qu'on aime qu'en le renonçant. Ce serait un livre aussi long que les *Mille et une Nuits* peut-être, mais tout autre. Sans doute, quand on est amoureux d'une œuvre, on voudrait faire quelque chose de tout pareil, mais il faut sacrifier son amour du moment, ne pas penser à son goût, mais à une vérité qui ne vous demande pas vos préférences et vous défend d'y songer. Et c'est seulement si on la suit qu'on se trouve parfois rencontrer ce qu'on a abandonné, et avoir écrit, en les oubliant, les 'Contes arabes' ou les '*Mémoires* de Saint-Simon' d'une autre epoque. (III, 1043–4)

Proust's narrator implies that a correlative truth intimates itself through all great literary works from all ages, because that 'truth' is a reflection of the common essential nature of human reality. It is not surprising, therefore, that the harmony of structure, characterization, imagery, and symbols which we perceived in Proust's masterpiece should recall to mind (or macrometaphorically connect itself with) Heraclitus' theory of the 'beautiful harmony' resulting from the combination of dissimilar entities. Heraclitus proposed that conflict is the source of all life: 'The unlike is joined together, and from differences result the most beautiful harmony, and all things take place by strife.'² Marcel Proust's *A la recherche du temps perdu* indicates that the internal reality of things is a reality superior to external appearance. Almost twenty-five hundred years earlier, Heraclitus similarly proclaimed that 'the hidden harmony is better than the visible.'³ In the course of our investigation of the intertwined themes of the *Recherche*, we saw that apparently contradictory entities (the 'two ways,' homosexuality/heterosexuality, male/female, good/evil, names/presences, art/life, external appearance/internal reality) frequently reveal themselves to be reversible, internal doubles of each other. Just as Proust illustrates that the apparently irreconcilable 'two ways' and all they represent are in fact joined together both geographically and socially, so Heraclitus hypothesized that 'they do not understand how that which separates unites with itself. It is a harmony of opposition, as in the case of the bow and the lyre.'⁴ The common ideas which express themselves through Heraclitus' *On Nature* (530-470? BC) and Proust's *A la recherche du temps perdu* (1913-27) suggest the existence of a 'life principle' in literature which transcends time and the distinctions between different languages, cultures, and literary genres which 'time' brings.

Approximately one hundred years after Heraclitus wrote his famous book *On Nature* on the city of Epheseus in Ionia, Aristotle (384-322 BC) wrote a treatise on *The Art of Poetry* in Athens, wherein he proposed that a 'complex' tragic plot distinguishes itself by the precipitation of catastrophe through 'reversal,' 'discovery,' or both. He stressed that these devices arise out of the very structure of the plot. A 'reversal' ('peripeteia') is a change of a situation into its opposite (from good fortune to bad fortune, for example, or from bad fortune to good). To illustrate his definition, he provided an example of 'reversal' from *Oedipus*: the messenger who comes to gladden Oedipus and to release him from his fears about his mother actually produces the opposite effect by revealing to him the secret of his birth.⁵ Aristotle defined 'discovery' as a change from ignorance to knowledge, and suggested that the best kind of 'discovery' is the one combined with 'reversals,' like the previously mentioned 'reversal' in the *Oedipus*.⁶ Such discoveries combined with reversals in tragedy will arouse either 'fear or pity' in the audience, in such a way as to accomplish a purgation ('katharsis') of such emotions: 'Tragedy, then, is a representation (mimêsis) of an action (praxis) that is serious, complete and of a certain magnitude; in language pleasurably and variously embellished suitably to the different parts of the play; in the form of actions directly presented, not narrated; with incidents arousing fear and pity in such a way as to accomplish a purgation (katharsis) of such emotions.'[7]

Aristotle implied that the spectator is relieved of the emotions of fear and pity through the transference of those emotions onto the tragic character depicted on the stage: 'katharsis' occurs when the spectator sympathizes (identifies himself) with the tragic hero. Because this 'doubles' relationship linking the spectator to the hero engenders itself as a direct result of the processes of 'reversal' and 'discovery' – the essential structures of tragic plot – Aristotle's theoretical treatise on art infers that the processes of 'reversal' (the reverse polarity of opposites) and 'discovery' (transcendence to a state of enlightenment) are forces which characterize the inherent nature of human reality; and by incorporating in itself structures which engender these forces, a good tragedy functions as a mirror in which the spectator can see himself.

Aristotle never compared Greek tragedy to a metaphor, but the mechanisms which he identified with a good tragedy (reversals, discoveries, katharsis) closely resemble the forces engendered by a metaphorical phrase. In the *Art of Poetry*, Aristotle defined metaphor in terms of transference: 'Metaphor consists in the transference of a name (from the thing which it properly denotes) to some other thing, the transference being either from genus to species or from species to species, or by analogy and proportion.'[8] A 'reversal' in tragic plot (the change of a situation into its opposite) is also a transference (or substitution) of one term for another. By suggesting that the best kind of 'discovery' (a change from ignorance to knowledge) in tragic plot is one combined with 'reversals,' Aristotle implied that knowledge (enlightenment, transcendence) is intrinsically related to 'reversals.' He did not utilize the term 'knowledge' in relation to poetic diction, but he did propose that the purpose of 'rare, metaphoric, ornamental' and other such special forms of speech is to 'raise language above the commonplace.'[9] If 'knowledge' in tragedy signifies enlightenment, and if enlightenment denotes transcendence above the commonplace, then the combination of reversal and discovery in tragic plot accomplishes on a macroscale what metaphor engenders at the level of language (diction).[10]

Friedrich Nietzsche's perception of Greek tragedy – of its origins and the forces it brings into play – had much in common with Heraclitus' vision of harmony springing from the reconciliation of opposites, and with Aristotle's explication of the processes of 'reversal' and 'discovery' in tragic plot, and the consequent 'katharsis' which results. In *Die Geburt der Tragödie* (1872), Nietzsche proposed that the cornerstone of ancient Greek tragedy and the cause of its cathartic effect is its establishment of a play of doubles between two diametrically opposed forces – the Apollonian and the Dionysian: 'But now follow me to witness a tragedy, and sacrifice with me in the temple of both deities!'[11] The purpose of Greek tragedy, according to Nietzsche, was the reconciliation of Apollonian beauty and imagery with its source and its opposite – the terror of undifferentiation (Dionysian 'oneness').[12] Within the representation of tragedy, according to his theory, the Apollonian and the Dionysian become each other through a play of doubles, resulting in the abrogation of their duality and their momentary experience of oneness. Being the objectification of a Dionysian state, however, Greek tragedy does not represent Apollonian redemption through mirror appearance, but on the contrary, the shattering of the individual and his fusion with primal being. The shattering of the individual spectator occurs through a series of reflections engendered by the structure of the tragedy itself. The satyr chorus, for example, which Nietzsche perceived as the Apollonian representation on stage of the original geniuses of nature, functions as a mirror in which the inner 'Dionysian man' of the spectator can see himself:

> In the light of this insight we may call the chorus in its primitive form, in proto-tragedy, the mirror image in which the Dionysian man contemplates himself. This phenomenon is best made clear by imagining an actor who, being truly talented, sees the role he is supposed to play quite palpably before his eyes. The satyr chorus is, first of all, a vision of the Dionysian mass of spectators, just as the world of the stage, in turn, is a vision of this satyr chorus ...[13]
>
> ...
>
> In this magic transformation the Dionysian reveler sees himself as a satyr, *and as a satyr, in turn, he sees the god*, which means that in his metamorphosis he beholds another vision outside himself, as the Apollinian complement of his own state. With this new vision the drama is complete.[14]

Nietzsche's perception of the play of doubles engendered by an ancient Greek tragedy bears a marked resemblance to Proust's narrator's theory of the literary work as a mirror in which we can see our internal reality reflected (III, 911, 1033). The reflective relationship which links their theories emphasizes that, in twenty-five hundred years, the structure and function of a work of art/literary work has not changed drastically; a novel of the twentieth century may bring into play the same forces that were engendered by an ancient Greek tragedy, because both works of art from both time periods reflect the true nature of human reality, which intimates itself to us through structural principles which mirror the nature of that common internal reality.

Nietzsche perceived the tragic hero as the representation of the god Dionysus experiencing the agonies of individuation,[15] and noted that Dionysus represents the origin of man and the gods: 'From the smile of this Dionysus sprang the Olympian gods, from his tears sprang man.'[16] By contemplating the suffering of the 'god' (tragic hero), therefore, the spectator of an ancient Greek tragedy also contemplates his own origin, and by doing so, he momentarily transcends through art the suffering of individuation which is man's lot and experiences oneness, or the original state which preceded individuation:

> And it is this hope alone that casts a gleam of joy upon the features of a world torn asunder and shattered into individuals; this is symbolized in the myth of Demeter, sunk in eternal sorrow, who *rejoices* again for the first time when told that she may *once more* give birth to Dionysus. This view of things already provides us with all the elements of a profound and pessimistic view of the world, together with the *mystery doctrine of tragedy*: the fundamental knowledge of the oneness of everything existent, the conception of individuation as the primal cause of evil, and of art as the joyous hope that the spell of individuation may be broken in augury of a restored oneness.[17]

The tragic experience of 'oneness' that allows the unsayable and the unhearable to be intimated through the language of images is like the beautiful harmony resulting from the union of dissimilars to which Heraclitus alluded, and the internal reality or essence of things which Proust perceived extricating itself from the combination of externally dissimilar phenomena in the links of a metaphorical phrase. Proust stressed, however, that the revelation of an internal truth through metaphor is not a process which occurs only in art, as a work of art/literary work duplicates through the use of metaphor the structural conditions which allow the internal reality of things to reveal itself to us in nature: 'La nature ne m'avait-elle pas mis elle-même, à ce point de vue, sur la voie de l'art, n'était-elle pas commencement d'art elle-même, elle qui ne m'avait permis de connaître, souvent, la beauté d'une chose que dans une autre, midi à Combray que dans le bruit de ses cloches, les matinées de Doncières que dans les hoquets de notre calorifère à eau?' (III, 889-90).

I proposed that, through their common structural nature, Proust's narrator's definition of metaphor connected itself macrometaphorically in the novel with his definition of 'the law of life' as 'the coupling of contrary elements'('l'accouplement des éléments contraires,' III, 108). The metaphors inherent in a work of art which allow us to perceive internal reality are simultaneously allowing us to perceive the 'law of life' which is our internal truth: the inexpressible 'oneness' (the life force) which resides in and results from the coupling of opposites.

Chapter 1 of this book asked a question that Paul Ricoeur posed in 'Metaphor and the Main Problem of Hermeneutics': to what extent may a work be considered as an expanded metaphor? Part I (Chapters 2-3) and Part II (Chapters 4-5) demonstrated that Marcel Proust answered Ricoeur's question and illustrated it in novelistic form through the macrometaphorical architectonics of the *Recherche*.

While asserting that metaphor is the building block of art in general and of literary works in particular, Proust chose to express his theory of the work-of-art-as-metaphor through the novel. We must determine, therefore, if there is something unique about the novel which renders it more 'metaphor-like' than other literary genres. Harry Levin, in *The Gates of Horn*, suggested that all of the imaginative arts, by Aristotle's primary definition, strive to imitate nature in their respective ways, but literature, because it makes use of what can be the most expressive medium, can give rise to the most convincing imitation. Because the novel has become the most resourceful of literary forms ('the most independent, most elastic, most prodigious,' in the words of Henry James), Levin proposes that the novel has come closest to the 'real thing.'[18]

We must ask ourselves just what is the 'real thing,' and why it should express itself more accurately through the novel than through other art forms. It is ironic that Levin should include Proust in a work dedicated to the study of 'realism' in literature, as the 'realistic' school of literary expression was precisely the kind of writing which Proust deemed to be the furthest removed from 'reality':

> Comment la littérature de notations aurait-elle une valeur
> quelconque, puisque c'est sous de petites choses comme celles
> qu'elle note que la réalité est contenue (la grandeur dans le
> bruit lointain d'un aéroplane, dans la ligne du clocher de Saint-
> Hilaire, le passé dans la saveur d'une madeleine, etc.) et
> qu'elles sont sans signification par elles-mêmes si on ne l'en
> dégage pas? (III, 894–5)

In lieu of the cinematographic depiction of objects of which 'realistic' writers were so fond, which reduced reality to a 'miserable collection of lines and surfaces' (III, 885), Proust advocated through *A la recherche du temps perdu* a literary style which would duplicate in writing the conditions in nature which allowed the inarticulate rapport between phenomena – the 'true' reality of things–to intimate itself. Proust's narrator recognized metaphor as the device which would allow a writer to express the essential nature of things through his work.

As if to put in relief the transcendent effect of 'metaphorical' literature (of which his own novel is a superb illustration) Proust included in the *Recherche* a pastiche of a passage from one of the Goncourt's 'unpublished journals' (III, 709–17), which becomes for the narrator an example of what true literature is not (III, 885, 889). The selection entails a boring, cinematographic account of Goncourt's visit to the Verdurin mansion and impresses the narrator with its inaccurate depiction of the Verdurins and their environment as he knew them. Whereas he can remember 'les vulgarités sans nombre' (III, 718) of which the Verdurins and their guests were in reality composed, Goncourt (who views them from the superficial point of perspective of a new acquaintance) is very impressed with the 'finesse' of Dr Cottard (III, 716), with the great delicacy of M. Verdurin who is 'l'amoureux de tous les raffinements' (III, 709), with the 'intelligence tout à fait supérieure' of Princess Sherbatoff (III, 711), with the charm of Mme Verdurin (III, 712).

Interestingly, the 'Goncourt' passage contains several poetic similes which recall comparisons drawn by the narrator in the course of his own reminiscences. A smoking room of Verdurin's mansion, we are told, was transported 'telle quelle,' as in a tale from the *Thousand and One Nights*, from a celebrated 'palazzo' whose name Goncourt forgets, but which boasted a well-head decorated with a Coronation of the Virgin – one of Sansovino's finest creations (III, 710). Because terms such as the *Thousand and One Nights* are also associated with events in the *Recherche*, the 'Goncourt' pages superimpose themselves in the reader's mind upon the narrator's 'reminiscences' and their ensuing comparison allows the reader to perceive the difference between a 'realistic' written work which utilizes poetic devices only in the service of banal representation, and a 'metaphorical' literary work which realizes in its totality the transcendent effect which a poetic metaphor attempts to engender. Although the 'Goncourt's' *Thousand and One Nights* comparison initially brings together two dissimilar realities (a room in Paris transported piece by piece from Venice/a magical 'transportation' which occurs in a tale from the *Thousand and One Nights*) the common essential nature (transportation in time and space) linking those different realities is not given a chance to truly reveal itself as such to the reader, because it is immediately linked in the text with a different kind of 'transportation' which is diametrically opposed to 'transcendence': the transformation of an 'objet d'art' into a utilitarian article. The decorated well-head by Sansovino appears to represent through itself the fate of poetic metaphor as utilized by Goncourt in his 'realistic' cinematographic depictions of reality: it ceases to be a work of art, and assumes instead the utilitarian function of an ashtray:

> la causerie continue dans la voiture qui doit nous conduire quai Conti où est leur hôtel, que son possesseur prétend être l'ancien hôtel des Ambassadeurs de Venise et où il y aurait un fumoir dont Verdurin me parle comme d'une salle transportée telle quelle, à la façon des *Mille et une Nuits* d'un célèbre 'palazzo' dont j'oublie le nom, 'palazzo' à la margelle du puits représentant un couronnement de la Vierge que Verdurin soutient être absolument du plus beau Sansovino et qui servirait, pour leurs invités, à jeter la cendre de leurs cigares. (III, 709–10)

In the wake of Proust's 'unvoiced' condemnation of poetic devices used in a purely representative sense in writing (a censure aptly expressed through the macrometaphorical bond which establishes itself between the 'Goncourt journal' and the narrator's reminiscences), let us summarize what 'metaphor' means for Proust, keeping in mind the privileged position he grants it in relation to the basic structure of a literary work. After analysing in Chapter 3 the chain of events which led the narrator to his realization of the power of metaphor, and after observing in Chapters 4–5 his usage of the term 'metaphor' in other parts of the novel (he described Elstir's paintings as metaphors, for example, because their composition entailed the visual superimposition of apparently incompatible terms one upon the other), I concluded that Proust utilized the term metaphor to designate a general structural mechanism, rather than to signify a poetic trope, even though metaphor-understood-as-a-poetic-trope is one manifestation (at the linguistic level) of the metaphorical process. As if to illustrate his definition of metaphor as the combination of dissimilar phenomena in the links of a 'beautiful style,' Proust's narrator reminds us that nature put him on the path of art: he only knew the beauty of a noontide at Combray, for example, through the sound of its churchbells (III, 889). 'Noontide' and 'the sound of bells' being dissimilar phenomena (the former is a mark in time, the latter is a physical sensation) whose superimposition in time and space reveals to the narrator a common beauty which they enshrine in themselves, their time/space contiguity constitutes a metaphorical structure.[19] This 'natural' metaphor also suggests to us that the time/space contiguity of different objects, abstract ideas, milieus, symbols, or characters co-existing in the totality of the novel may give rise to metaphor-like bonds which would reveal the common essential reality of these phenomena. Elstir's paintings illustrated that the metaphor-like superimposition of dissimilar phenomena in a work of art does not limit itself to literature; that a metaphor may realize itself just as effectively in a pictorial medium, through the superimposition of colour upon colour, image upon image. In the case of the Vinteuil Sonata, we saw that its 'dialogue' between violin and piano constituted a metaphor-like superimposition of sound upon sound, engendering an effect which transcended the boundaries of sound itself and allowed Swann to perceive the music as colours and images of the primeval origin.

In view of this evidence which suggests that any art form may be metaphorical in nature, why have I restricted this investigation of the text-as-macrometaphor to the novelistic genre? Perhaps it is the multi-levelled network of characters, milieus, times, images, ideas, and symbols which a single novel can bring together in a single work of art which allows it to duplicate, more accurately than any other art form, the rapport between multiple times, images, ideas, people, milieus, symbols which simultaneously comprise a single moment of life experience. Through its intertwined network of characters, milieus, ideas, symbols, physical objects, imagery, and space/time relationships which the novelistic genre allows, Proust's novel presents a comprehensive, metaphor-like reflection of life experience to us, which allows us to recognize – through the play of reflected doubles which the work engenders – the inarticulate, internal reality common to ourselves and to the work, which transcends the distinctions between time, life, and art: the life force.

This book has demonstrated that there is a trend in literature extending from the time of the ancient Greeks to the present day which distinguishes itself by a similar, metaphor-like structure of the text (a play of oppositions, mirror reversals of those opposed terms, and the consequent 'intimation' of an inarticulate reality which transcends the play of oppositions through which it reveals itself) which can best be described as 'macrometaphor.' 'Macrometaphorical' fiction depicts on a large scale the metaphorical quality of language, and of the human 'existential crisis' which represents itself in the lack of correspondence between language and its signified concept. If metaphor really is the 'lot of thought at the moment at which a sense attempts to emerge of itself, to say itself, to express itself, to bring itself into the light of language,'[20] and if one of man's greatest problems is his inability to express accurately in language those profound impressions which frequently appear to us as indefinable 'intimations' or manifestations of our most essential being which eludes direct expression through daily speech, then it follows that, when a writer attempts to depict in a literary work the true, indefinable reality of things, his work will duplicate unconsciously on a macroscale – in its characterizations, milieus, ideas, symbols, imagery – the original metaphor-like opposition between language and thought (signifier and signified) through which meaning realizes itself.

Nietzsche perceived that the differentiated Apollonian world of tragic images recalled the Dionysian realm of oneness back into itself through a play of doubles which abrogated their difference and allowed the spectator to see the unseeable, hear the unhearable. Marcel Proust proposed that, by incorporating 'general laws' about human reality into itself – into its characterizations, milieus, symbols, ideas, imagery – a literary work functions as a mirror wherein the reader can perceive his true internal self. Proust also perceived metaphor as the only device available to a writer which would allow him to express the internal reality of things through his literary work. That internal reality can only reveal itself as such, however, through the macrometaphorical, reflective bond which establishes itself between a reader and his text. Binary oppositions in literary works – which manifest themselves in characterizations, milieus, imagery, symbols, ideas, and the relationships which establish themselves between all of these textual elements – thus perform a function analogous to the role which Nietzsche accredited to the play of doubles engendered by an Attic tragedy and which Marcel Proust accredited to metaphor in particular and to the literary work in general: they allow the reader/spectator/participant to transcend the limits of language and thought, and glimpse into an inarticulate, primordial realm of truth, where opposites find their common origin in each other.

Notes

CHAPTER ONE: INTRODUCTION

1 Paul Ricoeur, 'Metaphor and the Main Problem of Hermeneutics' 100
2 Ricoeur's investigation of the relationship between text and metaphor is conducted along purely theoretical lines. He refers to other theories about metaphor proposed by other theorists (Max Black, *Models and Metaphors*; and Monroe Beardsley, *Aesthetics: Problems in the Philosophy of Criticism*), but he does not back up his hypothesis with any explications or analyses of working models; that is to say, he does not demonstrate how his theory may be applied to the interpretation of literary texts.
3 Ricoeur, 'Metaphor and the Main Problem of Hermeneutics' 110
4 A brief list of some works on Proust's poetic imagery which the reader may find useful and interesting includes Inge Karalus Crosman, *Metaphoric Narration: The Structure and Function of Metaphors in 'A la recherche du temps perdu,'* Stephen Ullmann, *The Image in the French Novel*, and Victor Graham, *The Imagery of Proust*.
5 Gérard Genette has conducted a study of the work as a whole in *Discours du récit, Figures III*, but not from the perspective of the metaphorical structure of the text. Likewise, Gilles Deleuze discusses the totality of the novel as an apprenticeship of signs, in *Proust et les signes*.
6 Roger Shattuck, *Proust's Binoculars: A Study of Memory, Time and Recognition in 'A la recherche du temps perdu'* 123–7
7 Paul de Man, 'Reading (Proust)' in *Allegories of Reading* 77
8 Paul de Man, 'Semiology and Rhetoric' in *Allegories of Reading* 13
9 de Man, 'Reading (Proust)' 72
10 Jean Ricardou, 'La métaphore d'un bout à l'autre,' *Nouveaux Problèmes du Roman*
11 Jean Ricardou, 'Pour une lecture rétrospective,' *Revue des Sciences Humaines*

12 Ibid. 59–60
13 Ibid. 60
14 Ibid. 60–1
15 Gérard Genette, 'Discours du récit,' *Figures III* 68
16 Marcel Proust, *Le temps retrouvé, A la recherche du temps perdu*, 1041. Further references to all volumes of *A la recherche du temps perdu* and quotations from them will appear in parentheses in the text. The Pléiade edition of the *Recherche* entails three volumes, which will be designated by the following numerals: I, *Du côté de chez Swann, A l'ombre des jeunes filles en fleurs*; II, *Le côté de Guermantes I, Le côté de Guermantes II, Sodome et Gomorrhe*; III, *La prisonnière, La fugitive, Le temps retrouvé*.

PART ONE

CHAPTER TWO: METAPHOR

1 Gilles Deleuze, 'Les signes de l'art et l'essence,' *Proust et les Signes* 59
2 Gérard Genette, 'La Rhétorique restreinte,' *Revue Internationale de Philosophie*, 23 année, No. 87 (1969) Fasc. 1, pp 58–69. This paper is also included in the collection *Figures III*, by Gérard Genette 21–40, and in *Communications* 158–71.
3 'Le Groupe de Liège' or 'Le groupe μ' consists of several academicians (Jacques Dubois, F. Edeline, J.M. Klinkenberg, P. Minquet, F. Pire, H. Trinon) affiliated with the 'Centre d'études poétiques' of the University of Liège, who grouped together to study questions which are being reconsidered by the 'naguère méprisée et jadis glorieuse' discipline of Rhetoric. They have taken as their sign the Greek letter 'μ' – the first initial of the word which signifies in Greek 'la plus prestigieuse des métaboles' (metaphor). (Le groupe μ, *La Rhétorique générale* 7)
4 Michel Déguy, 'Pour une théorie de la figure généralisée,' *Critique* 841–61
5 Jacques Sojcher 'La Métaphore généralisée'
6 The above-mentioned texts are not the only works that define metaphor in a general sense. As early as 1873, Friedrich Nietzsche stretched the limits of metaphor to such an extent that he attributed metaphorical power to every use of sound in speaking, which comes down to 'treating every signifier as a metaphor for the signified, while the classical concept of metaphor denotes only the substitution of one signified for another so that the one becomes the signifier of the other.'

A nerve stimulus, first transformed into a percept! First metaphor! The percept again copied into a sound. Second metaphor! (The discourse between quotation marks is from a commentary by Jacques Derrida entitled 'White Mythology: Metaphor in the Text of Philosophy.' The Nietzschean text referred to above is from 'On Truth and Falsity,' *Early Greek Philosophy and Other Essays* 178.)

7 Aristotle, 'The Art of Poetry,' *Aristotle* 316
8 Aristotle, *Rhetoric and Poetics*, 'Rhetoric,' Book III, 173
9 Genette, 'La Rhétorique restreinte' 158
10 For other works on Aristotle's generalized view of metaphor, see Derrida, 'White Mythology,' and Gérard Kamber and Richard Macksey, 'Negative Metaphor and Proust's Rhetoric of Absence' 858.

Although Genette does not explain at this time the exact manner in which Aristotle's definition of metaphor is general, Richard Macksey and Gerald Kamber (in another paper written in 1970, 'Negative Metaphor and Proust's Rhetoric of Absence') suggest that Aristotle, like Proust, seems to consider stated comparison or simile as a subordinate part of his metaphor (863).

Derrida, in 'White Mythology,' acknowledges that Aristotle uses the word metaphor in a general sense because metaphor in Aristotle is always connected with a theory of diction, which implies that metaphor is like the difference between thought and speech, and for this reason is at the heart of tragedy (32). Like Nietzsche, he suggests that 'Thought happens upon metaphor, or metaphor is the lot of thought at the moment at which sense attempts to merge of itself, to say itself, to express itself, to bring itself into the light of language' (32).

In a footnote which explains his contention that Aristotle used metaphor in the general sense, Derrida explains how Aristotle's usage of the term was general, and how it was regarded as such even by other ancient authors:

> This generality gives rise to problems, which, as we know, have in a way recently become reactivated. [We shall come back to them at the end. At all events] ... Aristotle was the first to consider metaphor as the general form of all figures of speech, or speech, whether by including them (as in the case of transfer by metonymy or synecdoche), or by having one of them as its own best form, as in the case of an analogy or 'proportional metaphor' (*Rhetoric* 1411a ff.). No doubt this generality is in proportion to the degree to which metaphor remains unspecified. Aristotle was already being accused or excused at an early date. André Dacier wrote (in

his introduction to 'La Poétique d'Aristote,' 1733): 'Some ancient authors condemned Aristotle for including under the term metaphor these first two cases, which are properly speaking only synecdoches: but Aristotle spoke in general, and he wrote at a time when refinements about figures of speech did not exist, either in distinguishing them, or in giving each of them a name which would have more clearly explained its nature. Cicero gives a sufficient justification of Aristotle when he writes in the *De Oratore*: "Aristotle in his *Poetics* uses metaphor in this extended sense, for any figurative meaning imposed upon a word: as a whole put for the part, or a genus for the species. But it would be unjust to tax this most acute writer with any inaccuracy on this account; the minute subdivisions, and various names of Tropes, being unknown in his days, and the invention of later rhetoricians".' (31 n27, 'White Mythology')

11 In *Des Tropes*, Dumarsais defines metaphor in the following terms: La métaphore est une figure par laquelle on transporte, pour ainsi dire, la signification propre d'un nom à une autre signification qui ne lui convient qu'en vertu d'une comparaison qui est dans l'esprit. Un mot pris dans un sens métaphorique perd sa signification propre, et en prend une nouvelle qui ne se présente à l'esprit que par la comparaison que l'on fait entre le sens propre de ce mot et ce qu'on lui compare.

12 Genette, 'La Rhétorique restreinte' 158
13 Ibid. 161
14 Ibid. 160
15 Ibid. 161
16 Roman Jakobson and Morris Halle, *Fundamentals of Language* 76
17 Ibid. 81–2
18 Genette, 'La Rhétorique restreinte' 165
19 Sojcher, 'La Métaphore généralisée' 58
20 Genette quotes from Michel Déguy's 'Pour une théorie de la métaphore généralisée' 841, 852, 861, on p 67 of his own text, 'La Rhétorique restreinte.'
21 Ibid. 168, 169
22 Ibid. 166
23 Sojcher, 'La Métaphore généralisée' 58–69
24 Ibid. 68
25 Genette, 'La Rhetorique restreinte' 163
26 Ibid. 165
27 Ibid. 166. The article referred to ('Métonymie chez Proust') has been

published in *Figures III* and also in *Poétique*. In 'Negative Metaphor and Proust's Rhetoric of Absence,' Gerald Kamber and Richard Macksey also drawn some conclusions about the general sense in which Proust uses the term 'metaphor' and his confusion of the terms 'metaphor' and 'metonymy.' Kamber and Macksey commence their paper with the assertion that Proust frequently transforms the vocabulary of traditional rhetoric to suit his own purposes: 'Although the intricate fabric of Marcel Proust's *Recherche* is shot through with references drawn from the vocabulary of traditional rhetoric, the terms are transformed frequently by the author's persistent need to bend or refract conventional usage to his own private purposes' (858).

To illustrate their proposal, Kamber and Macksey briefly examine Proust's utilization of the word 'metaphor' in three separate passages of the text. In his usage of metaphor as a means of describing the perspective of Elstir's seascapes, for example, Kamber and Macksey comment that the 'trope which seems more exactly to characterize Elstir's method in his paintings of reversing marine and contiguous terrestrial details would, in fact, be metonymy. But as we shall see, a number of other rhetorical figures are intimately related to Proust's notion of metaphor' (859). Although Kamber and Macksey never specify what other rhetorical devices and tropes are embraced by Proust's definition of metaphor, they do suggest that 'Proust uses the term generically for almost as broad an array of comparisons as Aristotle.' In Aristotle, as in Proust, 'the operative verbal idea is transfer – the application of a strange term across normal logical lines ... Like Proust, he seems to consider stated comparison or simile as a subordinate part of his metaphor' (863).

28 'La Rhétorique restreinte' 163
29 Sojcher, 'La Métaphore généralisée 68
30 Ibid. 68
31 Proust, like Antonin Artaud, denounced reason and logic as responsible for separating man from his true self (III 882). Antonin Artaud, in 'Le Théâtre et son double,' attempted the creation of a theatrical form which would prevent the force of life or inspiration from being stolen from himself through its descent into speech or representation; that is to say, he desired a theatre of pure presence that would avoid the absence of the signified concept; absence being a fundamental condition of any system of representation. In order to realize this project, Artaud advocated the use of hieroglyphics, or a concrete language of the stage, which was to take the form of thousands of masks and cries which were supposed to be a more authentic expression of human

emotions than words and conventional theatrical gestures. Artaud's project was a failure because he never realized that his totalitarian codification and rhetoric of forces was more oppressive to the force which eludes language than the devices of traditional language which, although it first robs speech of its 'breath' through translation into representation, is also capable of acting as a restorative aperture, which paradoxically, through limitation and selection, can project the mind onto vistas which exceed itself.

CHAPTER FOUR: STRUCTURE AS MACROMETAPHOR

1 The 'natural' metaphorical processes referred to are the past/present intimations, the obscure impressions, and the interaction of the narrator with the natural analogies presented to him.
2 It is worth noting here that the underlying assumption of Proust's novel as I interpret it, and of Proust's view of the function of metaphor differs fundamentally from one of the most contemporary theories about the effect of doubling and reflection – that expressed by Jacques Derrida. Whereas Proust sees successive metaphorical reflections in a work of art or in life as transparent envelopes which clarify their common denominators rather than concealing them, the fundamental premise of most of Derrida's work is that all representation gives rise to a play of reflected doubles which irrevocably obscures the origin of speculation:

La représentation s'enlace à ce qu'elle représente, au point que l'on parle comme on écrit, on pense comme si le représenté n'était que l'ombre ou le reflet du représentant. Promiscuité dangereuse, néfaste complicité entre le reflet et le reflété qui se laisse narcissiquement séduire. Dans ce jeu de la représentation, le point d'origine devient insaisissable. Il y a des choses, des eaux et des images, un renvoi infini des unes aux autres mais plus de source. Il n'y a plus d'origine simple. Car ce qui est reflété se dédouble en soi-même et non seulement comme addition à soi de son image. Le reflet, l'image, le double dédouble ce qu'il redouble. L'origine de la spéculation devient une différence. (Jacques Derrida, 'Linguistique et grammatologie' 55)

3 For further discussion about the innate metaphorical quality of all language, please see the following references: Friedrich Nietzsche, 'On Truth and Falsity,' 178; Jacques Derrida, 'White Mythology: Metaphor in the Text of Philosophy' 5–74; and Gérard Genette, 'La Rhétorique Restreinte' 168–9.

4 Gaston Bachelard, in *Lautréamont* and *La Psychanalyse du feu*, briefly outlines a project for a meta-poetics, and suggests proceeding by groups and diagrams in order that we may ultimately perceive the shape and form of the syntax of metaphors which constitute our thought and speech process. In *Lautréamont*, he postulates that all poetic images project themselves upon each other and are ultimately the same image:

> Quand on a médité sur la liberté des métaphores et sur leurs limites, on s'aperçoit que certaines images poétiques se projettent les unes sur les autres avec sûreté et exactitude, ce qui revient à dire qu'en poésie projective, elles ne sont qu'une seule et même image. Nous nous sommes aperçus, par exemple, en étudiant *La Psychanalyse de feu*, que toutes les 'images' du feu interne, du feu caché, du feu qui couve sous la cendre, bref du feu qu'on ne voit pas et qui réclame par conséquent des métaphores, sont des 'images' de la vie. Le lien projectif est alors si primitif qu'on traduit sans peine, sûr d'être compris de tous, les images de la vie dans les images du feu et vice-versa. ('Le Bestiaire de Lautréamont' 55)

Similarly, in his conclusion to *La Psychanalyse du feu*, Bachelard suggests that the work of a single poet could be reduced to a single diagram which would indicate the meaning and symmetry of his metaphorical co-ordinations, this diagramming being possible because the poetic mind is purely and simply a syntax of metaphors:

> Si le présent travail pouvait être retenu comme base d'une physique ou d'une chimie de la rêverie, comme esquisse d'une détermination des conditions objectives de la rêverie, il devrait préparer des instruments pour une critique littéraire objective dans le sens le plus précis du terme. Il devrait montrer que les métaphores ne sont pas de simples idéalisations qui partent, comme des fusées, pour éclater au ciel en étalant leur insignifiance, mais qu'au contraire les métaphores s'appellent et se coordonnent plus que les sensations, au point qu'un esprit poétique est purement et simplement une syntaxe des métaphores. Chaque poète devrait alors donner lieu à un diagramme qui indiquerait le sens et la symétrie de ses coordinations métaphoriques, exactement comme le diagramme d'une fleur fixe le sens et les symétries de son action florale. Il n'y a pas de fleur réelle sans cette convenance géométrique. De même, il n'y a pas de floraison poétique sans une certaine synthèse d'images poétiques. ('Lautréamont' 79)

5 In a letter to Madame Strauss (end of August 1909) Marcel Proust exclaimed that he had just 'begun and finished all of a long book.' He

also mentioned, however, that, although he had begun and finished his long book, he was still not finished. It appears, therefore, that the 'unfinished work' consisted of the middle of his long work:

> Et avant vous me lirez – et plus que vous ne voudrez – car je viens de commencer – et de finir – tout un long livre. Malheureusement le départ pour Combourg a interrompu mon travail, et je vais seulement m'y remettre. Peut-être une partie paraîtra-t-elle en feuilleton dans le *Figaro*, mais une partie seulement. Car c'est trop inconvenant et trop long pour être donné en entier. Mais je voudrais bien finir, aboutir. Si tout est écrit, beaucoup de choses sont à remanier. (*Correspondance de Marcel Proust* 163)

At this time, Marcel Proust had intended his work to be three volumes long. In another letter to Madame Strauss (Autumn 1912), he tells her that his manuscript is now ready, recopied, corrected, and he suggests to her the titles he has selected for the first and third volumes: 'le Temps perdu' and 'le Temps retrouvé':

> Pour moi mon manuscript est prêt, recopié, corrigé, etc.
>
> Ce que vous dites d'une 'Conquête sur le Passé' est une preuve de plus comme vous dites que nos sensibilités étaient accordées, et je ne peux pas vous en donner une meilleure preuve qu'un des titres auquel j'ai pensé pour mon livre est pour le premier volume *le Temps perdu*, et pour le troisième *le Temps retrouvé*. (ibid. 241)

In his book, *Comment Marcel Proust a composé son roman*, Albert Feuillerat examined the chronological sequence of the additions to the 'first edition of Marcel Proust's *Recherche* (accepted for publication by Grasset in 1913), and commented on the kind, quality, and sense of Proust's subsequent expansion of his work, which evolved from a proposed three-volume novel (*Du côte de chez Swann, Le côte de Guermantes, Le temps retrouvé*) of approximately 1500 pages in 1913, to an eight-volume work of approximately 4117 pages in 1927 (cf. 15–17). Feuillerat's study indicates that the middle volumes of the work (*Le côté de Guermantes II, Sodome et Gomorrhe, La prisonnière, Albertine disparue*) were written after the first three volumes, between 1913 and 1927.

In the 'Conclusion' to his study of Proust's manuscripts, Feuillerat quotes from a letter which Marcel Proust wrote to Benjamin Crémieux, in which he defends himself against criticism that his work was 'unconstructed,' by proclaiming that the last page of *Le temps retrouvé* was written before the rest of the work, and for this reason, the last page of his novel coincides with, or closes on the first page:

> On méconnaît trop, a-t-il dit, que mes livres sont une construction, mais à ouverture de compas assez étendue pour que la composi-

> tion rigoureuse et à quoi j'ai tout sacrifié, soit assez longue à discerner. On ne pourra le nier quand la dernière page du *Temps retrouvé* (écrite avant le reste du livre) se refermera exactement sur la première de Swann (255). (Originally quoted in *Du côté de chez Proust* by Benjamin Crémieux, 80)

Proust repeated this argument and his description of his method of composition in other letters to Paul Souday, Madame Strauss (see above), and others.

6 In 'Architecture of Time: Dialectics and Space,' Richard Macksey comments briefly on the elements common to the first and last volumes of the *Recherche* (a social gathering, the magic lantern, *François le Champi*, past/present reminiscences) which cause the work to turn upon itself, as its 'end' repeats its beginning:

> The two evocations are completed and the circle closed by a return to the distant bedroom and the narrator recollecting. But in a real sense the circle of 'Combray' forms a pier which will arch the entire work. As Proust remarked, the last chapter was written immediately after the first. The matinée at the Princesse de Guermantes' responds to and completes the initial soirée of Swann's fateful visit. Even more precisely the last chapter repeats the author's initial experiences and concludes his long education. Like so many of the characters, Golo of the magic lantern and François le Champi reappear. The narrator, at the lowest point in his affective life, is revived and sustained by the intervention of three experiences of involuntary memory. At last he understands the importance of the first invasion of this sort, the episode of the madeleine which resurrected the 'solid' Combray. With this sense of vocation found and confirmed he moves on to the matinée itself, which becomes the enormous fête masquée of time crowning the book. In an order which reverses that of 'Combray,' three moments in which the narrator turns back on his profound center, freed from time, are followed by the confrontation of a drama where time in all its transformations of appearance, station, and character are most acutely felt. The Marcel who suffered through the novel at last joins the Marcel who evoked him from his memory, when, like *Finnegans Wake*, the fictive novel is about to be born. (115)

CHAPTER FIVE: REPETITION AND CROSS-REFERENTIALITY AS MACROMETAPHOR

1 In 'Techniques of Fiction' (Chapter 2 of this book, *The Shape and Style of*

Proust), John Porter Houston comments on the 'double person' who is frequently depicted in Proust. He specifically mentions, among his examples, the double personality of Rachel. However, whereas this dissertation interprets the dichotomous nature of Proust's characters as a sign of the metaphor-like quality of the human personality (two dissimilar natures joined in one being, like the two dissimilar phenomena joined in a metaphor), Houston declares that 'metaphor' is too weak a term to characterize such a style of character development, and suggests that Proust was moving in the direction of the 'phenomenological description' which Sartre attempted somewhat later in *La Nausée*, which is the 'irreducible individuality of vision upon which Proust makes art rest' (58). Although I agree with Houston that the character portrayals in the *Recherche* are frequently conducted from a phenomenological vantage point (we have only to keep in mind the multiple visions of Albertine which the narrator perceives as his relationship with her progresses), I wish to clarify that it is the textual superimposition of these different 'phenomenological' personalities one upon the other in the course of the narration which is metaphor-like; as the layering of the innately similar personalities clarifies their common 'essence' – their constantly changing, 'phenomenological' natures.

2 In the third chapter ('The Stored Consciousness': Marcel Proust) of *Literary Architecture*, Ellen Eve Frank proposed that this first sentence of the book establishes an equation between self, church, quartet, and history, which possibly implies an identification between each member (self equals church, but church also equals quartet):

> Of course, in one sense, the dream-book is *A la recherche*, and perhaps the subject of the book is all four – self, church, quartet, history. But is each individually the subject? Does the equation propose identification between each member (self equals church, but church also equals quartet, etc.)? And are self, church, quartet, history therefore interchangeable? Finally, if the structure of the book is that of a church, as Proust and his narrator claim, are subject and structure – church – the same? Is the subject of the book architectural/literary structure?

Although Frank does not establish any connection between the nature of sleep/dreams, metaphor, and the four terms which are linked together during the narrator's dream, her 'equation' aligns itself well with my own study of the *Recherche*, as I am attempting to establish the common ground shared by 'une église' (the steeple and the church of Combray), 'un quatuor' (the Vinteuil Sonata), and 'la rivalité de

François 1er et de Charles Quint' (le Côté de Méséglise et le Côté de Guermantes) which would allow them to function as interchangeable terms of a reciprocal equation.

3 I, 9, 48, 171, 820; II, 419; III, 382, 539, 735, 884

4 Georges Poulet, in *L'Espace proustien*, draws parallels between the 'wavering and momentary stained glass window' ('un vitrail vacillant et momentané') created by the superimposition of Golo upon the reality of the room and numerous other circumstances in the *Recherche* that are characterized by a similar wavering effect. Included in his list of 'wavering' experiences are three circumstances that I am analysing in this book: the narrator's awakening from sleep, his sight of the three trees on the road near Balbec, and his initial reaction to the third 'intimation,' which he experiences in the Guermantes' dining room in *Le temps retrouvé*. Although Poulet does not connect the wavering effect engendered by diverse experiences in the *Recherche* with the metaphorical process, he does perceive the former as a sign of displacement in time and space, which occurs when a place tries to substitute itself for another place (cf. pp 15–16). Because displacement of sense is one of the primary conditions and effects which characterize the metaphorical mechanism, we can easily extend Poulet's argument and take his examples of displacement of time and space in Proust's novel as examples of spontaneous, metaphor-like processes.

5 In *A l'ombre des jeunes filles en fleurs*, the narrator previous classified Elstir's paintings as 'metaphors' because they frequently depicted the comparison of two different phenomena (the land and the sea, for example) in such a way that all lines of demarcation between them were eliminated (I, 836).

6 In 'Proust et les Noms' (1967), Roland Barthes proposed that the proper name in the *Recherche* functions as the linguistic form of reminiscence. He also suggested that it was Proust's discovery of 'names' which engendered the writing of the *Recherche*: names functioned as an 'event' and then a system from which and around which the work constructed itself:

> Les deux discours, celui du narrateur et celui de Marcel Proust, sont homologues, mais non point analogues. Le narrateur va écrire, et ce futur le maintient dans un ordre de l'existence, non de la parole; il est aux prises avec une psychologie, non avec une technique. Marcel Proust, au contraire, écrit; il lutte avec les catégories du langage, non avec celles du comportement. Appartenant au monde référentiel, la réminiscence ne peut être directement une unité du discours, et ce dont Proust a besoin, c'est d'un élément

proprement poétique (au sens que Jakobson donne à ce mot); mais aussi il faut que ce trait linguistique, comme la réminiscence, ait le pouvoir de constituer l'essence des objets romanesques. Or il est une classe d'unités verbales qui possède au plus haut point ce pouvoir constitutif, c'est celle des noms propres. Le Nom propre dispose des trois propriétés que le narrateur reconnaît à la réminiscence: le pouvoir d'essentialisation (puisqu'il ne désigne qu'un seul référent), le pouvoir de citation (puisqu'on peut appeler à discrétion toute l'essence enfermée dans le nom, en le proférant), le pouvoir d'exploration (puisqu'on 'déplie' un nom propre exactement comme on fait d'un souvenir): le Nom propre est en quelque sorte la forme linguistique de la réminiscence. Aussi, l'événement (poétique) qui a 'lancé' la *Recherche*, c'est la découverte des Noms; sans doute, dès le *Saint-Beuve*, Proust disposait déjà de certains noms (Combray, Guermantes); mais c'est seulement entre 1907 et 1909, semble-t-il, qu'il a constitué dans son ensemble le système onomastique de la *Recherche*: ce système trouvé; l'oeuvre s'est écrite immédiatement. (124–5)

(The above essay was first published in *To Honour Roman Jakobson: Essays on the Occasion of His Seventieth Birthday*.)

In 'L'âge des noms' (*Mimologigues: voyage en Cratylie*), Gérard Genette draws a parallel between the investigation of names in Plato's *Cratylus* and Proust's investigation of names in *A la recherche du temps perdu*. He concludes his discussion with the assertion that Marcel the narrator, like Socrates, assumes two different roles: 'le héro cratyliste devient (et ce devenir est l'une des leçons de ce roman d'apprentissage) le narrateur hermogéniste, lequel aura nécessairement le dernier mot, puisqu'il "tient la plume." Critique du langage, triomphe de l'écriture.'

Like Socrates, Proust presents two apparently contradictory views of names (names reflecting a man-made, externally imposed convention; names reflecting a 'natural' convention – the internal correspondence between things), and then shows that the two attitudes are not contradictory, but complementary (Genette, *Mimologigues* 11, 315, 328).

7 J.E. Cirlot, *A Dictionary of Symbols* 28
8 Although there is no explicit proof offered in the *Recherche* that Morel is having a homosexual relationship with Charlus, many of the narrator's comments imply that the two men are engaged in a relationship which is more than platonic. In *Sodome et Gomorrhe*, for example, the narrator remarks that Morel says the same things to him in Charlus' absence that Rachel used to say to him about Robert (II, 1060),

implying that Charlus' relationship with Morel is both sexual and financially supportive, as Saint-Loup's was with Rachel. Similarly, in *La prisonnière*, the narrator remarks that the young woman who translated M. Vinteuil's musical masterpiece into legible form had a relationship with his daughter which paralleled that between Charlus and Morel (III, 264). We saw evidence in *Du côté de chez Swann* that Mlle Vinteuil had a sexual relationship with her girlfriend; therefore, the narrator's parallel implies that the relationship between Charlus and Morel is sexual also.

9 The contents of one of Marcel Proust's personal letters indicates that the narrator's future work is the novel which the reader has been living with Marcel the narrator, as he traverses the time and space of his life in *A la recherche du temps perdu*. In his description of his future literary work as a church, Marcel the narrator reflects Marcel Proust the author, who confided in a letter to Comte Jean de Gaigneron that the structure of the *Recherche* is like a cathedral:

> Et, quand vous me parlez de cathédrales, je ne peux pas ne pas être ému d'une intuition que vous permet de deviner ce que je n'ai jamais dit à personne et que j'écris ici pour la première fois: c'est que j'avais voulu donner à chaque partie de mon livre le titre: Porche, Vitraux de l'abside, etc., pour répondre d'avance à la critique stupide qu'on me fait de manquer de construction dans les livres où je vous montrerai que le seul mérite est dans la solidité des moindres parties. J'ai renoncé tout de suite à ces titres d'architecture parce que je les trouvais trop prétentieux, mais je suis touché que vous les retrouviez par une sorte de divination de l'intelligence ... (letter communiquée par le Comte Jean de Gaigneron; André Maurois, *A la recherche de Proust* 175)

Although the affinity which Proust establishes in his written correspondence between the structure of his literary work and the architectonics of a church might appear to undermine the parallel that I have been drawing between the structure of the *Recherche* and the structure of metaphor, there is, in fact, no incongruity between the two views, as gothic cathedrals are just as 'metaphorical' in their structure as the outlines of the steeples which indicate them.

Ellen Eve Frank, in 'The Stored Consciousness: Marcel Proust' (Chapter 3 of her book *Literary Architecture*), investigates Proust's images of fiction as architecture, cathedral, temple, even rooms. She asks herself, 'What relationship does architecture, as art analogue of fictional literature, have to Proust's conceptions and methods of literary structure, subject and style?' (119). She briefly draws a parallel between the communication among narrative incidents and characters in the *Recherche*, and suggests that both kinds of communication depend upon 'discontinuity,' the gap or space between, which may receive or transport a charge, which Ruskin calls 'tension' (128). (She documents the traces of Ruskin which manifest themselves in Proust's work, as Proust studied and translated Ruskin's architectural essay, 'Bible of Amiens.') She proposes that the communication of discontinuity in Proust's work is like the communication at the basis of Ruskin's concept of the gothic (cf. p 128). Frank notes that Proust had discovered from Ruskin and then proclaimed for himself in the prefaces to his Ruskin translations that 'cathedrals are books to be read' (cf. p 146). In the fourth part of her chapter on Proust – 'Memorial Architecture' – Frank likens the totality of the *Recherche* to a gothic cathedral which preserves the past and the beauty and individuality of its parts (cf. p 165). Although she does not mention metaphor in connection with cathedral structure, I propose that the coupling of dissimilar individual elements in the unity of a single architectural monument (a cathedral) is a metaphor-like process.

Maintaining the 'essence' of cathedral structure (the unification of fragments) and returning to the steeples which indicate it, Georges Poulet suggests that the steeple of Saint-Hilaire symbolizes the unity and connectedness of the *Recherche* because the steeple offers a view that connects fragments of the countryside. Poulet establishes a parallel between the 'metaphoric action of memory' in the *Recherche* ('between times, between intermittent and opposite qualities, the mind discovers identities, – a common root, its own essence') and the view from the top of the steeple (alluded to by the parish priest in *Du côté de chez Swann*) which brings together things which are normally seen separately:

> Or, cette action supra-temporelle, nous l'avons vu, c'est l'action métaphorique du souvenir. Entre les temps, les qualités 'intermittentes et opposites,' l'esprit se trouve capable d'établir des rapports qui ne sont plus maintenant des rapports négatifs. Entre les moments retrouvés de son existence il découvre des identités, il retrouve en chacun d'eux une racine commune, sa propre essence ... Or tel est le propre du souvenir métaphorique. Il est le clocher qui surmonte l'étendue temporelle, mais qui, en la dominant, loin de l'abolir, lui donne sa complétion. (Georges Poulet, 'Proust,' *Etudes sur le temps humain* 436)

10 In 'The Architecture of Time: Dialectics and Structure,' Richard Macksey described the 'two ways' as a 'spatial metaphor,' but did not explicate the qualities that caused them to function like a metaphor (cf. p 114).

As mentioned in Chapter 1 (see p 4), Roger Shattuck, in *Proust's Binoculars* (1963), offered a more satisfactory explanation of the metaphor-like function of the 'two ways' in the *Recherche*: 'The book's central metaphor, which arches over the entire action, interior and exterior, is contained in the "deux côtés," a division of the environs of Combray and of the universe into two parts later reconciled and recognized as one' (123).

Shattuck also perceived the 'two ways' as a symbol for the two controlling dualities in the action of the *Recherche*; the first duality being that of the two 'snobismes' that fascinate Marcel as he grows up – the lure of the aristocratic levels of society and the attraction of the most vulgar and depraved levels (124) and the second duality consisting of the two paths of knowledge that for years determine Marcel's response to any event or situation – the apparent triviality of the familiar and the apparent mystery and promise of the unknown (125). Shattuck comments that the immense geographical polarity of the 'deux côtés,' which turns out to be an optical illusion of childhood, subsumes both of these moral polarities, even though the correspondence is nowhere made explicit.

11 In 'La Chevelure,' the poet feels himself transported to another geographical region and all that it represents by the hair of a woman:
>   Cheveux bleus, pavillon de ténèbres tendues,
>   Vous me rendez l'azur du ciel immense et rond;
>
> (Charles Baudelaire, 'La Chevelure,' 'Spleen et idéal,' *Les Fleurs du mal, Oeuvres Complètes* I, 27)

12 In 'Parfum exotique,' the sensuous perfume of a woman transports the poet into a country of sun and bliss:
>   Guidé par ton odeur vers de charmants climats,
>   Je vois un port rempli de voiles et de mâts
>
> (Baudelaire, 'Parfum exotique,' *Les Fleurs du mal* I, 25)

13 Roger Shattuck in *Proust's Binoculars* (1963) and Georges Poulet in *L'Espace proustien* (1963) both perceived a correlation between Proust's image of the past/present 'stilts' placed at the end of his work, and the initial description of the 'magic lantern' situated at the beginning of the novel. Poulet stated: 'The body of Golo does not hide the doorknob. Similarly, would it not be possible to imagine a world in which the ordinary capacity of beings, of places, of moments, would have given place to a certain transparency, so that in plunging his gaze into the depths of his own being, one could see the various epochs of it rise tier upon tier like the cells in a beehive? Is not that somehow the final vision that those trembling giants have of themselves in *Le temps retrouvé*,

perched by Proust on the heights made of the successive and semi-transparent layers of duration? Whatever is the case, the theme of the magic lantern placed by Proust at the beginning of his work, like that of the puppets placed by Goethe at the beginning of his *Wilhelm Meister*, has, it seems, a definite mission, that of expressing a paradox on which the Proustian novel will rest: the simultaneity of the successive, the presence, in the present, of another present: the past' (Georges Poulet, *Proustian Space* 93–4. To refer to the above quotation in the original, see *L'Espace proustien* 116–17). Similarly, Roger Shattuck proposes that 'the magic lantern which transforms Marcel's room in the opening pages metamorphosizes at the end into the stereoscopic vision of a giant standing erect in life and thus commanding time' (Roger Shattuck, *Proust's Binoculars* 129–30).

14 Proust, *Jean Santeuil*, 'De l'Amour' (la petite phrase), 816
15 Michel Butor, *Les Oeuvres d'art imaginaires chez Proust* 10
16 In a similar vein to Butor, J.M. Cocking suggests that 'Proust created Vinteuil's sonata by superimposing on the Saint-Saens Sonata impressions of many other works, fusing these together as he did when he created characters, places, the paintings of Elstir, and so forth' ('Proust and Music,' *Proust: Collected Essays on the Writer and His Art* 111–12).
17 Ibid. 19
18 Ibid.
19 Ibid.
20 Ibid. 22
21 Leconte de Lisle's poetic doctrine, which he expounded in 'Préface des Poèmes Antiques,' asserted that personal themes and their overly repeated variations sap the attention. He suggested, instead, the adoption of an impersonal tone in poetry, in order to avoid 'la plèbe carnassière' and the banal subjectivity of the nineteenth century. He proposed turning towards the past (especially Greek antiquity) for imagery, in order to allow the purity of past ideas to re-emerge into the context of the present: 'Le génie et la tâche de ce siècle sont de retrouver et de réunir les titres de famille de l'intelligence humaine.' It is no longer a question of evoking the past through flights of the imagination and the addition of local colour, as the romantic period attempted to do, but bringing the past into the present through the use of documentation: 'les idées et les faits, la vie intime et la vie extérieure, tout ce qui constitue la raison d'être, de croire, de penser, d'agir, des races anciennes' (cf. 'Préface des Poèmes Antiques,' *Derniers Poèmes*, Pièces Diverses, *Poésies Complètes III–IV*, 206–13).
22 In view of the parallel established previously in this section between

the structure of Vinteuil's sonata and the structure of *A la recherche du temps perdu*, it is noteworthy that Richard Macksey suggested in 'The Architecture of Time: Dialectics and Structure' a correspondence between the 'septet' ('Septuor') of Vinteuil and the 'seven-volume septet' which the narrator would later write:

> The reappearance of the music of Vinteuil thus punctuates the careers of all of the novel's great lovers; for Swann, the 'petite phrase' signals the beginning and end of his love for Odette; for Charlus, the performance of the septet at the Verdurins' is the moment of his betrayal and crushing reversal, but for the narrator the music which, as the 'petite phrase,' had once seemed to promise something withheld, now suggest not the end of an affair, but the beginning of a vocation, release from the tyranny of time and a promise of the seven-volume septet to come. (118–19)

23 The 'unpublished Goncourt journals' included by the narrator in his reminiscences are interesting in themselves, as they represent a reversal of 'real' and 'imaginary,' as applied to works of art depicted in *A la recherche du temps perdu*. Whereas the paintings attributed to 'Elstir' are apparently 'imaginary works of art' which exist only in the context of the novel, their subject-matter and their method of composition suggest a composite picture of some schools of painting prevalent in the late nineteenth and early twentieth centuries, which existed 'in reality' outside of the context of the novel. In the case of Goncourt's 'unpublished journal,' however, totally the opposite occurs. Whereas the unpublished journal is purportedly the work of the Goncourt brothers, who were members of the realistic / naturalistic school of literary expression in France during the late nineteenth and early twentieth centuries, the passage is equally as imaginary as Elstir's 'Le Port de Carquethuit,' as only the style of the writing finds its counterpart in lived reality outside of *A la recherche du temps perdu*. The actual events and the characters depicted in the 'Goncourt pages' (the Swanns, the Verdurins, the Guermantes) exist only in the context of the novelistic reality depicted by Proust's work.

CHAPTER SIX: CONCLUSION

1 Sophocles, *Oedipus at Colonus*, *The Theban Plays* 89
2 Heraclitus, *On Nature*, trans. from the Greek text of I. Bywater, fragment XLVI, 96
3 Ibid., fragment XLVII, 96
4 Ibid., fragment XLV, 96

5 Aristotle, *The Art of Poetry* 304
6 Ibid.
7 Ibid. 296
8 Ibid. 315
9 Ibid. xxii, 'The Role of Poetic Diction' 317
10 Paul Ricoeur, in his paper, 'Metaphor and the Main Problem of Hermeneutics,' has established a similar parallel between the possible connection, in Aristotle's *Poetics*, between the function of imitation (mimesis) as making human actions higher than they actually are, and the structure of metaphor, as transposing the meaning of ordinary language into strange uses. See Ricoeur, 'Metaphor and the Main Problem of Hermeneutics' 95–110.
11 Friedrich Nietzsche, *The Birth of Tragedy* 144
12 Ibid. He hypothesized that the ancient Greeks' Apollonian divine order of joy and beauty – the highest manifestation of which is the Greek tragedy – is the direct result of their awareness of the terror of existence which he equated with Dionysian 'oneness':

> Now it is as if the Olympian magic mountain had opened before us and revealed its roots to us. The Greek knew and felt the terror and horror of existence. That he might endure this terror at all, he had to interpose between himself and life the radiant dream-birth of the Olympians ... It was in order to be able to live that the Greeks had to create these gods from a most profound need. Perhaps we may picture the process to ourselves somewhat as follows: out of the original Titanic divine order of terror, the Olympian divine order of joy gradually evolved through the Apollonian impulse toward beauty, just as roses burst from thorny bushes. (42–3)

13 Ibid. 63
14 Ibid. 64
15 Nietzsche, *The Birth of Tragedy*. According to Nietzsche, this symbolic dismemberment of Dionysius is like a transformation of the primal element into air, water, earth, and fire:

> In truth, however, the hero is the suffering Dionysus of the Mysteries, the god experiencing in himself the agonies of individuation, of whom wonderful myths tell that as a boy he was torn to pieces by the Titans and now is worshipped in this state as Zagreus. Thus it is intimated that this dismemberment, the properly Dionysian suffering, is like a transformation into air, water, earth, and fire, that we are therefore to regard the state of individuation as the origin and primal cause of all suffering, as something objectionable in itself. (73)

16 Ibid. 73
17 Ibid. 74
18 Harry Levin, *The Gates of Horn* 3
19 Proust's example of a 'natural' metaphor (noon/churchbells) reminds us of the large, general sense in which Proust was utilizing the term (see pp 14–16): the evocation of the beauty of a noon at Combray through the sound of its bells is a process which – from a 'traditional' (seventeenth- to early twentieth-century) perspective – is more metonymical than metaphorical. Having already determined how and where Proust's generalized usage of the term fits into the history of the concept of metaphor (see pp 14–16), let us view this 'natural' metonymy from a metaphorical perspective.
20 Jacques Derrida, 'White Mythology: Metaphor in the Text of Philosophy' 32

Bibliography

ORIGINAL LITERARY TEXTS

Proust, Marcel *Correspondance de Marcel Proust* Texte établi, présenté et annoté par Philip Kolb. Paris: Librairie Plon 1982
- *Jean Santeuil* Paris: Editions Gallimard 1971
- *A la recherche du temps perdu*. 3 vols. Vol. I: *Du côté de chez Swann, A l'ombre des jeunes filles en fleurs*. Vol. II: *Le côté de Guermantes I, Le côté de Guermantes II, Sodome et Gomorrhe*. Vol. III: *La prisonnière, La fugitive, Le temps retrouvé*. Texte établi et présenté par Pierre Clarac et André Ferré. Paris: Librairie Gallimard, Bibliothèque de la Pléiade 1954

LITERARY TEXTS IN TRANSLATION

Heraclitus of Ephesus *On Nature* Ed. Bywater. Trans. G.T.W. Patrick. Chicago: Argonaut 1969
Sophocles *The Theban Plays: Oedipus the King, Oedipus at Colonus, Antigone* Trans. and introduction E.F. Watling. Great Britain: Chaucer Press 1947, 1975

CRITICAL STUDIES ON METAPHOR, LANGUAGE, OR TEXT

Aristotle 'The Art of Poetry' *Aristotle* Trans. Phillip Wheelwright. New York: Odyssey Press 1951
- 'Rhetoric' *Rhetoric and Poetics* Trans. W. Rhys Roberts. New York: Modern Library 1954
Artaud, Antonin 'Le Théâtre et son double' *Oeuvres complètes* IV. Paris: Editions Gallimard 1978
Bachelard, Gaston *Lautréamont* Paris: Librairie José Cortí 1939
Deguy, Michel 'Pour une théorie de la figure généralisée' *Critique* 25 (1969) 841–61

Derrida, Jacques 'Force et signification' *L'Ecriture et la différence* Paris: Editions du Seuil 1967
- 'Linguistique et grammatologie.' *De la grammatologie* Paris: Editions de Minuit 1967
- 'White Mythology': Metaphor in the Text of Philosophy' *New Literary History* (1974) 5–74

Dumarsais-Fontanier *Les Tropes* Paris: Edition de Paris 1818, rpt Genève: Slatkine Reprints 1967

Le Group μ, (J. Dubois, F. Edeline, J.M. Klinkenberg, P. Minguet, F. Pire, H. Trinon) *La Rhétorique générale* Paris: Larousse 1970

Jakobson, Roman and Halle, Morris *Fundamentals of Language*'s Gravenhage: Mouton and Co. 1956

Leconte de Lisle 'Préfaces des poèmes antiques' *Poésies complètes* III–IV. Genève: Slatkine Reprints 1974

Nietzsche, Friedrich *The Birth of Tragedy* Trans. Walter Kaufmann. New York: Vintage Books 1967
- *Die Geburt der Tragödie* Stuttgart: Alfred Kröner Verlag 1964
- 'On Truth and Falsity' *Early Greek Philosophy and Other Essays* Trans. Maximilian A. Mugge. New York: Russell and Russell 1964
- 'Über Wahrheit und Lüge im ausser moralischer Sinn' *Werke*. III. Ed. Karl Schlechta. Munich: Hanser 1956

Ricardou, Jean 'La Métaphore d'un boût à l'autre' *Nouveaux problèmes du roman* Paris: Editions du Seuil 1978

Ricoeur, Paul 'Metaphor and the Main Problem of Hermeneutics' *New Literary History* 6 (1974) 95–110

Sojcher, Jacques 'La Métaphore généralisée' *Revue Internationale de Philosophie* 87 (1969) f. 1, 58–68

CRITICAL STUDIES INCLUDING COMMENTS
ON PROUST AND METAPHOR

Cocking, J.M. *Proust: Collected Essays on the Writer and His Art* Cambridge: Cambridge University Press 1982

Crosman, Inge Karalus *Metaphoric Narration: The Structure and Function of Metaphors in 'A la recherche du temps perdu'* Chapel Hill: North Carolina Studies in the Romance Languages and Literatures 1978

de Man, Paul *Allegories of Reading: Figural Language in Rousseau, Nietzsche, Rilke and Proust* New Haven and London: Yale University Press 1979

Genette, Gérard 'Métonymie chez Proust' *Figures III* Paris: Editions du Seuil 1972. Also published in *Poétique* 2 (avril 1970)
- 'L'âge des noms' *Mimologiques* Paris: Editions du Seuil 1976
- 'La Rhétorique restreinte' *Revue Internationale de Philosophie* 87 (1972) 58–69. Also published in *Figures III* and in *Communications* 16 (1970) 158–71

Graham, Victor *The Imagery of Proust* Oxford: Basil Blackwell 1966
Kamber, Gerald and Macksey, Richard 'Negative Metaphor and Proust's Rhetoric of Absence' *Modern Language Notes* 85 (1970) 858–83
Ricardou, Jean 'Pour une lecture rétrospective' *Revue des Sciences Humaines* 49: 177 (Jan.–Mar. 1980) 56–66
– 'Proust: A Restrospective Reading' *Critical Inquiry* 8 (1982) 531–41
Shattuck, Roger, Chapter 5 *Proust's Binoculars: A Study of Memory, Time and Recognition in 'A la recherche du temps perdu'* New York: Random House 1963
Ullmann, Stephen *The Image in the French Novel* New York: Barnes and Noble 1963

CRITICAL STUDIES OF 'A LA RECHERCHE DU TEMPS PERDU'

Barthes, Roland 'Proust et les noms' *Nouveaux essais critiques* Paris: Editions du Seuil 1972. First published in *To Honour Roman Jakobson: Essays on the Occasion of His Seventieth Birthday* La Haye: Mouton 1967
Butor, Michel *Les oeuvres d'art imaginaires chez Proust* University of London: Athlone Press 1964
Crémieux, Benjamin *Du côté de chez Proust* Paris: Editions Lemarget 1929
Deleuze, Gilles *Marcel Proust et les signes* Paris: Presses Universitaires de France 1964, 1971
– *Proust and Signs* Trans. Richard Howard. New York: George Braziller 1972
Feuillerat, Albert *Comment Marcel Proust a composé son roman* New Haven: Yale University Press 1934
Frank, Ellen Eve 'The Stored Consciousness: Marcel Proust' *Literary Architecture* Berkeley, Los Angeles, London: University of California Press 1979
Genette, Gérard 'Discours du récit' *Figures III* Paris: Editions du Seuil 1972
Houston, John Porter *The Shape and Style of Proust* Detroit: Wayne State University Press 1982
Macksey, Richard 'The Architecture of Time: Dialectics and Space' in *Proust: A Collection of Critical Essays* ed. René Girard. Englewood Cliffs, NJ: Prentice Hall 1962
Maurois, André *A la recherche de Proust* Paris: Hachette 1949
Poulet, Georges *L'Espace proustien* Paris: Editions Gallimard 1963
– *Proustian Space* Trans. Elliot Coleman. Baltimore and London: Johns Hopkins University Press 1977
– 'Proust' *Etudes sur le temps humain* Paris: Union Générale d'Editions (Plon) 1972. Originally published in French by Edinburgh University Press 1949, and then by Plon (Paris) 1950
– 'Proust' *Studies in Human Time* Trans. Eliot Coleman. Baltimore: Johns Hopkins University Press 1956

- 'Proust and Human Time' *Proust: A Collection of Critical Essays*. Ed. René Girard. Englewood Cliffs, NJ: Prentice Hall 1962

OTHER WORKS

Cirlot, J.E. *A Dictionary of Symbols* Trans. Jack Sage. New York: Philosophical Library 1962, 1976

Harss, Luis and Dohmann, Barbara *Into the Mainstream* New York, Evanston, and London: Harper and Row Publishers 1966

Levin, Harry *The Gates of Horn* New York: Oxford University Press 1966

Index

Albertine, 54–5; comparison to Gilberte, 58; comparison to Odette, 59; playing pianola, 79; comparison to magic lantern, 79
analogy: interaction with reader, 20; in the *Recherche*, 34–5, 50; natural, 19–20, 35; relation to metaphor, 12, 24–5
Aristotle: metaphor, 3, 11, 12, 203–4; tragedy, 191–2
Artaud, Antonin, 16, 205n31
art/life/metaphor, 24–6, 46, 142–52

Bachelard, Gaston: metapoetics, 207n4
Barthes, Roland: names, 211n6
Bergotte, 156–60
binary oppositions: function in literary works, 199–200; time lost/time regained, 32, 49; relationship to metaphor, 32, 49

Charlus: exterior/interior, 55–6; feminine nature, 55
Church of Combray, 39–40; apse, 40–2; belfry, 41; stained glass windows, 39, 111; tapestries, 40, 111
Combray: comparison to magic lantern, 75, 80

contiguity: relation to metaphor, 12, 18

Déguy, Michel: metaphor, 11, 13
de Man, Paul: reading and the *Recherche*, 4
Derrida, Jacques: metaphor 203–4 n10; reflected doubles, 206n2
de Saint-Loup, Mlle, 119–20
doubles: life/art, 46; relation to metaphor, 27, 32, 210n1; Swann/narrator, 47
dreams/sleep, 64–72
Dumarsais, Jacques: metaphor, 11, 12, 204n11

Eikhenbaum, Boris: on metaphor and metonymy, 12
Elstir's paintings, 77–8, 166–73, 183–5
exterior/interior/metaphor, 51–9
external appearance/internal reality: calleya blossoms, 45; Gilberte, 54; Jupien, 56; hawthorne blossoms, 41; Legrandin, 41; love, 45; Mlle Vinteuil, 41, 53; Morel, 57; Odette, 45, 53; Octave, 56; Saint Loup, 53–4, 59

flowers: links to homosexuality, 60–4;

226 Index

comparison to steeples, 100; geraniums/impressions, 102; the two ways, 109
Fontannier, Pierre: metaphor and modern rhetoric, 12
François le Champi, 23, 37, 83–4, 93, 107, 124, 154–5, 180

generalities in a work of art, 24–5; in the *Recherche*: *see* Genette, Gerard
Genette, Gérard: generalities in the *Recherche*, 6; history of metaphor, 11–15; Proust and metaphor, 12, 14–15
'Goncourts' unpublished journals,' 178–9, 196–7
Groupe de Liège: metaphor, 11
Guermantes, 74–6, 80–3, 87–9

homosexuality/flowers/writing/metaphor, 54–5, 57, 59–64

involuntary memory: common essence, 25; relation to art and metaphor, 17; to obscure impressions, 21

Jakobson, Roman: metaphor and metonymy, 12–14

macrometaphor: common structures of metaphor and text, 3, 5–6, 7, 11, 18, 199; comparison to poetic metaphor, 34; reader/text, 36, 51; relation to natural analogies, 35
magic lantern/art/metaphor, 37, 72–81
metaphor, reflection of life, 185; three-part process, 48

metonymy: relation to metaphor, 12, 13

names/art/presence/metaphor, 81–94
Nietzsche, Friedrich: birth of tragedy, 193–5; metaphor, 202–3

'obscure' impressions, 21–2

past/present/metaphor/art/life, 18–27, 121–41
plant: comparison to writing, 62
Proust on metaphor, 18

reader/text/metaphor doubles, 25–6, 36; relation to metaphor, 50–1; macrometaphor, 51
repetition and difference in metaphor, 27; in the novel, 176–7; in the *Recherche*, 50–181
Ricardou, Jean: metaphor and the *Recherche*, 4–5
Ricoeur, Paul: metaphor and text, 3, 201n2, 218n10

Shattuck, Roger: metaphor and the two ways, 4
sleep/dreams/art/life/metaphor, 64–72
Sojcher, Jacques: metaphor, 11, 13–16
Sophocles: *The Theban Plays*, 188–9
steeples/art/metaphor: bi-partite structure, 40; relation to art and metaphor, 94–105

tea and the madeleine, 38–9
Thousand and One Nights, 129, 133–4, 140, 150–1
transformational effects, 48; Japanese papers, 38–9

'two ways'/art/metaphor: apparently diametrically opposed yet similar, 42–4, 46–7, 105–21

Verdurins, 56, 110, 113

Vinteuil Septet ('septuor'), 90, 102, 173–5
Vinteuil Sonata, 44–5, 47, 160–5

works of art in the novel/the novel/metaphor/art, 152–82

UNIVERSITY OF TORONTO ROMANCE SERIES

1 **Guido Cavalcanti's Theory of Love**
   J.E. Shaw
2 **Aspects of Racinian Tragedy**
   John C. Lapp
3 **The Idea of Decadence in French Literature 1830–1900**
   A.E. Carter
4 **Le *Roman de Renart* dans la littérature française et dans les littératures étrangères au moyen âge**
   John Flinn
5 **Henry Céard: Idéaliste détrompé**
   Ronald Frazee
6 **La Chronique de Robert de Clari: Etude de la langue et du style**
   P.F. Dembowski
7 **Zola before the *Rougon-Macquart***
   John C. Lapp
8 **The Idea of Art as Propaganda in France, 1750–1759: A Study in the History of Ideas**
   J.A. Leith
9 **Marivaux**
   E.J.H. Greene
10 **Sondages, 1830–1848: Romanciers français secondaires**
    John S. Wood
11 **The Sixth Sense: Individualism in French Poetry, 1686–1760**
    Robert Finch
12 **The Long Journey: Literary Themes of French Canada**
    Jack Warwick
13 **The Narreme in the Medieval Romance Epic: An Introduction to Narrative Structures**
    Eugene Dorfman
14 **Verlaine: A Study in Parallels**
    A.E. Carter

15 An Index of Proper Names in French Arthurian Verse Romances 1150–1300
   G.D. West
16 Emery Bigot: Seventeenth-Century French Humanist
   Leonard E. Doucette
17 Diderot the Satirist: An Analysis of *Le Neveu de Rameau* and Related Works
   Donal O'German
18 'Naturalisme pas mort': Lettres inédites de Paul Alexis à Emile Zola 1871–1900
   B.H. Bakker
19 Crispin Ier: La Vie et l'oeuvre de Raymond Poisson, comédien-poète du XVIIe siècle
   A. Ross Curtis
20 Tuscan and Etruscan: The Problem of Linguistic Substratum Influence in Central Italy
   Herbert J. Izzo
21 *Fécondité* d'Emile Zola: Roman à thèse, évangile, mythe
   David Baguley
22 Charles Baudelaire. Edgar Allan Poe: Sa Vie et ses ouvrages
   W.T. Bandy
23 Paul Claudel's *Le Soulier de Satin*: A Stylistic, Structuralist, and Psychoanalytic Interpretation
   Joan Freilich
24 Balzac's Recurring Characters
   Anthony R. Pugh
25 Morality and Social Class in Eighteenth-Century French Literature and Painting
   Warren Roberts
26 The Imagination of Maurice Barrès
   Philip Ouston
27 La Cité idéale dans *Travail* d'Emile Zola
   F.I. Case
28 Critical Approaches to Rubén Darío
   Keith Ellis
29 Universal Language Schemes in England and France 1600–1800
   James Knowlson
30 Science and the Human Comedy: Natural Philosophy in French Literature from Rabelais to Maupertuis
   Harcourt Brown
31 Molière: An Archetypal Approach
   Harold C. Knutson

32 **Blaise Cendrars: Discovery and Re-creation**
   Jay Bochner
33 **Francesco Guicciardini: The Historian's Craft**
   Mark Phillips
34 **Les Débuts de la lexicographie française: Estienne, Nicot et le** *Thresor de la langue françoyse* (1606)
   T.R. Wooldridge
35 **An Index of Proper Names in French Arthurian Prose Romances**
   G.D. West
36 **The Legendary Sources of Flaubert's** *Saint Julien*
   B.F. Bart and R.F. Cook
37 **The Rule of Metaphor:**
   Multi-disciplinary Studies of the Creation of Meaning in Language
   Paul Ricoeur
38 **The Rhetoric of Valéry's Prose** *Aubades*
   Ursula Franklin
39 **Unwrapping Balzac: A Reading of** *La Peau de chagrin*
   Samuel Weber
40 **The French Fictional Journal: Fictional Narcissism/Narcissistic Fiction**
   Valerie Raoul
41 **Correspondance générale d'Helvétius:**
   Volume I: 1737–1756; lettres 1–249
   Edition critique préparée par Peter Allan, Alan Dainard, Jean Orsoni et David Smith
42 **The Narcissistic Text: A Reading of Camus' Fiction**
   Brian T. Fitch
43 **The Poetry of Francisco de la Torre**
   Gethin Hughes
44 **Shadows in the Cave: A Phenomenological Approach to Literary Criticism Based on Hispanic Texts**
   Mario J. Valdés
45 **The Concept of Reason in French Classical Literature 1635–1690**
   Jeanne Haight
46 **A Muse for Heroes: Nine Centuries of the Epic in France**
   William Calin
47 **Cuba's Nicolás Guillén: Poetry and Ideology**
   Keith Ellis
48 **Fictional Meals and Their Function in the French Novel 1789–1848**
   James W. Brown
49 **The Composition of Pascal's** *Apologia*
   Anthony R. Pugh

50 **Surrealism and Quebec Literature: History of a Cultural Revolution**
André G. Bourassa
51 **Correspondance générale d'Helvétius, Volume II: 1757–1760; lettres 250–464**
Edition critique préparée par Peter Allan, Alan Dainard, Jean Orsoni et David Smith
52 **Theatre in French Canada: Laying the Foundations 1606–1867**
Leonard E. Doucette
53 **Galdós and His Critics**
Anthony Percival
54 **Towards a History of Literary Composition in Medieval Spain**
Colbert I. Nepaulsingh
55 **José Bergamin: A Critical Introduction 1920–1936**
Nigel Dennis
56 **Phenomenological Hermeneutics and the Study of Literature**
Mario J. Valdés
57 **Beckett and Babel: An Investigation into the Status of the Bilingual Work**
Brian T. Fitch
58 **Victor Segalen's Literary Encounter with China: Chinese Moulds, Western Thoughts**
Yvonne Y. Hsieh
59 **Narrative Perspective in Fiction: A Phenomenological Mediation of Reader, Text, and World**
Daniel Frank Chamberlain
60 **Marcel Proust and the Text as Macrometaphor**
Lois Marie Jaeck